CULTURAL THEORY

University of the
Wes

BRISTOL

B

POLITICAL CULTURES

Aaron Wildavsky, Series Editor

Political cultures broadly describe people who share values, beliefs, and preferences legitimating different ways of life. This series will be distinguished by its openness to a variety of approaches to the study of political cultures; any defensible comparison, definition, and research method will be considered. The goal of this series is to advance the study of political cultures conceived generally as rival modes of organizing political and social life.

A single set of common concerns will be addressed by all authors in the series: what values are shared, what sorts of social relations are preferred, what kinds of beliefs are involved, and what the political implications of these values, beliefs, and relations are. Beyond that, the focal points of the studies are open and may compare cultures within a country or among different countries, including or excluding the United States.

Books in the Series

Cultural Theory
Michael Thompson, Richard Ellis, and Aaron Wildavsky

*The American Mosaic: The Impact of Space, Time,
and Culture on American Politics*
Daniel J. Elazar

District Leaders: A Political Ethnography
Rachel Sady

*The Science of Political Culture
and the Culture of Political Science*
Michael E. Brint

CULTURAL THEORY

Michael Thompson
Richard Ellis
Aaron Wildavsky

Westview Press
BOULDER, SAN FRANCISCO, & OXFORD

Political Cultures

Copyright © 1990 by Michael Thompson, Richard Ellis, and Aaron Wildavsky

Published in 1990 in the United States of America by Westview Press, Inc., 5500 Central Avenue, Boulder, Colorado 80301, and in the United Kingdom by Westview Press, Inc., 36 Lonsdale Road, Summertown, Oxford OX2 7EW

Library of Congress Cataloging-in-Publication Data
Thompson, Michael.
  Cultural theory / Michael Thompson, Richard Ellis, and Aaron
Wildavsky.
    p. cm. — (Political cultures)
  Includes bibliographical references.
  ISBN 0-8133-7863-X   ISBN 0-8133-7864-8 (pbk.)
  1. Culture. I. Ellis, Richard (Richard J.). II. Wildavsky, Aaron
B. III. Title. IV. Series.
HM101.T5135 1990
306—dc20   89-21491
                                                                              CIP

Printed and bound in the United States of America

The paper used in this publication meets the requirements
of the American National Standard for Permanence of Paper
for Printed Library Materials Z39.48-1984.

10   9   8   7   6   5   4   3

To
Mary Douglas

Contents

Figures and Tables

Figures

Tables

Preface

The subject of this book is meaning. We are interested in how individuals confer meaning upon situations, events, objects, relationships—in short, their lives. How do people come to believe that physical nature is one way rather than another? How does one view of human nature come to seem more sensible than another? Why are some people alarmed at the use of nuclear energy while others are sanguine about it? Why does the destruction of the tropical rain forests in South America drive some individuals to the brink of despair while leaving others apparently unmoved? This book explores the different perceptual screens through which people interpret or make sense of their world and the social relations that make particular visions of reality seem more or less plausible.

Throughout this book, we use the vocabulary of subjectivity, of social construction, of the interpretation of meaning. These words have, unfortunately, become the almost exclusive province of those who insist that an explanatory social science in search of regularities is impossible. Proponents of hermeneutics, ethnomethodology, critical theory, and the like assert that understanding human beings, because humans confer meaning upon their lives, is inconsistent with theorizing in the spirit of the natural sciences. Understanding human beings is said to be more like textual interpretation (or even art) than it is like a science.

Our view is that this rigid dichotomy between interpretation of meaning and scientific explanation is unjustified. It is true that human beings create meaning. But it is also true that it is possible to make statements of regularities that help in explaining and even predicting (or retrodicting) the human construction of meaning. Subjectivity need not rule out regularity as long as different sorts of people feel subjective in similar ways with regard to similar objects. In this book by way of precept, in prior works by way of demonstration, and in future works by way of comparing rival theories to cultural theory, we hope to maintain against all comers the proposition that social science and the interpretation of meaning are not only compatible but essentially also the same subject.

Michael Thompson
Richard Ellis
Aaron Wildavsky

Acknowledgments

This book is dedicated to our teacher and friend Mary Douglas, upon whose pioneering work we build our theoretical edifice. Our gratitude for her inspiration and encouragement in what has become a joint intellectual program does not imply her agreement with what we have done. She will speak for herself. Here we wish to acknowledge her helpful comments on our chapter on Durkheim. We also wish to thank those who are engaged in a similar enterprise for the many things we have learned from them. Their names and works are noted in the bibliography.

At various stages in writing *Cultural Theory,* we solicited the critical comments of numerous colleagues in the social sciences: Gabriel Almond, Robert A. Atkins, Sam Barnes, Jonathan Bendor, Raymond Boudon, Harvey Brooks, Susan Buck, G. A. Cohen, Dennis Coyle, Terry Clark, Robert Dahl, Lewis Dexter, Gus diZerega, Dan Elazar, Jon Elster, Michael Faia, Ernest Haas, Andrew Janos, Robert Klitgaard, Martin Landau, Jan-Erik Lane, Stanley Leiberson, Arend Lijphart, Charles Lindblom, Duncan McRae, Duane Oldfield, Sam Popkin, Dirk Berg-Schlosser, Per Selle, Arthur Stinchcombe, Jonathan Turner, Ken Waltz, Joe White, Harold Wilensky, Frederick Wirt, and Sheldon Wolin. This book is better for their advice. Our thanks also go to the Spencer Foundation, which supported this project, and to the Lynde and Harry Bradley Foundation, which supported Richard Ellis under its Bradley Fellows Program.

Developing the foundations of a large-scale theory requires the formulation and scrutiny of bedrock premises usually left unexamined. The unexamined life may not be worth living, but as parents and politicians know, it certainly does avoid a lot of argument. When three quite different people set about agreeing on a common set of premises, going further to specify the connections and consequences among them, that takes a lot of doing. We think this often exhilarating but sometimes painful process of discovery has been worthwhile and that the result is a richer body of theory than each of us could have concocted on his own.

M. T.
R. E.
A. W.

Sociocultural Viability:
An Introduction

It is not our intention to bombard the reader with the myriad definitions of culture that have been tried and discarded, only to reappear without agreement among scholars.[1] Suffice it to say that two families of definitions vie for supremacy. One views culture as composed of values, beliefs, norms, rationalizations, symbols, ideologies, i.e., mental products.[2] The other sees culture as referring to the total way of life of a people, their interpersonal relations as well as their attitudes.[3] Rather than arguing for one definition over the other and vainly trying to pry people apart from their customary usage, we hope to gain clarity by distinguishing three terms—cultural biases, social relations, and ways of life. *Cultural bias* refers to shared values and beliefs. *Social relations* are defined as patterns of interpersonal relations. When we wish to designate a viable combination of social relations and cultural bias we speak of a *way of life*.

Causal priority, in our conception of ways of life, is given neither to cultural bias nor to social relations. Rather each is essential to the other. Relations and biases are reciprocal, interacting, and mutually reinforcing: Adherence to a certain pattern of social relationships generates a distinctive way of looking at the world; adherence to a certain worldview legitimizes a corresponding type of social relations. As in the case of the chicken and the egg, it is sufficient to show that cultural biases and social relations are responsible for one another, without confronting the issue of which came first.[4]

In this book we present a theory of sociocultural viability that explains how ways of life maintain (and fail to maintain) themselves.[5] The problem we have set for ourselves is not one of origins—when and how did ways of life emerge? It is instead a problem of persistence—how, having come into being, does a way of life sustain itself (and change)? How is it that the strength of ways of life waxes and wanes?

The viability of a way of life, we argue, depends upon a mutually supportive relationship between a particular cultural bias and a particular pattern of social relations.[6] These biases and relations cannot be mixed and matched. We call this the *compatibility condition*. A change in the way an individual perceives physical or human nature, for instance, changes the range of behavior an individual can justify engaging in and hence the type of social relations an individual can justify living in. Shared values and beliefs are thus not free to come together in any which way; they are always closely tied to the social relations they help legitimate.

A way of life will remain viable only if it inculcates in its constituent individuals the cultural bias that justifies it. Conversely (for we do not want to assign priority one way or the other), individuals, if they wish to make a way of life for themselves, must negotiate a set of values and beliefs capable of supporting that way of life. Our aim is to show that across a wide range of phenomena—whether ways of attributing blame, interpreting apathy, or perceiving risk—social relations generate preferences and perceptions that in turn sustain those relations. Instead of a social science that begins at the end—assuming values and beliefs— our theory makes why people want what they want and why people perceive the world the way they do into the central subjects of social inquiry.

The need to explain the preferences and perceptions of individuals opens up the need for a functional mode of explanation, i.e., an explanation "in which the consequences of some behavior or social arrangement are essential elements of the causes of that behavior."[7] Functional analysis directs attention to the social restrictions that hedge in the individual and thereby bolster a particular set of social institutions. Ways of life are made viable by classifying certain behaviors as worthy of praise and others as undesirable, or even unthinkable. Although it is individuals who construct, bolster, contest, and discredit ways of life, from the standpoint of any single individual the social world appears largely as a given. We side with Karl Popper's view that "it is to be stressed that this world exists to a large extent autonomously; that it generates its own problems . . . and that its impact on any one of us, even on the most original of creative thinkers, vastly exceeds the impact which any of us can make upon it."[8]

While we insist that ways of life channel the thought and behavior of individuals, we agree with Anthony Giddens that functionalism too often fails to acknowledge that many times an individual knows "a great deal about the conditions of reproduction of the society of which he or she is a member."[9] The extent to which individuals are aware of providing support to their way of life depends on their level of cultural consciousness. Intended functions, in our view, play as important a role as do latent functions in sociocultural viability.

Were it true that functional explanation is defective in principle, rather than only in past practice, our theory would collapse. We have to show, therefore, that it is only the singers, not the song itself, that are defective. By reviewing in Part 2 the use and abuse of functional explanation by major theorists—from Montesquieu to Merton—we show that functional analysis is indispensable to explaining how social life coheres. (After all, if a social system is not generating ways of behaving in the world, ways that sustain that system, how can one account for system maintenance except as a fortuitous occurrence?) The abuses are largely due to attaching functions to society as a whole. By breaking down societies to their constituent ways of life, and tying functions to those ways, we rehabilitate functional explanation.

Supplementing our claim that the viability of ways of life is constrained by the need for congruence between social relations and cultural biases is a second, more ambitious, claim: Five and only five ways of life—hierarchy, egalitarianism, fatalism, individualism, and autonomy—meet these conditions of viability.[10] We call this, rather grandly, our "impossibility theorem."[11]

Although five may seem to some readers an impossibly small number of ways of life, this number more than doubles the amount of conceptual variety available in existing theories of social organization. Part 2 makes good this sweeping claim. Whatever their singular merits may be, and these are considerable, the great social theorists of the past rarely went beyond the development from hierarchy to individualism, thereby leaving out fatalism, egalitarianism, and autonomy. Without these latter three types, theories of social organization lack, as Ross Ashby put it, requisite variety.[12]

Introducing more than two modes of organizing social life makes social change both more difficult and more interesting to explain. If there are just two ways of life, being dislodged from one necessarily means landing in the other. Allowing for changes between five ways of life, we maintain, produces a more powerful and discriminating theory of change.

Change occurs because the five ways of life, though viable, are not entirely impervious to the real world. That human perception is everywhere culturally biased does not mean that people can make the world come out any way they wish. Surprise—the discrepancy between the expected and the actual—is of central importance in dislodging individuals from their way of life. Change occurs when successive events intervene in such a manner as to prevent a way of life from delivering on the expectations it has generated, thereby prompting individuals to seek more promising alternatives.

At the same time that the five ways of life are in competition for adherents, so too, our theory insists, are they dependent on one another. Each way of life needs each of its rivals, either to make up for its deficiencies, or to exploit, or to define itself against. To destroy the other is to murder the self. Were egalitarians to eliminate hierarchists and individualists, for instance, their lack of a target to be against would remove the justification for their strong group boundary and thus undermine their way of life. Or, to take another example, were individualists ever to rid the world of hierarchy, there would be no extra-market authority to enforce the laws of contract, thus producing the breakdown of the individualists' way of life. If, as we are arguing, each way of life depends upon each of the four rival ways of life for survival, then it follows that for one way of life to exist there must be at least five ways of life in existence. This we refer to as the *requisite variety condition,* that is, there may be more than five ways of life, but there cannot be fewer.

That no way of life can exist alone does not mean that every way of life will be equally represented within a single country at a given point in time. Societies may be constituted so as to countenance certain ways of life and to discourage others. "American exceptionalism," for instance, in bringing individualism and egalitarianism together, has conspired to weaken hierarchy;[13] in Britain, by contrast, hierarchy and individualism have allied in such a way as to largely exclude egalitarianism. We do not mean by this that regimes such as these are in some sort of static equilibrium. On the contrary, we will show that recurrent patterns, such as those that distinguish American and British regimes, are possible only if the ways of life from which they are put together are in relationships of disequilibrium, so that they perpetually change their relative strength without ever settling down to some steady dynamic state. The differences between regimes, therefore, are to be found in the differing configurations of this perpetual dynamic imbalance between the five ways of life.

The study of culture, however defined, has characteristically emphasized uniqueness. Cultures, in this conception, are as varied as nations, ethnic groups, companies, clubs, any and all collections of people that think a bit differently, employ somewhat different signs, or whose customary practices and/or artifacts have something special about them. French culture is different from British culture is different from American culture; the corporate culture of Audi is different from Ford is different from Toyota; Presbyterian culture is different from Quaker culture is different from Baptist culture; and so on. Anyone who seeks to draw parallels between one culture and another (or, loftier still, to formulate a universal generalization about human behavior) is liable to have those whose stock-in-trade is the deep-seated particularities of a society or organization immediately step in with the anthropologist's veto: "Not in my tribe." Our aim is to override this veto by showing that although nations and neighborhoods, tribes and races, have their distinctive sets of values, beliefs, and habits, their basic convictions about life are reducible to only a few cultural biases. By limiting the number of viable ways of life, we contend, one can rescue the study of culture from the practitioners of "spiteful ethnography,"[14] who conceive of culture solely as a means to invalidate social science theories.

That a theory is new, to be sure, need not signify that it is true. (We are reminded of the social science adage: If true, not new; if new, not true.) In Part 3, we reanalyze some of the classic works in the political culture literature, from Almond and Verba on *The Civic Culture* to Banfield on *The Moral Basis of a Backward Society* to Pye on Chinese political cultures, in order to show what a difference a theory makes. We aim first to bolster our contention that there is more to social life than hierarchy and individualism by illustrating through extended examples—the Cultural Revolution in China and the amoral familism of southern Italy—that egalitarianism and fatalism are alive in our time. Our second aim in surveying these works is to demonstrate that even though the authors look for a single national culture, their empirical work reveals the universality (albeit in differing proportions) of competing ways of life within each society.

OUR POINT OF DEPARTURE: THE GRID-GROUP TYPOLOGY

Our theory has a specific point of departure: the grid-group typology proposed by Mary Douglas. She argues that the variability of an individual's involvement in social life can be adequately captured by two dimensions of sociality: group and grid. *Group* refers to the extent to which an individual is incorporated into bounded units. The greater the incorporation, the more individual choice is subject to group determination. *Grid* denotes the degree to which an individual's life is circumscribed by externally imposed prescriptions. The more binding and extensive the scope of the prescriptions, the less of life that is open to individual negotiation.[15]

The group dimension, Douglas explains, taps the extent to which "the individual's life is absorbed in and sustained by group membership." A person who joined with others in "common residence, shared work, shared resources and recreation" would be assigned a high group rating. The further one moves along the group dimension, the tighter the control over admission into the group and the higher the boundaries separating members from nonmembers.[16]

Although the term *grid,* as used here, may be unfamiliar to social scientists, the concept it denotes is not. In *Suicide* Durkheim presented much the same idea in his discussion of social "regulation."[17] A highly regulated (or high-grid) social context, Douglas writes, is signified by "an explicit set of institutionalized classifications [that] keeps [individuals] apart and regulates their interactions." In such a setting, "male does not compete in female spheres, [and] sons do not define their relations with fathers." As one moves down grid, individuals are increasingly expected to negotiate their own relationships with others.[18]

Modes of social control are the focal point of grid-group analysis. Individual choice, this mode of analysis contends, may be constricted either through requiring that a person be bound by group decisions or by demanding that individuals follow the rules accompanying their station in life.

Social control is a form of power. In the grid-group framework individuals are manipulated and try to manipulate others. It is the form of power—who is or is not entitled to exercise power over others—that differs.

Strong group boundaries coupled with minimal prescriptions produce social relations that are *egalitarian.* Because such groups lack (as a consequence of their low grid position) internal role differentiation, relations between group members are ambiguous. And since no individuals are granted the authority to exercise control over another by virtue of their position, internal conflicts are difficult to resolve. Individuals can exercise control over one another only by claiming to speak in the name of the group, hence the frequent resort to expulsion from the group in resolving intragroup differences. The drastic nature of these solutions, however, tends to drive disagreements underground, hence the presence of covert factions vying for control.[19]

When an individual's social environment is characterized by strong group boundaries and binding prescriptions, the resulting social relations are *hierarchical.* Individuals in this social context are subject to both the control of other members in the group and the demands of socially imposed roles. In contrast to egalitarianism, which has few means short of expulsion for controlling its members, hierarchy "has an armoury of different solutions to internal conflicts, [including] upgrading, shifting sideways, downgrading, resegregating, redefining." The exercise of authority (and inequality more generally) is justified on the grounds that different roles for different people enable people to live together more harmoniously than alternative arrangements.[20]

Individuals who are bound by neither group incorporation nor pre-scribed roles inhabit an *individualistic* social context. In such an environment all boundaries are provisional and subject to negotiation. Although the individualist is, by definition, relatively free from control by others, that does not mean the person is not engaged in exerting control over others. On the contrary, the individualist's success is often measured by the size of the following the person can command.[21]

People who find themselves subject to binding prescriptions and are excluded from group membership exemplify the *fatalistic* way of life. Fatalists are controlled from without. Like the hierarchists, their sphere of individual autonomy is restricted. They may have little choice about how they spend their time, with whom they associate, what they wear or eat, where they live and work. Unlike hierarchists, however, fatalists are excluded from membership in the group responsible for making the decisions that rule their life.[22]

For a few individuals there is a fifth possible way of life, one in which the individual withdraws from coercive or manipulative social involvement altogether. This is the way of life of the *hermit,* who escapes social control by refusing to control others or to be controlled by others.

In order to give the reader a richer understanding of these categories, we have chosen to present flesh-and-blood vignettes illustrating each of the five types. A high-caste Hindu villager and a member of a self-sufficient Western commune both have strongly positive group contexts. At the other end of the scale, a self-made Victorian manufacturer and an ununionized weaver employed at his mill both have strongly negative group contexts (Figure 1).[23] What separates the Hindu villager from the Western communard, and the mill owner from his hired hand, is the extent of prescriptions: the grid dimension. The high-caste Hindu villager and the ununionized mill worker both have strongly positive grid contexts in that their freedom is everywhere constrained by a socially imposed gridiron of things they cannot do and moves they cannot make. At the other extreme, the self-made Victorian manufacturer and the self-sufficient communard both have strongly negative grid contexts in that each rejects coercion; they both consider themselves free to act as they please—the one to hire and fire as he sees fit, the other to act as the equal in all respects of his fellow communards.

The self-made manufacturer has gotten to where he is by the full-blooded exercise of his rugged individualism. Always his own man, blunt and forthright, given to measuring success in material terms, and much impressed by the free operation of the market as a mechanism for increasing wealth and welfare, he follows a personal strategy that is both defiantly individualistic and unashamedly manipulative.

Figure 1. The five vignettes mapped onto the two dimensions of sociality

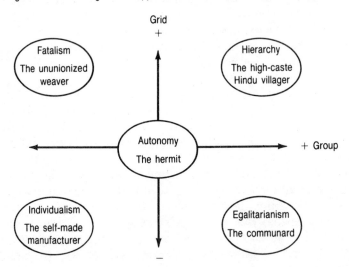

He is a pragmatic materialist; he will build networks by persuading others he is a good risk; the world, he believes, is a tough place and if he doesn't get there first, somebody else will. And, anyway, it's all for the best. Though not much given to moralizing, he will, if pressed, insist that it is this unbridled competition that actually transforms the raw materials of our external world into resources we can take command of. He prospers, he tells us, if and only if he serves others. Meeting other peoples' wants in a better way than competitors is his game. Human skill, enterprise, and daring, he insists, create a positive-sum game in which all the players—factory owners and factory workers—can become better off than they were at the start. The title (and content) of Julian Simon's book, people as *The Ultimate Resource,* and the novels of Ayn Rand describe well this individualistic bias.

The mill owner's hired hand finds himself on the receiving end of all this, not in the sense that his life is a misery of exploitation (though at times it may be), but in the sense that he finds himself the object of his employer's manipulation. His social context scores negatively on the group dimension but positively on the grid dimension: He is highly prescribed. Good times and bad times come to him, or so he thinks, regardless of his skill, character, and diligence. Ununionized, he is in a direct one-to-one relationship to his employer, but the crucial difference is that he has only one such relationship, while his employer has many. Elizabeth Gaskell exactly caught his predicament when she described his life as being "like a lottery."[24] His environment does things to him, sometimes good and sometimes bad, but he is unable to do anything (or, at any rate, anything consistent) to it. The unpredictability of his environment, and the lack of any feedback from it in response to his actions, or so he believes, mean that he cannot build much by way of a mental model of it. Sometimes it delivers, sometimes not, and he copes with it as best he can. He may even do well, but never, as long as his orientation is fatalistic, through his own efforts. Coping is what this social context is all about, and in the absence of any association (any bounded group that could negotiate with the mill owner on behalf of all hired hands), his strategy is inevitably one of personal survival.

The high-caste Hindu enjoys, by virtue of his membership in his bounded group, considerable rights to land, water, priestly duties, and the deference of his fellow villagers. Unlike the mill worker, the prescriptions that impose such a heavy behavioral gridiron on the high-caste Hindu are not the consequence of his being manipulated by others; they are the means by which he collectively manipulates others. These prescriptions are not imposed on his group by a higher group in order to keep him down; they are self-imposed to keep his group up—to ensure that its boundaries are not blurred and its rank differentials are not eroded as a result of lax observances that would allow transactions to spill out of their proper channels. The result is an environment in which all has been regulated; with a place for everything, the problem becomes one of keeping everything in its place. Scrupulous observation of the rules that protect each level of the hierarchy from contamination by the levels below it is his way to resolve this problem.[25] The high-caste Hindu follows a manipulative strategy in which he effaces himself by the observance of all the impersonal rules—dietary, occupational, matrimonial, and devotional—appropriate to his collectivity.

The member of a self-sufficient Western commune rejects the assumptions of inequality that inevitably accompany a caste system. He is a member of a group that is, above all else, egalitarian and that gains its definition not by its carefully negotiated and ranked relationships with other groups but by the critical rejection of that wider society with its coerciveness and inequality. His egalitarian collectivity cuts itself off from the nasty, predatory, and inegalitarian outside world by a "wall of virtue" that protects those on the inside and, in doing so, provides them with their sole principle of organization. The organizational problems that result from combining positive group with negative grid include: how to rule without authority; how to legitimate internal conflict when all adherents are good; how to retain membership without coercion (à la hierarchy) or selective benefits (viz. individualism). Although such outcomes would spell disaster for both individualists and hierarchists, egalitarians are not in the business of delivering. Their business is criticizing. Fervor, not market clearance or organizational refinement, is what matters to them. Fission is endemic but not disastrous; small, after all, is beautiful.

The hermit deliberately withdraws from the coercive social involvement in which the other four social beings, in their different ways, are caught up.[26] This autonomous way of life can flourish whenever withdrawal from coercive social involvement is possible, by a hermit either pulling back into a mountain fastness or finding overlooked corners closer to hand that none of the engaged ways of life is able to reach (or is interested in reaching). The hermit chooses to avoid the sorts of manipulation that are imposed on the mill worker and on the member of the self-sufficient commune, and at the same time, the hermit resists the sorts of temptations that might lead him to exercise manipulation in the manner of the mill owner or the high-caste Hindu. If he follows an occupation (such as taxi driving or marginal farming or the caretaking of a small office building) that is most effectively conducted in an individual rather than a group mode, and that does not offer much in the way of increasing returns to success (owner-drivers, no matter how successful, can only drive one taxi; caretakers can take care of only one set of offices[27]), these requirements will not be too difficult to satisfy. His strategy is aimed at autonomy: a relaxed and unbeholden self-sufficiency.

These five *social beings* are the elements of cultural theory. Each, in supporting a particular pattern of social relationships, and in cleaving to a distinctive set of convictions about how the world is and people are, is able to live, share, and justify just one of the five ways of life. Realists, however, will be dissatisfied with this formulation. They will argue that because we all inhabit a single world and share a single genome, the multiple natures that are needed to keep these five social beings viable are not available to us. But of course, there is always enough irreducible uncertainty in the world for us to be able to bias our convictions about it this way or that. For instance, the facts that would decide once and for all whether or not sin is original have yet to emerge, and the risks and benefits of nuclear power are still remarkably coy about revealing themselves in unequivocal terms. All that cultural theory requires is that there always be some uncertainty of this kind.

Resources, despite all the efforts that have been devoted to pinning down just what they are, still remain multiple in their definition. Those (the egalitarians) who speak of "natural resources," and who see mankind as trapped in a downward spiral of resource depletion, are in irresoluble conflict with those (the individualists) who speak of "raw materials," and who locate resourcefulness in the intangible and ever-expanding skills that we humans bring to bear on those raw materials. Nature, for egalitarians, is *strictly accountable*; for individualists, it is a *skill-controlled cornucopia*. Neither of these ideas of nature is of much use to hierarchists. If resources were everywhere depleting, it would not be easy to justify unequal access, and if resources could spring up like mushrooms in response to unregulated individual experimentation, there would be no need for the hierarchists' carefully planned frameworks for resource development and allocation. Nature for the hierarchists needs to be *isomorphic* with the social realm: its rich differentiation ensuring that it is forthcoming when approached in the right way by the right people but retributive when pushed beyond these carefully learned bounds.

For fatalists, the world can be cornucopian (sometimes its abundance even comes their way), but unlike the individualists' experience, nothing the fatalists do seems to them to make much difference. Nature's cornucopia is controlled, in the fatalists' vision, not by skill, but by a *lottery*. Hermits take no thought for the morrow (unlike egalitarians, who take thought for little else) because their aim is neither to manage nature, nor to exploit it, nor to accommodate themselves to its stern limits. Hermits, in sloughing off all these engagements that the other social beings fashion for themselves, seek to become one with nature. They do this, not in a misery of self-imposed privation, but in joyous participation in nature's fruitfulness. For them, nature's cornucopia is *freely available*.

THE PATTERNS BEHIND THE DIMENSIONS

Group is defined by Mary Douglas as "the experience of a bounded social unit." *Grid* "refers to rules that relate one person to others on an ego-centered basis."[28] Her two dimensions of sociality thus capture the fundamental mathematical distinction in patterns of relationships: groups and networks. If relationships are organized into a group pattern, then, no matter which individual you happen to choose to begin your mapping, you will end up with the same pattern of relationships linking the same set of individuals (and separating them from all the other individuals who are not members of that group). But if relationships are organized into networks, the pattern you trace out will be unique to the individual you have chosen. In terms of graphics, one diagram will serve to depict the relationships of all the group members, while there will have to be as many diagrams as there are individuals if the network patterns are to be fully depicted.

In social science (as we will show in Part 2), this distinction has been interpreted as one of pattern versus nonpattern. Groups, clearly, are patterned, but networks (because they spread all over the place, have no boundaries, and are as numerous as the individuals who build them) have been seen as what you get when the patterns—the groups—break down. The dimensions of grid and group ultimately derive from the recognition, first, that both groups and networks are patterns and, second, that they can intersect with one another to create networks of groups (hierarchies) and groups of networks (markets). Things are changing along two dimensions as we go back and forth between these familiar ways of organizing.

The group members' single diagram means that they can readily share the experience of their pattern of relationships but the members of a network, having each his or her own diagram, cannot. What is shareable about network involvement, however, is the common experience of network centrality (for those who have been forceful or lucky enough to forge relationships without serious restriction) and network peripherality (for those who have found many of the relationships they might have forged "foreclosed" by the prior incorporation of these possible "relatives" into the networks of others). In short, the experience of network involvement is perceptible and shareable in terms of the breaking of symmetry it entails.

If you were to set up a social system in which individuals had to maximize their transactions but were forbidden to form themselves into groups, you would end up with two quite distinct categories: network centralists (individualists) and network peripheralists (fatalists). These categories would, however, be altogether different from those that would be found if you set up your system on the contrary rule that transactions were to be maximized without the formation of individual networks. The breaking of symmetry in that case would be between two kinds of groups: those (egalitarians) whose members were maximizing their transactions by keeping their group apart from others and those (hierarchists) whose members were maximizing their transactions by arranging their group (not themselves) into orderly and ranked relationships with other groups.

Egalitarians, by keeping their group unrelated to the outside, are able to maximize transactions by connecting every insider to every other insider (institutionalized equality). Hierarchists increase their transactional involvement by connecting themselves to other groups, but as they do this, they inevitably impose some restrictions on the density of transactions within their group. Goods and services that are provided for them by others can no longer be provided by the group members and vice versa; otherwise there would be no way of differentiating between the groups (institutionalized inequality).

Hermits, as we might expect, are the odd ones out. Instead of maximizing their social transactions (which is what the members of the other four categories, each in their distinctive way, are doing), hermits move in the opposite direction: They minimize their transactions. In moving away from all forms of coercive involvement, they arrive at the one part of the grid-group diagram—the center—that is inaccessible to all those who are caught up in either groups or networks.

One major advantage of revealing these different patterns of relationships is that we can now see that the grid-group space is not evenly inhabited. In maximizing their transactions (or, in the hermits' case, minimizing them), people tend to end up clustered in the four corners and at the center. The cultural theory argument, therefore, is that people, by their interactions, organize themselves into these five clumps. But regardless of whether people are seen as organizing themselves or as being put in their places by cultural theorists, this fivefold scheme does seem to raise a serious problem: the denial of individual freedom.

HOW FREE TO CHOOSE WHAT?

Placing people in categories seems to many observers to do violence to the individual. For, they ask, if ways of life act as programs telling people what to prefer and how to behave, aren't individuals little better than automatons, robots, ciphers, mere windup toys moved by unseen hands? Solving the problem of preference formation seems to come at the expense of individual choice.

Plural ways of life, we respond, give individuals a chance for extensive, if finite, choice. The existence of competing ways of organizing gives individuals knowledge of other possibilities, and the opportunity to observe how the people who live according to these other ways are doing. Individuals use their powers of reasoning to compare existing social arrangements with alternatives. Thus we read in the papers how a quarter century of Burmese and Polish dictatorships has led these peoples to a favorable view of capitalism and democracy. Conversely, in some of the most privileged enclaves that capitalist systems have produced, we find cliques (like "The Apostles" at prewar Cambridge) dedicated to moving their society in the opposite direction.

The categories of social life generated by the grid and group dimensions possess the dual advantage of holding on to the best in previous research, thus cumulating findings, while opening up relatively unexplored, but important, avenues of cultural expression. Any theory of viable ways of life must be able to account for the two modes of organizing—hierarchy and markets—that dominate social science theories. Political scientist Charles Lindblom[29] and economist Oliver Williamson[30] are only two of the many scholars who have based entire bodies of theory on this fundamental distinction. Sensing that there may be more than markets and hierarchy, some organizational theorists occasionally mention "clans,"[31] or "clubs,"[32] or "collegiums,"[33] but these types do not come from the same matrix, built out of the same dimensions, as markets and hierarchies. One of the great contributions of Douglas's grid-group typology is to derive the egalitarian and fatalist modes of organization from social dimensions that can also produce the more familiar categories of individualism and hierarchy.

A further virtue of the grid-group framework is that the categories are formed from dimensions rather than being derived ad hoc from observation. Categorical ad hocracy—creating types to fit observations—tends to generate uneven typologies, that is, categories that are formed from different sorts of dimensions. One may be biological, another geographical, and still another technological. "Basing classification of 'objects' in a given domain upon a series of criteria that vary in this manner," as Arthur Kalleberg points out, "fails to satisfy the logical requirements of classification, for it fails to produce a mutually exclusive and jointly exhaustive set of classes for the domain under consideration."[34] That is to say, if the categories are based on different sorts of criteria, one may (logically, at least) be able to place objects in more than one category (therefore the categories are not mutually exclusive) and some objects may fit into none of the categories (thus the categories are not jointly exhaustive).

The grid-group typology discriminates between categories on the basis of common criteria. All five categories (ways of life) can be placed in relation to each other with respect to the degree of group involvement and degree of social prescription. By generating a mutually exclusive and jointly exhaustive set of categories for the domain of social life, this typology meets the logical requirements of classification.

Given that the categories of social relations described by cultural theory are *logically* coherent, we ask, how is it that they cohere *socially*? How do the ways of life sustain themselves? How is it that the categories remain separate rather than merging into an indistinct mix at the center of the typology? Following Edna Ullmann-Margalit we ask, "given that a certain social pattern or institution exists, why is it in existence?"[35]

The test of any theory is its effectiveness: Does it explain better than alternatives? A glance at the bibliography we have appended to this book will confirm that many practitioners (ourselves included) are convinced that it does. This wide and impressive body of applications that has built up over the past fifteen or so years prompts the further question: *Why* does it work? This is the question to which we have addressed ourselves.

NOTES

1. A. L. Kroeber and Clyde Kluckholm, *Culture: A Critical Review of Conceptions and Definitions* (Cambridge: Harvard University Press, 1952); Clyde Kluckholm, "The Concept of Culture," in Ralph Linton, ed., *The Science of Man in the World Crisis* (New York: Columbia University Press, 1945), 78–105.

2. This usage prevails among political scientists. See, for example, Gabriel A. Almond and Sidney Verba, *The Civic Culture: Political Attitudes and Democracy in Five Nations* (Princeton: Princeton University Press, 1963); and Lucien W. Pye, "Political Culture and Political Development," in Pye and Sidney Verba, *Political Culture and Political Development* (Princeton: Princeton University Press, 1965), 3–26.

3. American anthropologists have tended toward this more inclusive conception of culture. See, for instance, Ruth Benedict, *Patterns of Culture* (Boston: Houghton Mifflin, 1934).

4. On the logic of reciprocal causation, see Morris Rosenberg, *The Logic of Survey Analysis* (New York: Basic Books, 1968), 8–9; and Hubert M. Blalock, Jr., *Causal Inference in Nonexperimental Research* (Chapel Hill: University of North Carolina Press, 1961).

5. The term *sociocultural viability theory* has the advantage of indicating to the reader that ways of life are composed of both social relations and cultural biases (hence sociocultural) and that only a limited number of combinations of cultural biases and social relations are sustainable (hence viable). These words, however, are a mouthful. Because "sociocultural viability theory" is stylistically awkward and does not convey the instant recognition we seek, we shall often refer to our theory by the shortened designation "cultural theory."

6. To say that a way of life is viable does not mean that particular manifestations of a way of life may not be destroyed or transformed. Cataclysmic events, such as war, famine, or plague, may wipe out entire societies but do not set theoretical limits on the possible forms of social life. We are interested instead in the limits to viability posed by the limited number of ways in which one can justify social relations to oneself and to others.

7. Arthur L. Stinchcombe, *Constructing Social Theories* (New York: Harcourt, Brace & World, 1968), 80.

8. Karl Popper, "Epistemology Without a Knowing Subject," in Jerry H. Gill, ed., *Philosophy Today, No. 2* (New York: Macmillan, 1969), 272.

9. Anthony Giddens, *Central Problems in Social Theory: Action, Structure and Contradiction in Social Analysis* (Berkeley: University of California Press, 1979), 5.

10. The validity of this second claim is independent from the validity of the first. Even if it is not the case that (1) only these five ways of organizing life meet the conditions of viability, it may still be true that (2) in order to

be viable, ways of life must match patterns of social relations with cultural biases and that (3) the five ways of life we identify meet these conditions of viability.

11. The logic of "impossibility principles" is discussed in Giandomenico Majone, *Evidence, Argument and Persuasion in the Policy Process* (New Haven: Yale University Press, 1989), 70–75.

12. W. Ross Ashby, "Variety, Constraint, and the Law of Requisite Variety," in Walter Buckley, ed., *Modern Systems Research for the Behavioral Scientist* (Chicago: Aldine, 1968), 129–36.

13. Aaron Wildavsky, "Resolved, That Individualism and Egalitarianism Be Made Compatible in America: Political Cultural Roots of Exceptionalism," prepared for a conference on American Exceptionalism at Nuffield College, Oxford, April 14–16, 1988.

14. The phrase is from Clifford Geertz, "Politics Past, Politics Present: Some Notes on the Contribution of Anthropology to the Study of the New States," *European Journal of Sociology* 8 (1967): 1–14; quote on 4. Reprinted as Chapter 12 in Geertz, *The Interpretation of Cultures* (New York: Basic Books, 1973).

15. Mary Douglas, "Cultural Bias," in Douglas, *In the Active Voice* (London: Routledge and Kegan Paul, 1982), 190–92, 201–203.

16. Ibid., 191, 202.

17. See Emile Durkheim, *Suicide: A Study in Sociology* (Glencoe, Ill.: Free Press, 1951), especially Chapter 5.

18. Douglas, "Cultural Bias," 192, 203. Attempts to operationalize the grid and group dimensions can be found in Jonathan Gross and Steve Rayner, *Measuring Culture* (New York: Columbia University Press, 1985); James Hampton, "Giving the Grid/Group Dimensions an Operational Definition," in Mary Douglas, ed., *Essays in the Sociology of Perception* (London: Routledge and Kegan Paul, 1982), 64–82; and Robert A. Atkins, "Making Grid-Group Analysis Operational for New Testament Study," paper presented at the 1988 Annual S.B.L. meeting, Chicago, Illinois.

19. Douglas, "Cultural Bias," 206.

20. Ibid., 206–07.

21. Ibid., 202–03, 207–08.

22. Ibid., 202–03, 207.

23. Putting each way of life inside a "clump" so that it is separated off from the others alerts us to the fact that the centers of each of the clumps act as attractors and the separatices of the clumps act as repellers. This can be made graphically comprehensible by including a third dimension: grip (as it has been called by Nils Lind, an engineer who has shown that this dimension is an inevitable concomitant of the other two, that is, it is not a true dimension). *Grip* depicts the interaction of the various ways of organizing and disorganizing that go with the five ways of life. Fatalists, for instance, are the discards from the patterns of relationships that are put together by individualists, hierarchists, and egalitarians. Egalitarians, in organizing themselves against both individualists and hierarchists, inevitably end up long on purity and short on power.

There is a kind of action and reaction by which each way of life, in defining itself in relation to the others (our requisite variety condition), ends up with either positive or negative grip. This is true of all ways of life except for that of the hermit, which, in defining itself in contradistinction to the others, ends up at the one ordinal position that is not occupied by any of them: zero grip. Each way of life, as it were, gets going by getting some sort of grip on the others, and it is this mutual action and reaction that gives rise to the positive and negative directions to the grid and group axes and to the accompanying differentiations along the grip axis. The result of all this is a morphogenetic field (as it is called by dynamical systems theorists) that has just five flat areas: two hilltops (corresponding to the individualist and hierarchist clumps), two valleys (corresponding to the fatalist and egalitarian clumps), and a saddlepoint (corresponding to the hermit clump).

Readers who are interested in these graphic refinements, which are not essential to what we have to say in this book, are referred to Michael Thompson, "A Three-Dimensional Model," in Douglas, ed., *Essays in the Sociology of Perception,* 31–63.

Though we have tried to speak of grid and group as running from negative to positive, we have at times found it less of a mouthful to use Mary Douglas's weak/strong terminology. In these cases "weak" should properly read "negative" and "strong," "positive."

24. Elizabeth Gaskell, *North and South* (1855) and *Mary Barton* (1848), both republished in London by Penguin in the Penguin Classics (in 1971 and 1970 respectively).

25. Though we use the example of the high-caste Hindu (because the prescriptions he is subject to are so pronounced), we do not wish to give the impression that only those at the top of a hierarchy are hierarchists. The Hindu, whether he be high or low caste, is very much a member of the hierarchy. What varies as we go up or down is the degree of exclusivity of the rules that regulate transactions between levels (and the degree of scrupulousness with which they are observed: It is those some distance short of the top—the goldsmiths, for example—who tend to be the most scrupulous). However, there are always some among the out-castes who are not a part of this supposedly all-embracing framework. For the principle of all-inclusiveness, see Louis Dumont, *Homo Hierarchicus* (London: Paladin, 1970). For a masterly account of how cultural pluralism is unavoidable, and of how this pluralism coexists with and modifies the caste hierarchy, see McKim Marriot, "Hindu Transactions: Diversity Without Dualism," in Bruce Kapferer, ed., *Transaction and Meaning* (Philadelphia: Institute for the Study of Human Issues, 1967).

26. Mary Douglas has used this distinction to take the hermit "off the social map," but we prefer to keep him on it. Indeed, we prefer to place him at the very center of our map, at the place where he will inevitably end up as he withdraws from each of the four corners that are occupied by the engaged social beings.

27. See Michael Thompson and Aaron Wildavsky, "A Poverty of Distinction: From Economic Homogeneity to Cultural Heterogeneity in the Classification of Poor People," *Policy Sciences* 19 (1986): 163–99.

28. Mary Douglas, *Natural Symbols: Explorations in Cosmology* (London: Barrie and Rockliff, 1970), viii. These are her "root definitions"—the bases

from which the other definitions she provides (and that we have already used in explaining the grid and group dimensions) are derived.

29. Charles Lindblom, *Politics and Markets: The World's Political-Economic Systems* (New York: Basic Books, 1977).

30. Oliver Williamson, *Markets and Hierarchies, Analysis and Antitrust Implications: A Study in the Economics of Internal Organization* (New York: Free Press, 1975).

31. William G. Ouchi, "Markets, Bureaucracies, and Clans," *Administrative Science Quarterly*, March 1980, 129–41.

32. Williamson, *Markets and Hierarchies*.

33. The term is used by Giandomenico Majone.

34. Arthur L. Kalleberg, "The Logic of Comparison: A Methodological Note on the Comparative Study of Political Systems," *World Politics* 19, 1 (October 1966): 69–82, especially 73–74. Also see Carl G. Hempel, *Fundamentals of Concept Formation in Empirical Science* (Chicago: University of Chicago Press, 1952), 51.

35. Edna Ullmann-Margalit, "Invisible Hand Explanations," *Synthese* 39 (1978): 282–86; quote on 284.

THE THEORY

Introduction to Part One: Against Dualism

Social science is steeped in dualisms: culture and structure, change and stability, dynamics and statics, methodological individualism and collectivism, voluntarism and determinism, nature and nurture, macro and micro, materialism and idealism, facts and values, objectivity and subjectivity, rationality and irrationality, and so forth. Although sometimes useful as analytic distinctions, these dualisms often have the unfortunate result of obscuring extensive interdependencies between phenomena. Too often social scientists create needless controversies by seizing upon one side of a dualism and proclaiming it the more important. Cultural theory shows that there is no need to choose between, for instance, collectivism and individualism, values and social relations, or change and stability. Indeed, we argue, there is a need not to.

A recurring debate among social scientists is whether institutional structures cause culture (defined as values and beliefs, i.e., mental products) or culture causes structure.[1] As our definition of ways of life makes clear, we see no reason to choose between social institutions and cultural biases. Values and social relations are mutually interdependent and reinforcing: Institutions generate distinctive sets of preferences, and adherence to certain values legitimizes corresponding institutional arrangements. Asking which comes first or which should be given causal priority is a nonstarter.

In recent decades, the social sciences have witnessed a dissociation between studies of values, symbols, and ideologies and studies of social relations, modes of organizing, and institutions.[2] Cultural studies proceed as if mental products were manufactured in an institutional vacuum, while studies of social relations ignore how people justify to themselves and to others the way in which they live. One of the most important contributions of our sociocultural theory, we believe, is bringing these two aspects of human life together.

21

Nor do we feel it necessary to take sides in the dispute between adherents of methodological individualism, who hold that "all social phenomena are in principle explicable in ways that only involve individuals," and partisans of methodological collectivism, who argue that "there are supra-individual entities that are prior to individuals in the explanatory order."[3] Institutional arrangements do, as methodological collectivists contend, constrain individual behavior, but it is also true, as methodological individualists insist, that institutional arrangements are held together and modified by individual action. Individuals do find themselves in an institutional setting not of their making, as Marx says, but it is individuals who create, sustain, and transform that setting. Put another way, the individual (unlike the behaviorist's rats) shapes the maze while running it.[4]

We refuse also to cordon off stability from change. Cultural theory unites mechanisms of maintenance and transformation. If, as Marshall Sahlins says, change is failed reproduction,[5] then a theory of change must also be a theory of stability. Moreover, this dualism obscures the enormous amount of change that is required to secure stability. Individuals continually confront novel situations requiring a great deal of effort to maintain their familiar pattern of social relations. British Tories, for instance, in the face of considerable socioeconomic and political change, maintained their dominant position within society as well as their preferred pattern of deferential social relations by changing their policies regarding welfare state measures and suffrage reform.[6]

The fact-value distinction, although analytically defensible, obscures the extensive interpenetration of facts and values in the real world. Precious few are the claims that do not contain both value and factual components. Ways of life weave together beliefs about what is (e.g., human nature is good) with what ought to be (e.g., coercive institutions should be abolished) into a mutually supportive whole. Cultural biases are protected by filtering facts through a perceptual screen.[7] Contra Weber, however, normative beliefs about how life ought to be lived are not necessarily immune to facts.[8] When the promises that adherents of a way of life make to each other (or to supporters of other ways of life they wish to recruit) are not borne out by repeated experience, the discrepancy between the expectation and the result can dislodge individuals from their existing view of how the world ought to be and thrust them into another.

Rather than counterpoising rationality and irrationality, we refer to competing social definitions of what will count as rational. No act can be classified as in and of itself rational or irrational. What is rational depends on the social or institutional setting within which the act is embedded. Acts that are rational from the perspective of one way of life may be the height of irrationality from the perspective of a competing way of life. For instance, individualists, who believe they can increase both their wants and their resources, will deem fatalistic resignation utterly irrational. But for fatalists, who tell themselves that both needs and resources are beyond their control, resignation is eminently rational.

Often superimposed upon the dichotomy between rational and irrational is the division between primitive and modern. Although this distinction highlights the vast differences among societies that exist in technological development, we find it of no use in classifying ways of life. Contra Durkheim, we insist that the march of technological progress does not release modern man from the social control of cognition. Regardless of time or space, we argue, individuals always face (and, as long as human life exists, always will) five ways of relating to other human beings. This provides the foundation for the essential "unity in diversity" of human experience.

NOTES

1. See, for instance, Brian Barry, *Sociologists, Economists and Democracy* (London: Collier-Macmillan, 1970); and Carole Pateman, "Political Culture, Political Structure and Political Change," *British Journal of Political Science* 1, 3 (July 1971): 291–306.

2. S. N. Eisenstadt has recently called attention to this disturbing trend in "Culture and Social Structure Revisited," *International Sociology* 1, 3 (September 1986): 297–320.

3. Jon Elster, *Making Sense of Marx* (Cambridge: Cambridge University Press, 1985), 5–6. The debate is thoroughly vetted in the essays collected in John O'Neill, ed., *Modes of Individualism and Collectivism* (London: Heinemann, 1973).

4. Much the same idea is captured in Peter Berger and Thomas Luckman's epigram, "Society is a human product. . . . Man is a social product" (*The Social Construction of Reality* [Garden City, N.Y.: Doubleday, 1967], 61). Also see Robert Grafstein, "The Problem of Institutional Constraint," *Journal of Politics* 50, 3 (August 1988): 577–99.

5. Marshall Sahlins, *Historical Metaphors and Mythical Realities: Structure in the Early History of the Sandwich Island Kingdoms* (Ann Arbor: University of Michigan Press, 1981), cited in Sherry B. Ortner, "Theory in Anthropology Since the Sixties," *Comparative Studies in Society and History* 26, 1 (January 1984): 126–65, quote on 156.

6. This example is offered by Harry Eckstein, who terms this "pattern-maintaining change" ("A Culturalist Theory of Political Change," *American Political Science Review* 82, 3 [September 1988]: 789–804; quote on 794).

7. As Kenneth Burke formulated it, "A way of seeing is always a way of not seeing" (*Permanence and Change* [New York: New Republic, 1935], 70).

8. This point is elaborated in W. G. Runciman, *Social Science and Political Theory* (Cambridge: Cambridge University Press, 1963), Chapter 8.

CHAPTER 1

The Social Construction
of Nature

We begin our examination of the viability of ways of life with a bedrock question: What determines the models people use of human and physical nature? Ideas of nature, whether physical or human, we argue in this chapter, are socially constructed. What is natural and unnatural is given to individuals by their way of life.

To say that ideas of nature are socially shaped is not to say that they can be anything at all. Yet this is the relativist charge that is often leveled at those (the "strong programme" in the philosophy of science, for example, and the grid/group approach to the sociology of perception[1]) who have tried to account for the social construction of perception. "Okay, go and jump in front of the train," say the relativity rejectors, believing themselves to have achieved some sort of refutation when the relativist declines the challenge. But of course, no one is saying that perception is completely fluid, only that it is not completely solid. Rather, ideas of nature are plastic; they can be squeezed into different configurations but, at the same time, there are some limits. The idea of nature that would have us all leaping in front of trains is outside of these limits, that is, it is not a *viable* idea of nature.

This debate between realists (as they like to call themselves) and relativists (as they get called) is a pernicious trivialization of a serious issue and the time is long overdue for its replacement by a notion— we will call it *constrained relativism*—that firmly rejects both these polarized extremes. The difficulty, of course, lies not in saying this but in propounding the concepts to go with it, concepts robust enough to avert the deterioration of the debate to the dreary jump-in-front-of-the-train level. This, we claim, is precisely what our theory of sociocultural viability does.

FIVE MYTHS OF NATURE

In the course of studying managed ecosystems—like forests, fisheries, and grasslands—ecologists discovered that the interventions of the managing institutions in the ecosystems were wildly heterogeneous. That is, different managing institutions, faced with exactly the same sort of situation, did very different things (some, for instance, started spraying the forest with insecticide, others stopped). Whereas trees and budworms and other natural components of the ecosystem could be relied on to behave fairly consistently, the managing institutions could not. Yet the behavior of the institutions was not completely random. Though they did different things, they did not do just anything, and the ecologists discovered they could account for the diversity of institutional response by introducing into their analysis a number of *myths of nature.*[2]

These myths of nature are the simplest models of ecosystem stability that when matched to the different ways in which the managing institutions behave, render those institutions rational. However, unlike the explicit models that scientists usually deal with, these models are seen by those who hold to them as being built from largely unquestioned assumptions.

The myths of nature, in consequence, are both true and false; that is the secret of their longevity. Each myth is a partial representation of reality. Each captures some essence of experience and wisdom, and each recommends itself as self-evident truth to the particular social being whose way of life is premised on nature conforming to that version of reality.

There are five possible myths of nature: Nature Benign, Nature Ephemeral, Nature Perverse/Tolerant, Nature Capricious, and Nature Resilient. In order to simplify the exposition of the five myths, we leave the description of Nature Resilient, a sort of "meta-myth" that claims to subsume the other four, until later in this chapter. Each of the other four myths can be represented graphically by a ball in a landscape (Figure 2).

Nature Benign gives us global equilibrium. The world, it tells us, is wonderfully forgiving: No matter what knocks we deliver, the ball will always return to the bottom of the basin. The managing institution can therefore have a laissez-faire attitude. *Nature Ephemeral* is almost the exact opposite. The world, it tells us, is a terrifyingly unforgiving place and the least jolt may trigger its complete collapse. The managing institution must treat the ecosystem with great care. *Nature Perverse/ Tolerant* is forgiving of most events but is vulnerable to an occasional knocking of the ball over the rim. The managing institution must, therefore, regulate against unusual occurrences. *Nature Capricious* is a

Figure 2. The four primary myths of nature

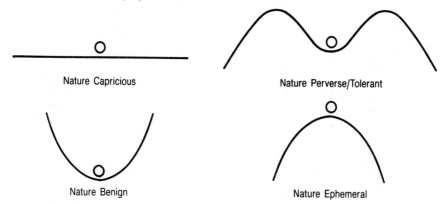

Nature Capricious

Nature Perverse/Tolerant

Nature Benign

Nature Ephemeral

random world. Institutions with this view of nature do not really manage or learn: They just cope with erratic events.

Nature Benign encourages and justifies trial and error. As long as we all do our exuberant, individualistic things, a "hidden hand" (the uniformly downward slope of the landscape) will lead us toward the best possible outcome. But such behavior becomes irresponsibly destructive if nature is ephemeral. Nature Ephemeral requires us to set up effective sanctions to prevent this sort of thing from happening, to join together in celebration of incuriosity and trepidity. Of course, the fact that we are still here, despite all our perturbations, would seem to make this myth a nonstarter. We need only to introduce a little friction into the landscape, however, for the ball to stay where it is, as long as we all hold our collective breath. This is the perfect justification for those who would have us all living in those small, tight-knit, decentralized communities that respect nature's fragility and make appropriately modest demands upon it.

Whereas Nature Benign encourages bold experimentation in the face of uncertainty and Nature Ephemeral encourages timorous forbearance, Nature Perverse/Tolerant requires us to ensure that exuberant behavior never goes too far, that the ball remains within the zone of equilibrium. Neither the unbridled experimentation that goes with global equilibrium nor the tiptoe behavior appropriate to global disequilibrium can command moral respect here. Rather, everything hinges upon mapping and managing the boundary line between these two states. Certainty and predictability, generated by experts, become the dominant moral concern.

With Nature Benign, Nature Ephemeral, and Nature Perverse/Tolerant, learning is possible, though each disposes its holders to learn different things (and, thereby, to construct different knowledges). But in the flatland of Nature Capricious there are no gradients to teach us the difference between hills and dales, up and down, better and worse. Life is, and remains, a lottery. It is luck, not learning, that from time to time brings resources our way.

These four thumbnail sketches (and the fifth to be dealt with presently) show that it is our institutions that supply us with our myths and, in so doing, systematically direct our attention toward certain features of our environment and away from others. Nature Benign is the myth that readily recommends itself to the competitor—the individualistic advocate of the free market—while Nature Perverse/Tolerant is the hierarchist's myth, Nature Ephemeral the myth of the egalitarian, and Nature Capricious the myth that reconciles those who find themselves squeezed out from all these institutional forms to their fatalistic ineffectuality.

The five myths of nature, derived from the work of ecologists, closely coincide with the ideas of nature (introduced in "Sociocultural Viability: An Introduction" and explored more fully in the next chapter), which we have deduced by asking how nature would have to be conceived for our five ways of life to be livable. To recap quickly, we suggested that for fatalism to be a viable way of life, nature must be constructed to appear as a lottery-controlled cornucopia. For egalitarianism to be a viable mode of existence, nature must be held strictly accountable. For individualism to be a viable way of life, nature must be a skill-controlled cornucopia. For hierarchy to be a viable way of life, nature must be bountiful within strictly accountable limits (the isomorphic idea of nature). The hermit's viability depends on nature's being seen as a freely available cornucopia.

Both the ideas of nature and the myths of nature thus map onto the very same institutional typology. The skill-controlled cornucopia and Nature Benign belong to the individualist; isomorphic nature and Nature Perverse/Tolerant belong to the hierarchist; accountable nature and Nature Ephemeral belong to the egalitarian; the lottery-controlled cornucopia and Nature Capricious belong to the fatalist; and the freely available cornucopia and Nature Resilient, we will show presently, belong to the hermit. The fact that despite their different points of departure, both the ideas and the myths end up with essentially the same typology suggests to us that our theory's dimensions and categories connect us, not to a transient relativity, but to something real and enduring: the diverse yet rational involvements of the followers of the different ways of life with the one world they all inhabit.

We need only to change a social being's myth of nature to confirm the validity of this functional relationship between a particular set of convictions about how the world is and a particular way of life. An individualist who came to believe that nature was ephemeral could hardly justify the continuous process of trial and error that is the essence of his self-regulating way of life, because any error would be likely to cause irreparable damage. Moreover, if nature were strictly accountable, there would be no possibility of everyone becoming better off. Only if nature were cornucopian would it be possible for the "hidden hand" to do its wonderful behind-the-scenes work and add to the welfare of the whole. Similarly, a hierarchist who came to believe, with individualists, that there was no limit on what nature could tolerate would no longer see any purpose in having experts to determine where those limits lie. On top of that, if those limits and the regulations by which their respect is enforced were to disappear (as they would if no one supported the experts), there would be no way of keeping the different ranks of humankind separate from one another. Aristocrats would have no defense against *arrivistes*. Worse still, the very possibility of making such distinctions would disappear once there was no longer any transaction-regulating framework to define people's stations in life for them. Furthermore, were egalitarians to believe that nature is cornucopian, there would be so much of everything valuable that there would be no point in sharing out. And if fatalists found patterns in nature, so they could get in sync with these predictable forces, they could do something to control their fate. What about the hermit, whom we have so far put off discussing?

THE HERMIT'S MYTH

The hermit's strategy is one of withdrawal; yet coercive social involvement is what the other ways of life are about—each seeks to maximize the transactions through its favored pattern of relationships, and thereby to minimize those through the other patterns of relationships. The hermit's strategy of minimizing his transactions is viable, therefore, only if everyone else is maximizing theirs. Whereas the viability of each of the four engaged ways of life depends on the presence of the other three (for only then can they set up between them the patterns of manipulation that tell them the world is indeed the way they see it—rewarding the individualist's skill and enterprise, for instance, and confirming the fatalist in his conviction that nothing he does makes much difference), the hermit's viability depends on the presence of all four. The hermit's bias is against the entire system that is sustained by the interdependencies of the other four biases.[3] It is not surprising, therefore, that the claim of transcendence—the oneness of man and nature, the unity of opposites, and the ultimate possibility of release from the cycle of suffering—is so much a part of the framework that stabilizes the hermit's precarious detachment from the coercive social world. But in withdrawing from this fourfold system, in which each of the engaged ways of life is endlessly chewing bits off the others, the hermit is sustained not by the unalloyed truth but by his own distinctive myth: Nature Resilient.

Of course, these myths are also contradictory in that they cannot all be true in the same time and place. Nature cannot be both cornucopian and fragile, for instance, except in regard to different objects, times, places, and conditions. Neither can any of the other myths be true all the time, everywhere, and under all conditions. That is why we refer to transcendence as a claim like the others, partial and imperfect. But it does serve to justify belief in an autonomous culture, and it does capture some essence of experience and wisdom that is not captured by the other myths of nature.

The hermit takes his cue from *The Tibetan Book of the Great Liberation*:

> There being really no duality,
> pluralism is untrue.
> Until duality is transcended and
> at-one-ment realized,
> Enlightenment cannot be attained.[4]

When the hermit looks at the myths of nature that go with the four engaged ways of life, he sees that despite their contradictions, they are all dualistic. They all assume the clear separation of ball and landscape. His distaste for this sort of dualism is now shared by many physical and social scientists.

Both natural and man-made systems now provide us with many instances in which the movement of the ball actually alters the shape of the landscape through which it moves. Ecologists, for instance, find that stability regions can suddenly implode, and economists are aware that the decisions of individual firms, in aggregate, can alter the overall environment within which each of those decisions makes economic sense.[5] Studies of fisheries and of farming systems in Canada have shown how policies that are based on the myth of Nature Perverse/Tolerant start well but end up increasing the "brittleness" (and, hence, the unmanageability) of those systems.[6] Keeping the ball away from the boundary works and goes on working until that unsuspected moment when the bowl, which has been getting steadily shallower, ceases to be a bowl and becomes a bump instead. All is then lost; the tolerant pocket, which was the key to the management of the system, has disappeared, and nature is suddenly everywhere perverse (a situation that is made sense of by the myth of Nature Ephemeral). Mathematicians refer to these sudden and discontinuous changes as "nonlinearities"; they are currently the focus of much attention. The earth's atmosphere, it is feared, may suddenly flip over into a new system-state in response to the changes we are making to its constitution. (Whether the earth's temperature will become hotter or colder, or either in different regions, and how soon, is very much the object of dispute.) On a more local level, there is growing concern that economic management is relying on a linear model to manage a nonlinear economy.

Nature Resilient, in transcending the duality of ball and landscape, captures the transformational properties of the world that are ignored by the other four myths. Since the hermit's myth is concerned with transformation, it is not so easily depicted as are the other four. The easiest way to visualize Nature Resilient is to consider what would happen to both ball and landscape if the ball sucked up the landscape as it moved through it. If we start off with a bowl-shaped landscape, we find that it changes first to a depression on a mesa, then to a flat surface, and then to an up-turned bowl. In the last situation, the ball will roll off, coming to rest only when it finds its way into another depression. This completes the transformational cycle, and the next one starts off from this new hollow. In this way the cycle—the myth of Nature Resilient—repeats itself but history does not. We come, not full cycle, but full spiral (Figure 3).[7]

Figure 3 is the graphical representation of the myth of Nature Resilient. In it the pictures that capture each of the myths that sustain the four engaged ways of life become "stills" in a sequence of transformations that takes us from Nature Benign, through Nature Perverse/Tolerant, and then Nature Capricious, to Nature Ephemeral. The hermit's myth, since it captures these transformational properties, which are missed by all four of the myths that keep the engaged ways of life engaged, certainly contains both truth and wisdom. Moreover, since the hermit's myth subsumes all the other myths within itself, we may be tempted to conclude (as do those who cleave to the hermit's way of life) that it contains all truth and all wisdom. Not so. (Or, at least, not so in any social sense. In attaining total enlightenment the hermit leaves the social map.)

Because the myths that guide the four engaged ways of life are mutually contradictory, they each define as rational behavior what the others define as irrational. This means that the myth of Nature Resilient can be reached only if these other myths are treated, not as bases for action (because, taken together, they could only furnish a basis for inaction), but as objects of contemplation. Hermits, therefore, do not

Figure 3. Transformational properties of ball and landscape

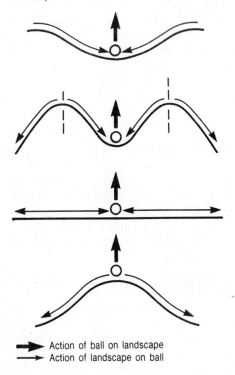

➤ Action of ball on landscape
→ Action of landscape on ball

transcend the other ways of life; they bias themselves away from them. It is this—their autonomous cultural bias—that makes their way of life livable, reproducible, and a part of the proper study of social science. What it does not do is give us (or them) access to a transcendental social science.

The hermit's myth, unlike the other four, shows us that change is inevitable. The argument is this: Since each myth captures some essence of experience and wisdom, and since the transformational properties of the world are the only features that the hermit's myth captures and the others do not, these properties must be there in the world at times and in places. If they were not, there would be no wisdom within the hermit's myth and it would cease to exist. To act in the world on the conviction that it is one particular way, this myth's existence tells us, is sooner or later to change the world to some other way.

Each myth comes with its own seeds of destruction and rebirth. Though, for ease of exposition, our early chapters in Part 1 are concerned with how people come to bias their cultures in ways that are socially viable and our later chapters in Part 1 (4 and 5) are concerned with how people change from one bias to another, this dualism—stability versus change—is not valid. Without change there could be no stability. Like the ball and the landscape through which it moves, each is a part of the other. In much the same manner, our myths of physical nature and our concepts of human nature reinforce and enter into each other.

Until now we have argued that the viability of a way of life depends on its ability to develop models of physical nature that justify that way. Obviously it is equally important that adherents of each way of life have a concept of human nature that fits in with how they wish to relate to one another. Discussion of human nature no doubt goes as far back as political philosophy itself. Even further. In what follows we hope to explain both why such discussions have proven unsatisfactory in the past (the lack of an institutional context) and what is necessary to make them worthwhile in the future (placement within a theory of viability).

THE SOCIAL CONSTRUCTION OF HUMAN NATURE

Why is it that "for two generations the . . . concept [of human nature] was officiously, if not officially, pronounced dead by many social scientists"?[8] Peter Corning's answer is that "empirically oriented social scientists" regarded the question "what is human nature" as leading to simplistic generalizations, while "normatively oriented scholars" believed that even asking the question was inherently biased toward conservative ends.

We believe that, by reformulating the question, the concept of human nature can be revived as a subject of social inquiry. Rather than ask, What is human nature? we ask, What are the social constructions of human nature? That is, what does social life have to be like to make a particular conception of human nature persuasive to people?

Social relations (ways of relating to others) and conceptions of human nature, we have maintained, according to the compatibility condition, cannot be mixed and matched. Views of human nature are inextricably tied to social relations. A change in the way an individual perceives human nature, we predict, will be accompanied by a change in the pattern of social relations that an individual can justify to himself and to others (and, by the same token, a change in an individual's social relations will alter the individual's conception of what human nature is). What has been missing from past conceptions, in sum, is the institutional context within which models of human nature make sense to the people involved.

Egalitarians believe that human beings are born good but are corrupted by evil institutions. This view of human nature is nicely expressed by Rousseau's famous pronouncement at the outset of *The Social Contract*: "Man is born free; and everywhere he is in chains" (and the less well known introductory sentence to *Emile:* "God makes all things good; man meddles with them and they become evil"[9]). From an egalitarian perspective, human nature is not only good but is also highly malleable, an optimism captured by Charles Reich's prediction in *The Greening of America* that "what is coming is nothing less than a new way of life and a new man."[10] Just as human nature can be made very bad by evil institutions (i.e., markets and hierarchies), so it can be made very good by constructing a noncoercive, egalitarian society.

This optimistic view of human nature is essential to the viability of egalitarian social relations (low levels of prescription within a communitarian setting). By making man (and woman) naturally good, egalitarians can persuade each other that (1) uncooperative behavior is a product of the false consciousness that coercive institutions have imposed on individuals (thereby justifying the efforts of egalitarians to raise the consciousness of others) and that (2) a noncoercive (low-grid) and cooperative (high-group) social environment is a viable way of organizing life. Were an egalitarian to become persuaded that human nature is irretrievably bad, he could hardly resist hierarchical arguments for increasing institutional restraints upon individuals, or deny the individualists' claim that there was no sense in trying to remake human nature.

For individualists, human nature, like physical nature, is extraordinarily stable. No matter what the institutional setting, individualists believe, human beings remain essentially the same: self-seeking. By making man self-seeking and unmalleable, individualists can justify a way of life that attempts to channel existing human nature rather than change it.

In *Federalist 10,* for instance, James Madison posits that the causes of faction are "sown in the nature of man." Human nature, Madison argues, is both self-seeking and unmalleable. Because no institutional arrangement (other than despotism) can prevent men from pursuing their self-interest at the expense of the larger community, Madison deduces that the political system should be structured so as to take advantage of the inevitable conflicts among self-interested individuals and groups. Pitting interest against interest, Madison reasoned, would create a political system that generated a beneficial collective outcome (limiting the scope of political power), which was no part of the intention of any of the participants.

It is only after one accepts the premise (human nature is self-seeking and unmalleable) that the conclusion (a competitive political system is best) becomes persuasive. Were one to reject the premise, as the egalitarian and the hierarchist do, the conclusion ceases to be compelling. If man is naturally cooperative and altruistic, why pit one against the other? If man's nature can be changed, why not construct institutions that try to bend man's nature to more noble ends? From the point of view of adherents of the other ways of life, Madison's view of human nature is only ideological justification for the individualist way of life.

Similarly, egalitarian and hierarchical institutions must (and do) teach their adherents to reject Adam Smith's proposition that "it is not from benevolence of the butcher, the brewer, or the baker, that we expect our dinner, but from their regard to their own self-interest. We address ourselves, not to their humanity but to their self-love, and never talk to them of our own necessities but of their advantages."[11] To accept this proposition is to accept that social relations should be founded upon "truck, barter, and exchange." The egalitarian and the hierarchist do not accept this social construction of human nature because it denies that individuals can be motivated by pursuing the good of the collective.

Hierarchists believe that human beings are born sinful but can be redeemed by good institutions. This conception of human nature helps sustain a way of life rich in institutional restraints. Hierarchy teaches its adherents to reject the egalitarian's sunny view of human nature because it would undermine the need for the painstaking regulation of human activities (and make all restraint appear as illegitimate coercion). Similarly, hierarchy has little truck with the individualist view that human nature cannot be modified.

The hierarchical view of human nature is more variegated than either the individualist or egalitarian view. The moral philosophers of the Whig party in the United States, historian Daniel Walker Howe found, "conceived of human nature as consisting of a hierarchically arranged series of powers or faculties." It was the task of the higher powers of conscience and reason to regulate, discipline, and restrain the lower, baser passions and impulses, which, left to themselves, would escape control and wreak havoc.[12]

For fatalists, human nature is unpredictable. Some people may be benevolent, offering an outstretched hand, but more are hostile, only shoving the defenseless fatalists further down. Never knowing what to expect from others, fatalists react by distrusting their fellow human beings. This suspicious view of human nature justifies their fatalistic acceptance of their exclusion from the other three ways of life.

These four views of human nature can be represented by the same diagrams that described the myths of nature. Just as the individualists' view of physical nature can be represented by a U-shape, so their conception of human nature is U-shaped: No matter what efforts are undertaken to modify human nature, man remains self-seeking. The egalitarians' view of human nature, as is the case with their view of physical nature, is best represented by an inverted U: Man is basically good but his nature is highly susceptible to institutional influences. The hierarchical construction of human nature, paralleling that of physical nature, is shaped like a curved and flattened M: Human nature is naturally evil but can be made somewhat better but only within the strict limits determined by the hierarchy. The fatalistic conception of human (and physical) nature is best represented by a horizontal line: Human nature is so unpredictable that it is essentially random in character.

What, then, is the hermit's conception of human nature? By the line of reasoning set out above, it should encompass and transcend all the ideas that are held to with such tenacity by the four engaged ways of life. That the hermit certainly believes in the inherent goodness of man is evident in his insistence that we must not do anything to others to (as the hierarchist or the egalitarian might say) save them from themselves. To do this to another human, in our inescapable ignorance of his or her condition, would be to interfere with his or her *lei* (as it is called in Tibetan): the proper course of his or her life, that is, the course it would follow in the absence of all coercive social involvement. But the hermit at other times appears to believe in the inherent sinfulness of man. Proudly vegetarian American Buddhists were dismayed to learn from their Tibetan teacher that there were weevils in the rice they were eating and that the taking of life was unavoidable even when one did everything one could to avoid it. The hermit, however, speaks not of sin but of ignorance, and this enables him to encompass the hierarchist's low opinion of human nature without having to share his coercive remedy. It is up to the individual, not others, to do what he can to lessen his ignorance (by meditating on the Whispered Chosen Truths, for instance, and thereby dissolving the hierarchist's "erring ignorance" into one of the Twelve Oblivions). He can ask others to help him do this (as long as his request does not coerce them), but they, for their part, should not force their attentions upon him.

The hermit, in subsuming all the rival myths of human nature, inevitably withdraws himself, to some extent, from the ravening desires that variously fuel the engaged ways of life. By then projecting this direction of withdrawal beyond the point he has reached, he is able to descry his unique goal: the state of enlightenment in which all desire is transcended. At that moment, of course, he escapes from the wheel of suffering *and* from the social map. Nirvana is someplace else.

Having changed the question from, What is human nature? to, How is human nature socially constructed? we no longer need, as social scientists, to choose between these competing conceptions. Rather than join in the fruitless debate over which conception of human nature is more realistic than the others, we prefer to show how each way of life makes a particular view of human nature seem more reasonable to its adherents than the other views.

NOTES

1. These two approaches are elegantly combined in David Bloor, "Polyhedra and the Abominations of Leviticus: Cognitive Styles in Mathematics," in Mary Douglas, ed., *Essays in the Sociology of Perception* (London: Routledge and Kegan Paul, 1982), 191–218.

2. Crawford S. Holling, "Myths of Ecological Stability," in G. Smart and W. Stansbury, eds., *Studies in Crisis Management* (Montreal: Butterworth, 1979); Holling, "The Resilience of Terrestrial Ecosystems," in W. C. Clark and R. E. Munn, eds., *Sustainable Development of the Biosphere* (Cambridge: Cambridge University Press, 1986); and Peter Timmerman, "Myths and Paradigms of Intersections Between Development and Environment," in Clark and Munn, eds., *Sustainable Development.* Since fatalists seldom find themselves in charge of major national and international agencies, one of the five myths—Nature Capricious—was not fully described by ecologists.

3. Whether these four engaged ways of life need the hermit's way of life to define themselves against is an open question. While it may be that hermits simply colonize transactional niches that are inaccessible to the followers of the other ways of life, it may also be the case that in providing a reservoir into which the excess pressures of the manipulative system can escape, the hermit is vital to the viability of that which he distances himself from.

4. W. Y. Evans-Wentz, ed., *The Tibetan Book of the Great Liberation* (Oxford: Oxford University Press, 1981), 206. Reprinted by permission of Oxford University Press.

5. To believe otherwise, Keynes pointed out in his *The General Theory of Employment, Interest and Money* (London: Macmillan, 1936), is to commit the logical fallacy of composition.

6. Timmerman, "Myths and Paradigms"; Jagmohan Maini (personal communication).

7. This spiral has now been demonstrated in a computer simulation. Michael Thompson and Paul Tayler, "The Surprise Game: An Exploration of Constrained Relativism," Warwick Papers in Management, no. 1, Institute for Management Research and Development (Coventry: University of Warwick, 1986).

8. Peter A. Corning, "Human Nature Redivivus," in J. Roland Pennock and John W. Chapman, eds., *Human Nature in Politics* (New York: New York University Press, 1977), 19.

9. Jean-Jacques Rousseau, *Emile,* trans. Barbara Foxley (London: Dent, 1974), 5.

10. Charles Reich, *The Greening of America* (New York: Random House, 1970), 350.

11. Adam Smith, *The Wealth of Nations,* ed. Edwin Cannon (New York: Modern Library, 1937), 14.

12. Daniel Walker Howe, *Political Culture of the American Whigs* (Chicago: University of Chicago Press, 1974), 29.

CHAPTER 2

Making Ends Meet

How people make a living is central to their lives. If we can show that there are different ways of "making ends meet," all of which are viable, we can rid ourselves of the stultifying view that there is only one way of economizing and that modern economics is equivalent to reason itself. Once we see how people can bring their resources and their needs together in different ways, we are in a position to ask what is required for social viability, that is, how people can live together so as to justify different arrangements of needs and resources and thereby support their preferred ways of life.

Social scientists generally assume that it is needs and resources, through the requirement that people make ends meet, that constrain behavior. This is not the case. Needs and resources, we insist, are socially constructed. The conceptions of needs and resources are, in effect, supplied to the members of a way of life, thereby enabling them to justify that way of life. The constraints on behavior are thus located in the ways of life, not in needs and resources themselves.

This chapter makes five claims:

1. Making ends meet is fundamental (a point on which we can agree with most, perhaps all, social scientists).

2. As social scientists we do not have to decide between the contradictory answers that can be given to the question, What is the nature of needs and resources and how can they be reconciled?

3. These conflicting answers can be accommodated by allowing for the social construction of needs and resources. "Objective reality" does not determine how people try to make ends meet; on the contrary, adherents of each way of life define needs and resources—human nature and physical nature—in such a way that the strategy they use to make ends meet supports their cultural bias and hence sustains their way of life. Making this allowance for the social malleability of needs and resources gives us three "degrees of freedom," which in turn give us

five, and only five, strategies that people can adopt in managing (and defining) their needs and resources.

4. By showing that people do adopt these five strategies and that they do not take up any other strategies, we call into question those theories that maintain there is just one way in which needs and resources can (or should) be reconciled and those theories that insist on an infinite number of ways of making ends meet. Both absolutist (the one right way) and relativist (all ways are possible and right) theories have to give way to a strictly limited pluralism.

5. Identifying the social constraints that bring different people to these different strategies enables us to establish a more discriminating basis for rational choice explanations. If there are several different ways of life with their various modes of making ends meet, then there cannot be just a single objective that the people involved are trying to maximize. What is rational to go uphill may not qualify as rational for going downhill.

RECONCILING NEEDS AND RESOURCES

The exuberant businessman who trots out that old quip about being unable to reconcile his net income with his gross habits is, in a rather backhanded way, boasting about his worldly success; we can be pretty sure that if he manages to push his income a few notches higher he will not take that opportunity to close the gap between needs and resources. No, he will just develop some even grosser habits, thereby maintaining both his insatiability and his expansive optimism. He will be propelled ever onward and upward until that unfair day when death (nature's way of saying, slow down) finally puts a stop to it all.

From this tale we might deduce (like many an economist, sociologist, and psychologist before us) that needs are effectively infinite and that economizing is brought about only by the finiteness of resources. Our needs will always exceed our limited resources, forcing us to set priorities on the things we want and to be continually weighing how much of this we must give up for so much of that. But if we adopt this view of the nature of needs and resources, what are we to make of Po Chu-i?

What I shall need are very few things.
A single rug to warm me through the winter;
One meal to last me the whole day.
It does not matter that my house is rather small;
One cannot sleep in more than one room!

It does not matter that I have not many horses;
One cannot ride on two horses at once![1]

Po Chu-i's needs are finite and they fit comfortably inside the confines of his quite modest resources. If we want to be able to explain his behavior, we will have to revise our idea of how needs and resources are related. Both resources and needs will have to be finite, with the needs fitting inside the resources. On this view, the exuberant businessman is seriously out of control and heading for trouble.

But then comes a knock on Po Chu-i's door. It is a small deputation of public officials come to tell him that he has been living below the poverty line; he does not have enough bedclothes; he is not eating enough; his mobility is inadequate; his small house is in contravention of current housing standards. He is to be moved into an old people's home where he will be properly clothed, fed, and housed. As he makes this involuntary transition to the old people's home, his needs are expanded for him until they reach their "correct" level.

If we want to be able to explain these public officials, we will have to revise again our ideas about the relationship between needs and resources. Needs, in this example, are being imposed by the social order. From the point of view of the public officials, both the exuberant businessman and the self-sufficient Po Chu-i are, in their different ways, irrational (pathological, even) cases that will have to be brought into line if their needs and resources are to be sustainably matched.

At this stage in our story, we have something like two centuries of social science dangling on the end of our line. Depending on whether you take the businessman, Po Chu-i, or the public official as your exemplar, you will come up with three fundamentally contradictory descriptions of the relationship between needs and resources. Which one is right? Our answer is that all three (and another two descriptions that we will come to in a moment) are right.

But how can all these descriptions be correct when they are fundamentally contradictory? The puzzle is easily resolved if we allow people to select the ends themselves, chosen to support their way of life, before they go on to the task of making them meet. Needs and resources, we are suggesting, are *socially malleable*. They can be eased this way, and they can be eased that way (which provides for the variety), but they cannot be eased just anywhere (thereby limiting the variety).

LIMITS TO RECONCILING NEEDS AND RESOURCES

People, we insist, do not just have needs, nor do they just have resources. They are, to some variable extent, able to manage their needs and their resources. Indeed they are able, within limits, to define what shall count as a need and a resource, a proposition that comports with the everyday observation that, under similar conditions, some people feel more needy and some more resourceful than others. Short of needs and resources relating to biological survival, with its unmistakable signs, as in famines, needs and resources do not define themselves; they are man-made.

The businessman and Po Chu-i now regain both their dignity and their rationality. We can now credit each of them, rather than being pathological cases, with the savvy to manage and to define needs and resources in accordance with the distinctive strategy each of them is following. Allowing for the social malleability of needs and resources enables us to deduce four logical and equally legitimate possibilities:

1. You can manage neither your needs nor your resources.
2. You can manage your needs but not your resources.
3. You can manage your resources but not your needs.
4. You can manage both your needs and your resources.

These four permutations allow for rationality to be plural. Behavior, these permutations tell us, is never rational or irrational in itself but only in relation to a particular need-and-resource-managing strategy, and a rational one bolsters one's way of life. For instance, what is rational for people who want to lower needs to match resources may be irrational for those who want to increase resources so they meet needs. The clue lies in the internal dynamics of each of the viable ways of life that leads its adherents to a need-and-resource-managing strategy that will support the kind of life they wish to lead. Our theory, therefore, is not a rejection of rational choice; rather we contend that rational choice explanations are deficient unless they are united with ways of life. Achieving that union is one of the objectives of our theory of sociocultural viability.

The fourth of these permutations—that in which you can manage both your needs and your resources—offers the individual who finds himself with these two freedoms an option that, in effect, is a third freedom: He can, if he so wishes, manage not his needs and resources but the size of the overlap between them.[2] For many individuals it is the size (and sign) of this gap and not the absolute dimensions of the needs and resources that define it, that is the crucial variable, viz.: "Annual income twenty pounds, annual expenditure nineteen nineteen and six, result happiness. Annual income twenty pounds, annual expenditure twenty pounds ought and six, result misery."[3] Of course, it was Mr. Micawber's comic tragedy never to be able to achieve this management goal that he perceived so clearly and described so pithily. But Po Chu-i was able to do it (at least until the public officials arrived on his doorstep), and therein lies the crucial distinction between these two social beings.

We can visualize the interactions between individuals as causing some of them to have one or more of these freedoms "frozen up" and others to have them "thawed out."[4] If they are all frozen up, then that individual has access to only the first possibility: Neither needs nor resources can be managed. As the three freedoms variously freeze up and thaw out, so the individual will find himself at one or the other of the four remaining permutations (the overlap-managing option now making a total of five). The more freedoms he enjoys, the more malleable his needs and resources become, and depending on what he finds he can and cannot do with them, he will quickly find his way to the particular need-and-resource-managing strategy that enables him to make the most of his predicament. The next step, therefore, is to describe these five strategies and the ways of life that each strategy sustains.

FIVE STRATEGIES MAPPED ONTO FIVE WAYS OF LIFE

Possibility 1

The individual who has no scope to manage his needs or his resources really cannot be said to have a management strategy. His concern is to cope as best he can with an environment over which he has no control. Po Chu-i, after being transferred to the old people's home, finds himself in this sort of situation. Both his needs and his resources—no longer in his control—have been assessed by the kind-hearted public officials. Po Chu-i can count himself lucky that the resources he is given are exactly equal to the needs he is given. The rational response if you find yourself at Possibility 1 is to keep your fingers crossed and hope that Lady Luck smiles on you—*survive by coping.*

This response is justified by a view of nature as essentially a lottery-controlled cornucopia. There are clearly plenty of resources out there, but the horn of plenty disgorges in your direction only when it is your lucky day. A matching response to environment can be achieved only by adopting an attitude of fatalism. Putting first things first, fatalists construct a view of nature that operates without rhyme or reason in order to sustain and dignify their way of life.

Possibility 2

Because you perceive resources to be fixed and you believe people can do nothing about them, your only available strategy is to decrease your needs so as to ensure a comfortable (or at any rate, a nonnegative) overlap. But it is no use doing this on your own. If resources are fixed and finite, then one person's gain is inevitably another's loss; to be effective, therefore, this need-reducing strategy will have to be followed by everyone.[5] Little chance of that, you might think, but in an egalitarian and strongly collectivized social context—that of the members of the Voluntary Simplicity Movement, for instance—individuals can all see the advantages of such behavior (not the least of which, as we will show, is the way it keeps them all equal and unites them in their opposition to those who do not adopt this behavior). For this to be rational behavior, nature cannot be viewed as cornucopian; it must be perceived to be strictly accountable. Only then can resources be shared out equitably so that, in the current American usage, all count as one and no one more than one. At Possibility 1 the a priori—the unquestioned gut conviction about how the world is—can be summarized in the phrase: If your number comes up . . . ; at Possibility 2 there can be no such thing as a windfall—nature is a zero-sum (or even a negative-sum) game. Indeed nature is so precarious that the least inequality in the distribution of its resources will bring calamity. Here the catch phrases refer to "fragile ecosystems," "unsustainable levels of consumption," "overloaded arks," and "global villages." By defining resources and raw materials as one and the same, those who follow this strategy are able to insist that all nonrenewable resources are inevitably being depleted and that even the renewable ones must be drawn on frugally. Abstemiousness and simplicity reinforce sharing. Thus we claim that egalitarians construct the world in such a way as to define resources as fixed. They then choose a needs-and-resources strategy (decrease needs) that justifies their cultural bias and sustains their way of life.

Possibility 3

If you cannot do anything about your needs, the only available strategy is to increase your resources so as to make sure that the overlap does not become negative; that increase requires resource mobilization. However, there is little point in going to an inordinate amount of trouble to increase the size of the overlap if your needs are fixed. Po Chu-i in his old people's home cannot fit this strategy because, though his needs are fixed, he is not in any position to manage his resources. But what about those who put him there—the public officials? They are from different departments and different grades within the kind of complex hierarchical organizations that maintain themselves by imposing numerous ranked patterns of needs upon the individuals who compose them. Individually, the members of such groups within a hierarchy have little manipulative ability; collectively (by working to rule, for instance, or by compulsory levies on members) they are able to increase their share of the cake as long as, in doing so, they do not overtake the group above them. If this collective strategy is being pursued at all the different levels of the hierarchy (and it will have to be if the hierarchy itself is to remain in existence), the result is *differential maintenance.*

This response is legitimated by a view of nature as holding up a mirror to society. Nature is seen as bountiful but within accountable limits. These limits are given by the imperative to maintain nature's isomorphism with society—differentials have to be maintained and we cannot allow the reflection to become blurred by levels merging or, worse still, changing places. Leopards, it is assumed, cannot change their spots. If leopards could change their spots, we simply would not know where we were; thus, to those individuals to whom knowing where they are (and where everyone else is relative to them) is very important, spotless leopards are unthinkable. Also taken for granted is that experts know best. If nature could be forthcoming, but only if it is approached properly by certified experts, a collective body must determine the credentials of those who know how to control nature.

Most people, we suspect, will have little difficulty with the idea that you can manage your needs upward and downward. What may be more difficult for them to accept is that some people are not in a position to do this. But those individuals whose lives are hedged about with all sorts of socially imposed prescriptions will find it very difficult to do anything to their needs; these are, in one way or another, just given to them.

For instance, a young subaltern in a smart British regiment will find that his time, his dress, his social relations, his recreations, even his eating, his drinking, and his sleeping (and his sleeping partners) are almost totally imposed by virtue of his fairly lowly position within a complex hierarchical organization. He has to wear a well-cut suit on an informal evening in the mess and he has to wear expensive mess dress on a dinner night. All sorts of compulsory items, ranging from donations to regimental charities to subscriptions to the Polo Loan Fund, are added to his mess bill. If he has no private income, and therefore no scope to increase his resources, he may be tempted to try to decrease his needs. He will find it almost impossible to do so. The additional items on his mess bill are compulsory, the dinner nights are compulsory, even the excessive drinking of champagne and the marvelously idiotic and dangerous games that go with it are compulsory. If he has a private income, he may be tempted to increase his needs: Hard drinking, hard gambling, and hard riding are the traditional avenues. But if his drinks bill, his bridge book debts, and his stable charges rise above a quite low threshold, he will be given a "talking to" by his superior officers and brought firmly back into line.

A complex hierarchical organization maintains itself by imposing equally complex and hierarchically patterned levels of needs upon the individuals who compose it. The result is that though his level of needs may be set quite high, he can neither manage it up or down. On the positive side, the young subaltern's lack of scope helps to sustain the collectivity to which he belongs. It also makes sense to him. It confirms him in his particular rank, defines the gradations between his station and those above and below him in the framework, enables those in these stations to recognize him and treat him accordingly, and impresses upon him the fact that he enjoys the privilege of holding a responsible position within a fine disciplined body of men.

If a hierarchy prescribes the needs of its members, even to the point of regulating their use of their private incomes, then it will also have to ensure that the resources are there to meet those needs. As they say in the military, "The Ordnance giveth and the Ordnance taketh away." Hierarchies, however, do prefer a positive-sum environment because they can then point to all the benefits that trickle their way down the pyramid. "You've never had it so good," said Harold Macmillan—the last great patrician prime minister—to the British lowerarchs in the expansive 1960s. In hard times, hierarchies go on the defensive. They demand sacrifices, institute rationing, and stress that their scrupulous fairness and their highly ordered system of distribution will protect those who otherwise would find themselves most at risk. And in the long run, the sun, they insist, will shine once more.

Possibility 4

Here both needs and resources are perceived to be manageable, and the individual has chosen to manage them in such a way that he also has the scope to manage the overlap between them. This means that, unlike our exuberant businessman, his needs will nestle comfortably inside his resources. If he manages his resources up, his needs then can follow at a safe distance; if he is managing his resources down (perhaps because he cannot manage them up,[6] perhaps because he does not want to), he will have to bring his needs down a little bit ahead of them. Po Chu-i, before he is taken into the old people's home, is in this situation. Though he could probably increase his resources, he chooses not to; there lies coercive social involvement and he has had enough of that.

> People when they are old are often burdened with ties;
> But I have finished with marriage and giving in marriage.
> No changes happen to jar the quiet of my mind;
> No business comes to impair the vigour of my limbs.
> Hence it is that now for ten years
> Body and soul have rested in hermit peace.[7]

This is the rational response to a nature that is essentially benevolent provided that (like nature mystics the world over) one makes oneself a part of it. Provided you do that, nature's cornucopia will be freely available to you. Po Chu-i became autonomous by choosing not to coerce while trying to avoid being coerced by others. For those whose needs are slight (and whose time horizons are short), nature will always provide. When Po Chu-i starts to take some thought for the morrow and to worry about what is to become of him in his failing years, he relies on the winter chrysanthemum to dismantle his alarming time structure.

> At this sad season why do you bloom alone?
> Though well I know it was not for my sake,
> Taught by you, for a while I will smooth my frown.[8]

Possibility 5

The exuberant businessman would consider himself to be in a bad way if he caught himself talking to chrysanthemums; they are for buying and selling. You don't waste your time talking to flowers; you talk to people—important people. The businessman wades straight into all that social involvement that Po Chu-i has been at such pains to avoid. He clearly has the scope to manage both his needs and his resources, and he chooses to reject the *overlap-managing* option and to manage his needs and his resources upward to the very limit of his entrepreneurial skills.

Unlike Po Chu-i, plenty of changes happen to jar the quiet of his mind. He is right in the middle of the turbulent stream of competitive individualism, where success comes to those who boldly and skillfully accept the risks—the opportunities—that present themselves there. Nature is cornucopian, but it is not a freely available cornucopia nor is it controlled by lottery—it is controlled by skill. It is a jungle out there; it is the survival of the fittest; it is nature red in tooth and claw.

Is nature really like that? It is, we would reply, sometimes like that. And if it is more like that than it is any other way, our individualists will do well. But only "if." The same holds for the other ways of life and for the natures they make for themselves.

ONLY FIVE MANAGEMENT STRATEGIES?

Needs and resources have a certain social malleability; they are underdetermined[9] by our own physiological properties and by the physical properties of the world in which we live. What, then, determines them? It is not the physical but the moral constraints, the availability of reasons acceptable to others for adopting and sustaining a strategy, that limits and shapes our strategies for making ends meet. These five strategies are shareable because they match the five distinctive ideas of nature by which they are morally justified. Thus the idea that the three freedoms are frozen up or thawed out according to variations in an individual's social context—according, that is, to the pattern of institutional relationships he or she is caught up in—provides us with a plausible way of connecting needs, resources, and management styles with the processes of social life.

The five need-and-resource-managing strategies allow us to pinpoint what it is, amidst a chaotic welter of values, beliefs, actions, and social relationships, that is conferring viability on some tiny proportion of all the combinations that are possible (thereby ensuring that they can reproduce themselves) and withholding viability from all the rest (thereby ensuring that they cannot maintain themselves). These five strategies for making ends meet are the only ones that contain views of economizing congruent with the models of nature that serve to justify the corresponding ways of life. Should egalitarians seek to expand resources, they could not justify sharing out. Should hierarchists attempt to decrease needs, they could not maintain the differentials required to support graded statuses. And so it goes. Supporters of each way of life construct their ends to make their cultural biases meet up with their preferred pattern of social relations. Their strategies do what is most important to them—uphold their way of life.

It is students of animal behavior, thanks to their focus on biological reproduction, who have made themselves the experts on these sorts of strategies (which they call "evolutionarily stable strategies").[10] They ask how it is that an entire population of animals comes to behave in a way that is conducive to the well-being of the species as a whole, even though individual animals could do much better for themselves by acting quite differently and, in effect, saying, "To hell with the species!"

Taking care not to confuse the actual mechanisms (genetic in the animal case, social and cultural in the human case) by which the reproduction is achieved, we hypothesize that the five need-and-resource-managing strategies are doing much the same for our five ways of life as the evolutionarily stable strategies are doing for the various species. The timeless quality of the examples we have given—lifting Po Chu-i out of the ninth century and putting him alongside contemporary entrepreneurs and bureaucrats—testifies to the long-run stability of the various strategies that these different social beings are following.[11] This long-run stability, we are arguing, comes about because only a small number of combinations of cultural biases and social relationships— those that have come together in such a way as to induce in their constituent individuals one of these five need-and-resource-managing strategies that meshes with their way of life—are capable of reproducing themselves.

Charles Darwin's explanation for the remarkably similar behavior of individual members of a species was that they did what they did "for the good of the species." This, of course, was a *functional* argument. Individual behavior was explained by the beneficial consequences it had for the totality. The trouble with this explanation, as John Maynard Smith has pointed out, is not that it is wrong but that it has a large hole in it. Since most animals are physiologically capable of behaving in ways that would be more advantageous to themselves than is the way they actually behave, an explanation for why they do not do this is necessary.

Maynard Smith's explanation is derived from game theory.[12] He shows that only certain ways of behaving (the aforementioned "evolutionarily stable strategies") are likely to be successful in the long run. That is, those individuals who happen to behave in the way that happens to be "good for the species" will pass on their genes more often than do those individuals who happen to behave in other ways. This means that if you were able to go to a desert island and release an entire population of animals programmed to behave in every physiologically possible way, you would find on returning to the island some centuries later that almost all of them (or, rather, their descendants) were behaving in much the same way. The population, over a number of generations, would have found its way, without any of its members knowing it or intending it, to an evolutionarily stable strategy. The successful behavior would have driven out the unsuccessful behavior— a tautological statement that is saved from circularity by selection among the relative efficacies of the various strategies individuals could adopt. This selection happens, Maynard Smith shows, because some strategies—the evolutionarily stable ones—turn out to be "uninvadable." At the end of this process of self-organization, the genes themselves are still as selfish as ever but the individual animals now look as if they are being altruistic. The question for us will be what we have to offer in place of the biological process of selection, and our answer will be a reformulated functional explanation called a theory of sociocultural viability.[13]

The five need-and-resource-managing strategies meet our compatibility condition in that their biases match the desired social relations of their adherents. Hence our theory of viability fills exactly the same hole in functional explanations of social forms as does Maynard Smith's for animal species. The five ways of life exist, and continue to exist, albeit in different proportions, because they alone are viable.

Our explanation is functional in character, but it differs in important respects from the functional explanations that have been advanced up to now. The gaping hole between individual behavior and its beneficial consequences for the aggregate is now filled by the five viable ways of life. Functions go with ways of life, *not* with entire societies. The intentions of individual actors (though they may well be there) are not necessary to functional explanation. For it is the socially constructed cultural biases (see Chapter 3) that generate preferences. If that was all there was to it, this coherence of the parts would be at the cost of the disintegration of the whole: The ways of life would fly apart from one another. But, as our requisite variety condition insists, it is the mutualities between the ways of life that establish the closure of the whole. The hostilities between the ways of life (see Chapter 5) are essential to their continued coexistence. Hence, functional explanation stands revealed as a form of causal explanation and functional explanation becomes a necessary part of rational choice explanation: Without functions, there can be no preferences, and thus no objectives for individuals to try to achieve through rational, i.e., goal-directed, choice.

Since there are more viable ways of life than previously suspected, both stability and change appear in different garb. Because there are so many ways of life, there is competition among them. Stability, therefore, becomes imbued with activity, running hard to stay in place. More than that, our idea that these five ways of life, for all their competition, ultimately require one another provides a plausible explanation for their continued coexistence. For the same reason, there are many more varied paths of change. Thus there is more change but also more patterned change. These five ways of life turn their conflict with one another into a source of reinforcement, thereby maintaining both the variety and the limits to that variety of social life.

The model for this sort of system—a system that is driven by the competition and the interdependence of its parts—is now well understood by students of prebiotic evolution; it is called the *hypercycle*.[14] A great many amino acids can be formed by the interactions of the simpler molecules that constitute the "primordial soup," but since these reactions are reversible, the amino acids can just as quickly break up. Since these amino acids are in competition with one another for the simpler molecules, the result is a zero-sum game in which none of the competitors ever gets permanently ahead of the rest. Or, at least, it would be a zero-sum game were it not for the fortuitous fact that some of the amino acids act as catalysts for the formation of some of the others. When one of these catalytic sequences happens to join up with its other end, its properties alter dramatically because it is now doing more to hold itself together than the amino acids on the outside are doing to pull it apart. Its game, in other words, has become positive-sum and this gives its components an advantage over all those amino acids that are not part of such a cycle.

It is by this sort of mechanism, so the theory of prebiotic evolution has it, that strong patterns emerge from within an initially patternless soup. The same sort of thing, we are arguing, is happening with viable ways of life. Ways of life are certainly in competition with one another (they need adherents), but if one of them were to disappear, that would break the positive-sum cycle and they would all end up back in the soup. This, of course, is our *requisite variety condition,* and we will have more to say about it once we have clarified the *compatibility condition* that gives us the ways of life, the social analogues of the advantaged amino acids.

Some readers may object that by sidestepping the question of what the innate drives and impulses of human beings are, we have left ourselves unequipped to explain why people want what they want. We deny this, arguing that individuals do not come into the world equipped with a set of preferences. Rather, individual preferences, we argue, come from involvement with others. The next chapter is devoted to demonstrating this proposition.

NOTES

1. Po Chu-i, "A Mad Poem Addressed to My Nephews and Nieces," trans. (ca. 1918) Arthur Waley, *Chinese Poems* (London: Allen and Unwin, 1918). Reproduced by kind permission of Unwin Hyman Ltd. Po Chu-i flourished circa 835.

2. If you are managing both your needs and your resources up, then you can, if you wish, opt for managing the size of the overlap between them. All you have to do is focus your attention not on the absolute rates at which your needs and resources are increasing but on the rate of one relative to the other.

The same holds for the situation in which you are managing both your needs and your resources down. Indeed, if you are to keep the overlap management going indefinitely, you will have to move back and forth between these two states. In the other two possible situations—managing needs up and resources down, and vice versa—the overlap-managing option is closed because in the first situation the overlap is bound to be getting smaller and in the second it is bound to be getting larger.

3. Charles Dickens, *David Copperfield,* chap. 12.

4. Taking this freezing and unfreezing metaphor literally, we can see that the "heat" in this system is defying the second law of thermodynamics. It is flowing from the "cold" bodies to the "hot" bodies in that those individuals who are able to create freedoms for themselves are doing so largely at the expense of those who are not able to do this. There is, in other words, a breaking of symmetry, in which tiny random imbalances, far from canceling one another out, are magnified into mutually sustaining differences of kind. It is this sort of disequilibrating mechanism—the more, the more; the less, the less—that is at the center of theories of self-organization generally. For the breaking of symmetry, see Réné Thom, *Stabilité Structurelle et Morphogénèse* (Paris: Benjamin, 1972). For self-organization, see Ilya Prigogene and I. Stengers, *Order out of Chaos: Man's New Dialogue with Nature* (New York: Bantam Books, 1984). For nonergodicity (the failure of small historical events to cancel one another out), see W. Brian Arthur, "Self-Reinforcing Mechanisms in Economics," in Philip W. Anderson and Kenneth J. Arrow, eds., *The Economy as an Evolving Complex System*. Santa Fe Institute Studies in Complexity (Reading, Mass.: Addison-Wesley, 1989); and W. Brian Arthur, "Competing Technologies, Increasing Returns and Lock-In by Historical Events," *Economic Journal* 99 (1989): 116–31.

5. It would, of course, be true that if resources are fixed, one person, in reducing his needs on his own, would free another from the necessity of reducing his. One person's loss, in other words, would be another's gain. However, since this line of reasoning overlooks the question of intergenerational transfers (not "mortgaging our children's future"), something that is always very much in the forefront of egalitarian concern, it is not morally defensible.

6. One of the advantages of a classical education, it used to be said, was that it enabled you to enjoy life without all the things such an education prevented you from getting.

7. Po Chu-i, "A Mad Poem."

8. Po Chu-i, "The Chrysanthemums in an Eastern Garden," in Waley, *Chinese Verse.*

9. We borrow this neologism from W.V.O. Quine, who has argued that "language is underdetermined by experience."

10. John Maynard Smith, *Evolution and the Theory of Games* (Cambridge: Cambridge University Press, 1982).

11. Anyone who thinks entrepreneurs and bureaucrats are exclusively modern phenomena should dip into the sixteenth-century fairy tale *Monkey,* by Wu Ch'eng-en. (London: Allen and Unwin, 1942, transl. Arthur Waley).

12. Maynard Smith, *Evolution and the Theory of Games.*

13. Studies of lions in the wild have confirmed that lions consistently follow one of Maynard Smith's evolutionarily stable strategies—the bourgeois strategy (so called because individual lions, other things being roughly equal, defer to lions who are already in possession of a resource). Moving closer to human social behavior, a nice example of the same sort of self-organization is provided by the computer tournaments that have been organized around the game of Prisoner's Dilemma. See D. R. Hofstadter, "Metamagical Themes: Computer Tournaments of the Prisoner's Dilemma Suggest How Cooperation Evolves," *Scientific American* 248, 5 (1983): 16–26; Anatol Rapaport, "Uses of Experimental Games," in M. Grauer, M. Thompson, and A. P. Wierzbicki, eds, *Plural Rationality and Interactive Decision Processes. Lecture Notes in Economics and Mathematical Systems 248* (Berlin: Springer, 1985), 147–61.

14. M. Eigen and P. Schuster, "Emergence of the Hypercycle," *Naturwissenschaften* 64 (1977): 541–65; Karl Sigmund and J. Hofbauer, *Evolution of Hypocycles* (Cambridge: Cambridge University Press, 1984).

CHAPTER 3

Preferences

Where do preferences come from? This is the great unanswered question in the social sciences. Indeed, for the most part, it is the great unasked question.

Economists take preferences as given, as external to the system being considered. They can, of course, handle the consequences of changes in preferences—that is what economics is about—but they cannot say anything about where these preferences come from.[1] Political scientists are interested in how people get what they want through political activity, but the prior question of why they want what they want is not normally posed. Similarly, decisionmaking theorists focus on the means used to achieve a given end but rarely ask how people come to prefer that end over some other end.

Unable to say much about where preferences come from, some social scientists have tried to catalog needs. Psychologists, for instance, posit a "hierarchy of needs"—basic needs: food, shelter, and procreation, leading to more derived needs: self-expression, spiritual fulfillment, smoked salmon, and Chateau Latour.[2] The more derived needs, they assume, are only striven for once the more basic ones have been met— an attractive theory that collapses once the anthropologist points out that as you go from one culture to another (or even from one social class to another), one person's basic need becomes another person's derived need and vice versa. Western aid-providers in Nepal, for instance, were horrified to see poor villagers spend their money, not on improving the productivity of their rice fields, but on refurbishing the village temple. The aid-providers (the World Bank, through its Basic Needs Program) had assumed that an adequate supply of rice was the basic need of the villagers. The villagers' basic need, however, was a good relationship with their gods; you cannot, they insisted, do anything about increasing your food supply until you have that.

In avoiding the problem of preference formation, social scientists have been following the unquestioned axioms of everyday life that tell us, "There's no accounting for tastes," "Chacun à son goût," "De gustibus non est disputandum." These ancient proverbs, with the authority they carry, warn us off from asking the unanswerable. Our argument is that, despite all these proverbial assurances to the contrary, a theory of tastes *is* possible.

ACCOUNTING FOR TASTES

> Jack Spratt could eat no fat,
> His wife could eat no lean,
> And so, between the two of them,
> They licked the platter clean.

Conventional wisdom tells us that the preferences of Jack Spratt and his wife are inherent to them as individuals. Both of them, on their own, know what they like and what they do not like; the complementarity of their preferences, once they are married, is just a fortuitous, and rather comical, feature of that relationship. We hypothesize, in contrast, that Jack Spratt and his wife, before they came together, did not really know what they liked and that they formed their preferences in the process of establishing their relationship. This is not to deny differences—their previous experiences with other people, their taste buds and genes—but to point out that, as the existence of "acquired tastes" shows, preferences are usually underdetermined by physiology.

The preferences of the Spratts, we contend, can be explained by the beneficial consequences these preferences have for their relationship. Preferences, in other words, can be accounted for (not always, but often) by their consequences for social relations. We are not claiming that fortuitous combinations of tastes never occur. What we are saying is that in many cases the things (and ideas) that people prefer—from plain food to nuclear energy to weak leadership—can be explained in terms of the consequences these preferences have for their social relationships.

People, we are suggesting, get their preferences from their involvement with others. Social relations are the great teachers of human life. They provide us with our conceptions of what is desirable, beautiful, horrible, normal, outlandish. There is no escaping this social imposition; self-dealing is a curse, not a context. Individuals are not isolated psycho-physiological entities but (in Durkheim's phrase) "social beings." "No man," as John Donne said, "is an island, entire of itself." All are, for better or worse, "involved in Mankind." It is this social involvement that makes it possible for social science to account for tastes.

If preferences inhered in individuals, there would have to be a separate explanation for each individual. Social science, not to mention society, would be impossible. Fortunately (for social scientists as well as society) preferences are never just randomly assembled; they are patterned, both within and between individuals. Choosing what to want is not like ordering à la carte, but rather is more like ordering prix fixe from a small number of set dinners. The task for the social scientist is to describe and explain this patterning of preferences. Whereas explanation in terms of personalities makes analysis too chaotic, explanation in terms of large aggregates (such as societies, tribes, or classes) cannot account for the significant variety that we observe within those sorts of entities. Our theory of sociocultural viability, which conceives of the individual as constrained by the social relations that form him, and of societies as constituted by ways of life, provides the long-sought-after middle way between too diverse individuals and too uniform societies.[3]

DERIVING PREFERENCES FROM WAYS OF LIFE

Preferences are formed from the most basic desire of human beings—how we wish to live with other people and others to live with us. "The real moment of choosing," as Mary Douglas puts it, "is . . . choice of comrades and their way of life."[4] From this choice about how to relate to other people are derived the myriad preferences that make up everyday life.

Preferences are "derived" from ways of life in two analytically distinct senses. First, by putting preferences and ways of life in a means-end reasoning chain, individuals can deduce their preferences from their way of life. Without knowing much about a new development, those who identify with a particular way of life can figure out whether its effect is to bolster or undermine their way of life. An egalitarian, for instance, need only ask whether a policy or practice will increase or diminish differences among people. Of course, people may be, and often are, mistaken. To seek is not necessarily to find a culturally rational course of action, i.e., a course of action that upholds one's way of life.

Second, preferences emerge as unintended consequences of attempting to organize social life in a particular way. In choosing how to relate to others, people unwittingly commit themselves to a number of other choices. Attempting to live a collective life without the sanctions to compel members to remain in the group, for instance, promotes apprehension of an evil outside infiltrating a vulnerable inside. Although no individual is likely to have consciously embraced a belief in an external conspiracy in order to further his or her way of life, the well-defined group boundary separating members from nonmembers—which is so essential to keeping members committed to the group—encourages just such a conspiratorial "us versus them" perception of the world (a perception that in turn justifies building the "wall of virtue" ever higher). Preferences in such a case are less a rational calculation about how to advance a way of life than an unintended and unrecognized reaction that our social relations, as Durkheim argued, impose upon us.

Those few social scientists who have tackled the question of preference formation have largely eschewed the Durkheimian path in favor of the more familiar one of inserting preferences into a means-ends chain of cognitive reasoning. Cognition, we think, has driven out social relations. The concept of schemas is an instructive example.[5] Like cultural biases, schemas are the tacit theories people hold about the world, enabling them to make sense of an otherwise bewildering array of information. They help people figure out what they prefer by interpreting new events in terms of old knowledge. Our theory differs, however, in that biases are not disembodied ideas; they are not merely cognitive. Mental activity is embedded in and justifies social relations.

Moreover, as Schank and Abelson comment, "it does not take one very far to say that schemas are important: one must know the content of the schemas."[6] Neither does it take one very far if schemas are multiplied ad infinitum until there is a schema for every situation or act. By infusing biases with content, and limiting the number of those biases, our theory provides what has been missing from schema theory.

While we do not wish to deny the importance of cognitive "reasoning chains,"[7] our theory pays special attention to the role of unintended and unanticipated consequences in forming preferences. If it were necessary to go back to the sociocultural source each time a new development occurs, building up to the actual preference through a chain of inference, many people could not manage the complexity. Preferences would be far less common or consistent than they are. The ubiquity of preferences presses us to look beyond the individual's chain of reasoning (a small number of premises generating a large number of preferences) to the unintentional choices that are created for people by certain modes of social interaction. Our interest is in exploring the ways in which social institutions generate preferences (to use Marx's phrase) "behind the back" of individuals.

In real life, of course, these two analytically distinct social processes are so closely intertwined that it is often difficult to tell where intention leaves off and unanticipated consequences begin. Consider, for instance, the Sherpa's reluctance to mention the names of the dead. This practice of continually dismantling the past has the consequence of sustaining the Sherpa's noncoercive autonomous social existence, because by bringing down a "curtain of amnesia," it becomes impossible to construct the sorts of genealogies that would provide powerful "charters" for claims to land and social obligations.[8] Do the Sherpas work their way, step by step, through this chain of reasoning, carefully calculating the benefits of following such a practice? Probably not; yet neither are the benefits of the behavior totally lost on them (particularly those acquainted with the anthropological literature on Sherpas). Some Sherpas make the connection all the way from the belief to its system-maintaining consequence, but most trace it only a small part of the way.

Just as when we walk down the street, we do not weigh up all the relationships we have and wish to have before putting one foot in front of the other, so the Sherpa does not have to make explicit his entire moral framework before he can decide what course of action to follow. Life, we concur, goes on, much of it on automatic pilot. Walking, once we have mastered it, looks after itself; much the same is true of many day-to-day decisions that (unlike walking) support certain relations and weaken others. Decision theorists call these automatic pilots "heuristics"; we call them cultural biases. These cultural biases—the shared meanings, the common convictions, the moral markers, the subtle rewards, penalties, and expectations common to a way of life—that become so much a part of us are constantly shaping our preferences in ways that even the brightest among us are only dimly aware of.

Beginning from the premise that it is cultural biases that teach people what to prefer and what to abhor, we can predict such critical matters as blame, envy, risk, growth, scarcity, apathy. These are the grand and eternal themes that any social theory worth its salt should address. We begin with the greatest and longest-running drama of all: whom to hold responsible.

Blame

When things go wrong, as they must, who is held to blame? Hierarchists cannot blame the collective. "System blame," blaming the relationship between the parts and the whole on which they pride themselves, would amount to self-destruction. Instead, hierarchies are famous for their blame-shedding techniques. Responsibility is hidden or (the same thing) diffused among numerous offices. Investigations are quashed or forbidden by Official Secrets Acts. Blame is shifted to deviants, who do not know their place and must be subject to reeducation or sent to asylums.

To egalitarians, who reject authority, it is the system (some combination of individualism and hierarchy) that is held to blame. If egalitarians had their way, suicides would be owed redress by the implacable institutions that drove them to their undeserved deaths. Were society differently organized, murderers would not want to kill their prey. Since good people are corrupted by evil institutions, the egalitarian task is to unmask authority by revealing the connection between apparently benign institutions and the harm they actually cause. Solidarity is maintained by portraying external forces as monstrous, and by accusing deviants of secretly importing evil ways ("hidden hierarchies" and "opportunism") to corrupt the membership. Consequently, egalitarians search for contamination from secret enemies within, the turncoats, the political radishes, the witches, the polluters, who have brought duplicity into their midst.

Individualists attribute personal failure to bad luck or personal incompetence or some combination thereof. Those who complain are told, "You have had your chance and will have it again if you work hard." The competitive system itself remains blameless. People may be dumb, as economic individualists say, but markets are always smart.

Fatalists prefer to blame (and credit) fate. Blaming or crediting the individual makes no sense, for events are not within the control of the individual. The world, as the fatalist sees it and experiences it, does things to you, sometimes pleasant and sometimes unpleasant, but there is no discoverable pattern to these erratic events. Unlike the egalitarian, the fatalist has no group to hold together and thus has no need to identify external enemies. Blame is instead diffused onto that amorphous entity "fate."

Hermits discipline themselves into a transcendence of the various frames of reference that the engaged ways of life draw on in pinning blame. When the renowned Tibetan hermit Milarepa is visited by an academic who wants to incorporate the sage's wisdom into a highly organized system of knowledge, he is firmly put down:

> Accustomed long to meditate upon The Whispered Chosen Truths,
> I have forgot all that is said in written and in printed books.
> Accustomed, as I've been, to study of the Common Science,
> Knowledge of erring Ignorance I've lost.[9]

Alone among adherents of the viable ways of life, hermits lay no blame because they take no part in the struggles of social life.

Envy

Why do so many egalitarians prefer the simple life—plain food, meals without main courses (especially without meat), simple clothes, bare furniture, unornamental "worker" housing? The answer lies in their need to control envy in the face of their belief that distinctions between people are illegitimate. Envy is not correlated with the size of social differences alone but rather with their acceptability. The crucial question is not whether there are large differences in individual or group resources—surely there are—but whether these are viewed as natural or unnatural, right or wrong, appropriate or illegitimate.

The humble life preferred by egalitarians is rejected by individualists, whose way of life depends on the ability of competitors to appropriate the benefits of the risks they take. Individualists prefer to flaunt what they have (a phenomenon Thorstein Veblen termed "conspicuous consumption") so as to show others where the power is and thereby expand their network for future ventures. Envy is the spur of ambition.

Hermits are satisfied with sufficiency, an accommodation that largely removes them from the frenzies of finger-pointing and self-justification that are entered into by the four engaged ways of life. To dedicate yourself to the conquest of desire, as hermits do, is to put some distance between yourself and the debate over what is most desirable.

Controlling envy is of paramount importance in hierarchy because its way of life institutionalizes inequality. Ostentation is reserved for the collectivity—grand palaces, public works, ornate buildings in which the complexity of design mimics the near-infinite gradations of social structure. Hierarchs may wear faded finery at home, but the army and the marching bands and the tombs of the founders are bedecked in splendor. As education inculcates the desirability of differences, envy is deflected by arguing the appropriateness of specialization and the division of labor: Experts do know best.

Economic Growth

Egalitarians have little interest in (that is, they do not prefer) economic growth because abundance makes it more difficult to maintain equality. Far better for egalitarians to concentrate on equal distribution, which keeps them together, than on unequal development, which pulls them apart.

Wealth creation is preferred by the "established" ways of life—hierarchy and individualism—but in different ways. The hierarchy's promise is that collective sacrifice will lead to group gain. It plans to reduce consumption now to create capital to invest for future benefits. Should its solidarity be threatened, the collective may adopt a limited redistributive ethic, buying off discontent, limiting exchange so as to limit losers. Not so competitive individualists. They seek new combinations in order to create new wealth so that there will be more for all and they can keep more of it.

Fatalists are happy enough to see more wealth around. Although they believe they cannot get wealth by their own work, chance may bring it their way. Nor do hermits mind getting in on a good thing, provided they do not have to join a group of some sort or someone else's network. Conviviality, provided it is not coercive, is very welcome.

Scarcity

Perceptions of scarcity can also be explained by the functions they serve for ways of life. The idea of resource scarcity is useful to hierarchists, who can then proceed to allocate physical quantities by direct, bureaucratic means. Resource depletion is a useful belief for egalitarians, who can blame "the system" for exploiting nature, as it does people, and who can then try to get the authorities to change their inegalitarian life-style. The idea that resources are limited is rejected by the individualist because it implies that exchange will make people worse off (and should therefore be curtailed). The individualist defines a resource as a raw material on which human skill, knowledge, and daring have been successfully focused. Since it is the ingenious, inquiring, and experimenting individual who is, quite literally, "resource full," nature's limitations scarcely enter into the individualist's definition of resources. Whereas the egalitarian tries to make natural resources last for all eternity, the individualist's aim is to use up the raw material while it is still worth something.

Being neither borrowers nor lenders, hermits make use of what nature provides. Thus hermits are especially good at scavenging. Milarepa, so the legends have it, lived on the nettles that grew wild around his cave, becoming bright green, and much revered, as a result.

Risk

Why do different people worry about different risks? Following the conventional view of preferences, we might seek an answer in psychology. Some personalities, this view would hold, are risk-averse, while others are risk-taking. Alternatively, one could proceed by grounding risk in the environment itself: Some situations are more risky than others. Both of these views have merit but fail to explain adequately variation in preference for risk. The view that risk preference is inherent in individuals cannot account for why the same individuals perceive grave risk in some situations, say nuclear power, and not in others, say AIDS. The view that the perception of risk is grounded in the environment cannot explain why different individuals react differently to that same objective reality. We have proposed a different view. The perception of risk is a social process. Preferences for risk, we argue, can be explained by the function those preferences serve for an individual's way of life.

For individualists, risk is opportunity. Were there no uncertainty or no danger of loss, there would be no prospect of personal reward and hence no scope for entrepreneurs. The long run will take care of itself; by that time, individualists believe, new combinations and new technologies will arise to mitigate unforeseen consequences.

Hierarchies are not at all squeamish about setting acceptable risk at high levels, as long as the decision is made by experts. Hierarchies inculcate respect for authority as long as decisions are made by the right people in the right place; experts are expected to do the right thing. To suggest that authorities acted out of ignorance or self-interest would be to delegitimize not only a single decision but also the system that authorized it.

By accentuating the risks of technological development and economic growth, egalitarians are able to shore up their way of life and discomfort rival ways. Any system that would impose hidden, involuntary, and irreversible dangers on people is not to be trusted. Egalitarians' predictions of imminent catastrophe—global warming, nuclear meltdowns, deforestation—not only enable them to discredit existing authority for ignoring the welfare of its citizens, but also help convince themselves anew that it is safer inside than outside the egalitarian group, thereby dampening its schismatic tendencies.

Fatalists do not knowingly take risks. What would be the point? All they could do, in their own estimation, is get hurt while having no chance of gain. But others, because of the fatalists' passivity, may try to impose unwanted dangers on them. "What you don't know can't harm you" tends to be the fatalist's accommodation to those risks that, willy-nilly, cascade down on him. Though those who cleave to the other ways of life can demonstrate the wrongheadedness of this rationalization, it serves fatalists well. It enables them not to worry over things they believe they can do nothing about, and it confers on them a sometimes awesome stoic dignity.

The risks that cascade down upon the fatalists alert us to the existence of a whole web of risk exchanges that lace the engaged ways of life into an elaborate (and in many ways counterintuitive) system of interdependency. Since each way of life is handling, in its distinctive way, only those risks that its cultural bias tells it are there, the risks that are missed can be picked up by others (if they see them as worth picking up) or shunted off somewhere else (if they see them as not worth picking up, and provided these others have the oomph to do the shunting). Individualists are good at spotting the opportunities others have missed. They are also good at shunting off those risks that they judge are unlikely to bring them any reward. Hierarchists strive hard to internalize their externalities—to manage the entire risk system (which explains their readiness to set acceptable levels of risk)—but, even so, hierarchists will always be missing something. Egalitarians, though they may sometimes cry wolf, do spot risks that the others have missed. However, since egalitarians tend not to see risk as opportunity, they then do everything they can to shunt off these risks by bringing them forcibly to the attention of the people they see as having generated them.

Economists call these unaccounted-for imports and exports "uncompensated risks" and "uncompensated benefits."[10] Our theory of cultural bias shows us, first, that such transfers are unavoidable and, second, that they constitute an entire exchange system that is operating behind the economic system that is so well described by economists in terms of compensated risks and compensated benefits. This behind-the-scenes system (without which the front-stage economic system would be a nonstarter), though it is far from symmetrical as far as its constituent parts are concerned (individualists, for instance, usually end up long on uncompensated benefits, fatalists long on uncompensated risks), is cyclical (in the sense that none of the ways of life is a circulatory dead end). Each way of life, in saying to the others, "We want (or in some cases are powerless to refuse) what you don't," takes up its place in the hypercycle that confers on these four ways of life their crucial advantage over any others that might try to enter into competition with them. Because of this circulatory system, they are, like Maynard Smith's evolutionarily stable strategies, uninvadable.

But what about the hermit? The hermit adopts a risk-handling style that is characterized by the eager acceptance of myopically perceived risk (a commitment so strongly biased that it is usually enough to deter any adherents of the other ways of life who might have been toying with the idea of becoming hermits). At the same time, his strategy of avoiding all socially coercive involvement results in the risks he takes remaining closely attached to him. Unlike, say, the individualist, he cannot shunt some of them onto someone else. On the positive side, his autonomous strategy insulates him from the unwelcome attentions of those risks that, having been exuded by some other way of life, are looking for a social sponge to absorb them. This strategy results in an impressive imperviousness when it comes to uncompensated risks— they cannot be squeezed out and they cannot be sucked in—and the hermit's way of life experiences neither an inflow nor an outflow of such risks. In this it differs from all the other ways of life.

We can now see how the hermit, by defining himself in relation to the primary hypercycle that is formed by the four engaged ways of life, makes his way of life livable. All it needs are the right conditions, a coercive transactional system from which to withdraw and a congenial niche to withdraw into. Sometimes the niche is geographically defined (as in the Himalayas); sometimes it consists of nothing more than a fortuitous absence of opportunities for economies of scale (as in the inner-city lives of self-employed taxi drivers and the caretakers of small office buildings). Either way, hermits are alive and well and perfectly capable of reproducing their distinctive way of life.[11]

Apathy

Adherents of each way of life select an interpretation of apathy (its causes, consequences, and extent) that supports their preferred social relationships. Egalitarians justify their rejection of established authority by arguing that there is no real participation. They "unmask" power by showing that fatalism is the true location of the mass of citizens. Like the wonderful Steinberg cover of the *New Yorker* where Manhattan has grown so large the rest of the country recedes from view, egalitarians see fatalists as most of the people; they see a nation metaphorically populated by 4,200 oligarchs, 2,000 egalitarians, and 200 million apathetics. All the while, egalitarians seek to recruit fatalists, who, the egalitarians claim, are apathetic because decisions are made for them by the establishment.

The counterclaim put forward by individualists and hierarchists is that apathy implies consent. Failure to vote, individualists would emphasize, indicates only that individuals find the costs of participating in this manner greater than the benefits. If the costs go down (making registration easier) or the benefits go up (a close race), they predict, people will turn out in greater numbers. There are many ways to participate that the individual may believe, individualists would remind us, are more beneficial to him.

Although hierarchists share the view that abstention implies consent, they are also prone to raise concerns that a lack of turnout reflects poorly upon the citizenry's sense of civic consciousness. Thus hierarchies try to inculcate, and sometimes even legislate, an obligation to vote. But participation, in the hierarchical view, should not go much further than the ballot box. What would worry the hierarchist much more than low voting rates is unconventional modes of participation in which individuals were acting outside the sphere of competence assigned to them.

Fatalists believe that apathy is due to the fact that an individual's vote can't make a difference and, even if it might, it doesn't matter who wins. Voting, like every other form of public participation, from this social vantage point, is an irrational act. Alternatively, fatalists may make it rational, in their terms, by seeing the election as a horse race and then trying to put their vote on the winner.

CONCLUSION

In answering the hitherto unasked question, Where do preferences come from? we have provided the first half of our answer to the question of how social relations are sustained. Social relations are sustained by generating preferences that in turn reproduce those social relations. Functional explanation shows that these two questions—how social relations are sustained (the question of viability) and how preferences are generated (the question of preference formation)—are the same question. Were these not the same question, human history would be so chaotic as to be virtually unknowable. Patterns of behavior would die off almost as quickly as they arose.[12]

Each way of life, we have argued, is a vigorous and precarious dynamic process. It constantly has to generate within itself the behavior and the convictions that will hold it together. Stability is not like being in limbo, suspended, motionless, with no energy required. Rather, stability requires constant energy, running, as it is said, just to stay in place. Change is thus stability's permanent accompaniment.

NOTES

1. An exception is George J. Stigler and Gary S. Becker, "De Gustibus Non Est Disputandum," *American Economic Review* 67 (December 1977): 76–90.

2. Abraham H. Maslow, *Motivation and Personality* (New York: Harper, 1954). Also see Ronald Inglehart, *The Silent Revolution: Changing Values and Political Styles Among Western Publics* (Princeton: Princeton University Press, 1977).

3. See Robert K. Merton, "On Sociological Theories of the Middle Range," in Merton, *Social Theory and Social Structure* (New York: Free Press, 1968), 39–72.

4. Mary Douglas, "How Identity Problems Disappear," in Anita Jacobson-Widding, ed., *Identity: Personal and Socio-Cultural,* A Symposium, Uppsala Studies in Cultural Anthropology 5, 35–46; quote on 45. (Uppsala: Academia Up-Saliensis, 1983)

5. See, for example, Robert Axelrod, "Schema Theory: An Information Processing Model of Perception and Cognition," *American Political Science Review* 67 (December 1973): 1248–66; S. E. Taylor and J. Crocker, "Schematic Bases of Social Information Processing," in E. T. Higgens et al., eds., *Social Cognition* (Hillsdale, N.J.: Lawrence Erlbaum, 1981); Susan T. Fiske and Donald

R. Kinder, "Involvement, Expertise, and Schema Use: Evidence from Political Cognition," in Nancy Cantor and John F. Kihlstrom, eds., *Personality, Cognition, and Social Interaction* (Hillsdale, N.J: Lawrence Erlbaum, 1981), 171–90; David O. Sears and Jack Citrin, *Tax Revolt: Something for Nothing in California* (Cambridge: Harvard University Press, 1982); and Pamela Johnston Conover and Stanley Feldman, "How People Organize the Political World," *American Journal of Political Science* 28 (1984): 93–126.

6. R. C. Schank and R. P. Abelson, *Scripts, Plans, Goals and Understanding* (Hillsdale, N.J.: Lawrence Erlbaum, 1977), 10.

7. See Paul M. Sniderman, Michael Hagen, Philip E. Tetlock, and Henry Brady, "Reasoning Chains: Causal Models of Policy Reasoning in Mass Publics," *British Journal of Political Science* 16 (1986): 405–30.

8. Michael Thompson, "The Problem of the Centre: An Autonomous Cosmology," in Mary Douglas, ed., *Essays in the Sociology of Perception* (London: Routledge and Kegan Paul, 1982).

9. From W. V. Evans-Wentz, *The Tibetan Book of the Great Liberation* (London: Oxford University Press, 1954), 20–21. Reprinted by permission of Oxford University Press.

10. See William D. Schulze, "Ethics, Economics and the Value of Safety," in Richard C. Schwing and Walter A Albers, Jr., eds., *Societal Risk Assessment* (New York and London: Plenum, 1980).

11. For details of how they actually do this, see Thompson, "The Problem of the Centre"; and Michael Thompson and Aaron Wildavsky, "A Poverty of Distinction: From Economic Homogeneity to Cultural Heterogeneity in the Classification of Poor People," *Policy Sciences* 19 (1986): 163–99.

12. One way of stating our impossibility theorem (stating theorems, mathematicians tell us, is often more difficult than proving them) is by way of our answer to the question, Where do preferences come from? People, we say, discover their preferences by establishing their relationships. "Establish" has two meanings: putting something in place and determining what is already in place. Until now we have concentrated largely on the second of these meanings, but our theory can also cope with the first—the linked emergence of sets of preferences and patterns of relationships. See Chapter 5, "Reprise: Cultural Theory Restated," in which we state the impossibility theorem in terms of transaction maximizing and minimizing and show how it is that individuals, in striving to make sense of their lives, will end up at one or the other of the five "singularities" that are possible.

CHAPTER 4

Ringing the Changes

The preceding chapters have shown that if a way of life is to endure it must instill values and beliefs among its adherents that sustain that way. Viability requires each social form to teach its adherents, among other things, to shut out perception of some dangers and highlight others, assign blame to some actors and absolve others, accept certain conceptions of physical and human nature and reject others. But if preferences and perception are socially constructed in such a way as to justify particular patterns of social relations, how does change ever occur? If ways of life are self-protecting, instructing people what to value, what to ignore and notice, shun and embrace, how is it that ways of life ever lose (or gain) adherents?

Much the same way, we suggest, as scientific theories lose and gain adherents: the cumulative impact of successive anomalies or surprises. Both theories and ways of life are resistant to change; anomalies are explained away, pigeonholed, ignored, or just not seen. Neither life nor science can stand still while each bit of evidence that might contradict an accepted idea is tested. Were every surprise or disappointment to send us scrambling for an alternative theory, both science and life would lack the necessary stability. Science would lose its cumulative character, and social relations would be characterized by a permanent state of anomie.

But ways of life, like theories, cannot exclude reality altogether. As evidence builds up against theories, or as ways of life do not pay off for adherents, doubts build up, followed by defections. A persistent pattern of surprises forces individuals to cast around for alternative ways of life (or theories) that can provide a more satisfying fit with the world as it is.

THINKING ABOUT SURPRISE

In Chapters 1 and 2 we showed that models of nature (both the ideas of and the myths of nature) are a major means by which organizational stability is secured. In each way of life just one model of nature is capable of providing the necessary stabilizing forces; all the others would result in that way of life's transformation. Just because one must act in the world in the conviction that it is one particular way, however, it does not follow that the world is that way. To the extent that a model corresponds to reality, adherents of that form of social organization will find things going their way more often than will those who are acting in the conviction that it is some other way. To the extent that the model diverges from reality, their organizational form will be at a considerable disadvantage compared to those whose idea of nature comports more closely with how the world actually is.

Each myth of nature is a *partial* representation of reality. If nature were everywhere and always one of those ways, then the other myths would never capture any essence of experience and wisdom. One myth of nature would win every time and the others would rapidly pass into extinction. That the models do not become extinct tells us that nature, sometimes and in some places, conforms to each of these myths.[1] But nature, for all its accommodating ways, does not meekly accept every cultural construction we try to impose on it, and, in fighting back, it generates a countervailing force: the natural destruction of culture. That Dr. Johnson was able to refute Bishop Berkeley by kicking a stone reminds us of nature's ability to point out the inadequacies of some beliefs. This sort of feedback does not, of course, always get through. In a social setting where everyone subscribes to the same idea of nature, there may be no skeptic around to kick the stone deliberately. But if the natural constraint is there, people will sometimes kick stones by accident. Of course, we still may not notice these accidents, but if they are frequent enough and painful enough, we eventually will. In this way, social action based on incorrect assumptions about nature runs up against the unsuspected vetoes that are the means by which natural constraints sooner or later make themselves felt.

The challenge is to understand how these natural and social constraints interact in shaping perception and reaction to surprise. Our theory of surprise has three axioms:

1. An event is never surprising in itself.
2. It is potentially surprising only in relation to a particular set of convictions about how the world is.
3. It is actually surprising only if it is noticed by the holder of that particular set of convictions.

The particular "invisible college" that is organized around the theory of surprise is, at present, much excited about the possibility of a

Figure 4. A typology of surprises

Actual World / Stipulated World	I Capricious	II Ephemeral	III Benign	IV Perverse/ Tolerant
I Capricious (Fatalist's myth)		Expected windfalls don't happen	Unexpected runs of good luck	Unexpected runs of good and bad luck
II Ephemeral (Egalitarian's myth)	Caution does not work		Others prosper	Others prosper
III Benign (Individualist's myth)	Skill is not rewarded	Total collapse		Partial collapse
IV Perverse/ Tolerant (Hierarchist's myth)	Unpredictability	Total collapse	Competition	

typology of surprises. Some have gone so far as to assert that the appearance of such a typology would signal the arrival of a new paradigm.[2] A grandiose claim, indeed, and one that we have our doubts about (a new paradigm is like style; those who go on about it usually have not got it), but it does at least suggest something of the importance that is currently attached to this problem.

A TYPOLOGY OF SURPRISES

Our candidate for a typology of surprises is the four myths of nature that are tied to (that is, are generated by and sustain) the four engaged ways of life.[3] In Figure 4 we let the rows be the actual worlds and the columns the stipulated worlds; we then fill in the cells by deciding what sort of surprise would hit the social being who, stipulating that the world was one way, acted in a world that was, in fact, some other way. For instance, if we have assumed a world in which learning is not possible (Nature Capricious), when in fact we occupy a world in which it is, then we will be slow to pick up the recurrent regularities that are being thrown up around us. And when we do begin to pick up those regularities—when we begin to learn—inevitably, we will find ourselves being eased away from the fatalist's idea of nature and being brought under the thrall of one of the others. Conversely, if we have stipulated a world—Nature Perverse/Tolerant—in which there is a clear boundary between equilibrium and disequilibrium, when in fact the world we occupy is flat and featureless, then try as we may (and we will), we will not be able to obtain the crucial information we need if we are to act rationally. Our information costs, as we put this strategy of certainty-creation to work, will shoot off to infinity and our resources will drain away into a plugless sink. This strategy may well lead us to switch resources to some other area of information needs, but if the world is everywhere flat, we will just be switching those resources from one plugless sink to another. Eventually, if we learn from these surprises that learning is not possible, we will find ourselves abandoned by the hierarchist's myth of nature as tolerant (if manipulated by the right people) and perverse (if manipulated by the wrong people) and embraced by the fatalist's vision of nature as capricious.

The same sort of logic applies to the remaining cells of the matrix; in every case (where the stipulated world conflicts with the actual world) surprises, as they build up, will eventually tip the appropriate social being out of one niche and into another. Along the top-left to bottom-right diagonal, however, there are no surprises because, in each of these instances, the world is indeed the way it has been stipulated to be. If the world, everywhere and always, were just one of these ways, then the surprises that befell all those who insisted that it was some other way would eventually tip them out of their delusions and into that one true world. That this does not happen—that people go on and on being surprised—tells us that the world is never just one way; it is constantly changing.

Without surprises, without expectations against which to compare what is happening, we would lose all contact with the world we both live in and change. Surprises—the mistakes we go on and on making—are profound truths, even though (indeed, precisely because) they cannot tell us what is true.

Since we usually think it smart to discard our mistakes as untruths, we will have to put ourselves through some unfamiliar intellectual contortions before we can see them in this more favorable light. Instead of throwing them away, we will have to collect our surprises (as if they were precious botanical specimens) and scrutinize them for their similarities and differences. This is what our typology—our matrix of actual and stipulated worlds—does. It not only tells us how many kinds of surprises there are and how they differ; it tells us how nice or nasty they are likely to be. To discover that you win life's lottery more often than you expected you would is to be quite pleasantly surprised; to experience total system collapse is to be very unpleasantly surprised.

Once we know how nice or nasty these various surprises are likely to be, our matrix is transformed into what game theorists call a payoff matrix. Thompson and Tayler have elsewhere devised a computer simulation of this "surprise game,"[4] but since such a simulation is a lengthy and rather technical business, we will restrict ourselves here to a more straightforward account of what this sort of game entails.

The game starts with the typology of surprises (Figure 4). We imagine, for the sake of concreteness, that we are the management of some substantial industrial enterprise with a fair number of competitors. What are the possibilities?

1. If we are individualists, we believe in the myth of Nature Benign, so we are very optimistic about our commercial chances. The main surprise for us is if we do not do very well. Other people's failures do not really worry us (they must be unlucky or lack our heroic spirit). Our own failure worries us more, though we would hope to try again. What may well shake our worldview would be a systemic failure, a collapse of the market.

2. If we are egalitarians, we believe in the myth of Nature Ephemeral, which tells us not to expect to prosper. Playing in a negative-sum game, we expect competing ways of life to fail and quite possibly, despite our protests, to drag us down with them. Thus, we are not at all surprised if we do not win. We will be surprised if we do well, even more surprised if our competitors do better than we do. Both outcomes would imply that the outside world is not as inhospitable as we had thought.

3. If we are fatalists, we believe in the myth of Nature Capricious. We cannot be sure how well or how badly we will do, but we do not expect to be able to do anything to improve our chances. Nor do we expect to see any consistent trends. The only thing we claim to know is that we cannot know anything about our environment. If, therefore, we and others do consistently well or consistently badly, we will be surprised by this new-found predictability of nature, so we will begin to suspect something is wrong with our myth.

4. If we are hierarchists, we believe in the myth of Nature Perverse/Tolerant, expecting to do fairly well as long as the experts our cultural bias tells us to rely on are entrusted with the critical choices. We will be surprised at doing badly, but we will also be surprised if we see

competitors doing substantially better without being as knowledgeable or as careful as we are.

Each surprise is relative to the convictions about the world that are held by the person who is surprised. Each time he is surprised, the hold he has on those convictions is inevitably weakened. Once he is sufficiently surprised, he loses his hold completely and ends up with some other set of convictions.

Keeping track of where all these surprises are taking the totality is not easy. Computer simulation is a great help, but a simple and more elegant way of showing the sorts of things that are going on is provided by the sequence of "stills" that constitutes the hermit's myth—Nature Resilient (see Figure 3).

1. Nature Benign—the state of the world that is most favorable to the individualist—is ushered in once there is an excess of opportunity over existing investment. It is this excess, plus the myriad actions of individual agents, that enables "the hidden hand" to emerge and do its wondrous works. Under such conditions, there is continuous learning by experimentation: continuous, that is, for as long as the excess persists. Nature Benign, therefore, matches the state of the world that is assumed by the neo-Austrian economic theorists.[5]

2. In the next state of the world—Nature Perverse/Tolerant—this excess has vanished (all good things come to an end) and there is no longer anything for the hidden hand to get hold of. Transaction costs rise steeply, innovation brings losses as often as it brings profits, markets fail, and we find ourselves in Oliver Williamson's transition to bureaucratically sustained transactions.

3. As we go into the next state—Nature Capricious—both hierarchy and individualism begin to lose their transactional grip. It is a time of contradiction and confusion, one in which small, egalitarian, and self-disciplined cells can prepare themselves for the recessive realities that are about to overwhelm the conventional institutional arrangements—the markets and the hierarchies.

4. As we enter the next state—Nature Ephemeral—we enter a world in which all scale increases bring punitive diseconomies and the economy itself, like the universe that contains it, winds down and down. Georgescu-Rogen's "entropy principle" and Schumacher's dictum "small is beautiful" make economic sense of this state of affairs.

5. In making sense of it, however, they pave the way for its transition back to the state we started with: the individualist's positive-sum world in which advantages for the bold and skillful, and increasing returns for those who are prepared to act expansively, make economic nonsense of the second law of thermodynamics.

Figure 5. The twelve microchanges

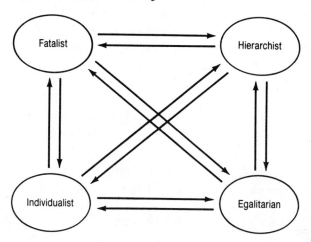

To recapitulate our answer to the question of change: People change their ways of life whenever successive events (that is, surprises) intervene in such a way as to prevent the preferred pattern of relationships from delivering on the expectations it has generated. In the remainder of the chapter, we pursue this question further by exploring the directions of change. How many types of change are possible, and under what conditions are each of these types of change most likely?

TWELVE KINDS OF CHANGE

Our answer to the question of the direction of change differs from those that have been given by the masters of social thought because we have three possible destinations for every displacement, whereas they offer only one. If, as Durkheim argues, there are only two forms of solidarity—mechanical and organic—then the weakening of one will inevitably result in the strengthening of the other. Similarly with Tönnies's gemeinschaft and gesellschaft, with Sir Henry Maine's historical transition from status to contract, with Marx's relocation of control over the means of production from the bourgeoisie to the proletariat, and with Weber's (and Lindblom's and Williamson's) dichotomy between markets and bureaucracies. If a theory allows only two states for people to be in, then if they move out of one, they must end up in the other.

Setting up four social contexts individuals can live in (five, if you include the autonomous, which we will not do here because hermits withdraw from transactional involvement) gives us twelve types of change (Figure 5).

Of course, just because you can draw these twelve transitions on a piece of paper, it does not follow that you can make them in real life. Some of them may be socially impossible. So a sensible first step is to run through all twelve and see whether we can spin recognizable stories around each of them.

1. From fatalist to individualist is the familiar "rags to riches" story. More gradually, it is "pulling yourself up by your own bootstraps."

2. The reverse, from individualist to fatalist, is the "downward spiral of poverty" or, in terms of New Guinea anthropology, from "big man" to "rubbish man." Transitions 1 and 2 together, when spread over a sizable span of family history is "clogs to clogs in three generations."

3. From egalitarian to hierarchist is Max Weber's "routinization of charisma." In more secular terms, it is the path taken by the troublesome outsider who finds himself co-opted by the establishment.

4. The reverse, from hierarchist to egalitarian, is the path taken by the schismatic: the loyalist who becomes the heretic. In more secular terms, it is the whistleblower.

5. From fatalist to hierarchist is Marx's "dictatorship of the proletariat." His description, of course, assumes this to be a macrochange (one that is taken by all people as they come together to cast off their chains), and it was Lenin who realized that if it was going to be dictatorial it would have to be hierarchical as well as collectivist. At the micro level it fits the no-hoper who gambles all on joining the French Foreign Legion and, in retrospect, sees it as having been the "making of him."

6. From hierarchist to fatalist is the most extreme form of a "fall from grace." It corresponds to "defrocking," being "drummed out of the regiment," "discharged with ignominy," "disbarred," "struck off."

7. From individualist to egalitarian is "Saul on the road to Damascus." One minute he is a "big man" in a growth industry—Christian persecution; the next minute he is the charismatic leader of an egalitarian and persecuted sect. British captains of industry who lose their achieved positions (through retirement or takeover) sometimes take this path, becoming prominent figures in activist groups (like the Soil Association or the Findhorn Community).

8. From egalitarian to individualist fits the person who, having been rudely expelled from his tight little group, "lands on his feet." Many small-scale entrepreneurs—in new energy technologies, in whole-food retailing, and in high-tech waste treatment, for instance—have followed this route. Their careers, if they prosper and become large-scale entrepreneurs, take us onto the first of the diagonals.

9. From individualist to hierarchist is Max Weber's "bureaucratization." At first, the ex-activist's business bowls along on casual but

Figure 6. A macrochange

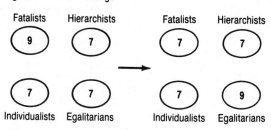

efficient first-name terms. Face-to-face and few in number, he and his employees just get on with it, sweeping up, serving, driving the truck, or whatever, in an agreeably higgledy-piggledy confusion of people and jobs to be done. As the firm grows, however, so the roles and the people who perform them crystallize out into job descriptions, separate departments, salary grades, and so on.

10. From hierarchist to individualist is the "gamekeeper-turned-poacher": the civil servant, for instance, who, having spent many years devising and implementing some regulatory framework, leaves his secure niche and sets himself up as a consultant. In recent years, many British tax inspectors have taken this route.

11. The other diagonal, from egalitarian to fatalist, fits the person who is rudely expelled from the activist group and does not land on his feet. Resourceless, unprepared, and suddenly quite alone, he has no choice but to go straight into ineffectuality.

12. The reverse, from fatalist to egalitarian, is the path taken by the isolated individual who, by chance, happens to display the characteristics that members of some tight-knit group are looking for. Squatting cooperatives in London, for instance, are always on the lookout for real, working-class, homeless families who are willing to join them and have their consciousnesses raised in the process.

That recognizable stories can be spun around each of these twelve transitions suggests they are all socially possible. Any change in the strength of one (or more) of the four ways of life (a macrochange) can therefore be understood as an aggregation of some or all of these twelve microchanges.

The disconcerting message (once there is conceived to be more than one possible destination) is that a macrochange, in itself, tells us very little about the microchanges by which it came about.[6] Take, for instance, the macrochange depicted in Figure 6 (an increase in egalitarianism and a decrease in fatalism): While this shift can certainly be brought about by two fatalists becoming egalitarians, it can just as easily be brought about by a mix of changes that involve no transitions

Figure 7. Two possible sets of microchanges

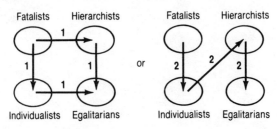

Figure 8. Another possible
set of microchanges

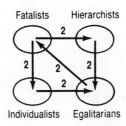

from fatalist to egalitarian (Figure 7). Indeed, it can even be brought about when the only movement of individuals between the two positions is in the opposite direction: from egalitarian to fatalist (Figure 8).

The discrepancy between individual- and aggregate-level change is well known to students of voting behavior, but it has rarely been countenanced within those grander theories that deal with alternative ways of life. Many of the master social theorists, because they work with only two social contexts and assume that change is unidirectional (from primitive to modern, gemeineschaft to gesellschaft, rural to urban, capitalism to communism, and so on), have had no need to worry much about the distinction between macrochange (shifts in the aggregate strength of ways of life) and microchanges (the movement of individuals from one way to another). In a dichotomous world in which change is unidirectional, change in the aggregate strength of a way of life must reflect an exactly parallel change at the level of individuals.

LOOSENING THE CONSTRAINTS

By allowing individuals to occupy four social positions and by allowing for change both in and out of the four ways, our scheme loosens, without abandoning, constraints on the direction of change. Allowing three routes in (and out) of every way of life reveals what is obscured when macro trends are described without specifying the paths of change by which that aggregate change is reached. An increase in hierarchy at the aggregate level, for instance, usually lumped together under the label "bureaucratization," can be produced by three distinct paths of change: (1) the increasing division of labor and the spiraling transaction costs described by Williamson (the individualist to hierarchist transition), (2) the dictatorship of the proletariat (the fatalist to hierarchist transition), and (3) the routinization of charisma (the egalitarian to hierarchist transition). Similarly, an increase in fatalism (what social scientists commonly refer to as "marginalization"), egalitarianism (a process that often goes under the name "radicalization"), or individualism (sometimes called "privatization") can each be reached by three different routes.

The benefits to be gained from this more variegated conception of change can be illustrated by considering contemporary Britain. Margaret Thatcher's avowed aim is to create an "enterprise culture" (individualism). The major obstacle, Thatcherites believe, to the establishment of such a culture is the clutter of institutional structures based on a careful balancing of privilege and obligation (hierarchy). If hierarchy and individualism were the only two viable social positions, it would follow that policies that dismantled hierarchy would produce an increase in individualism. But if, as we contend, there are four viable social positions (and thus three routes into and out of each of the quadrants), then, we would predict, radically shifting social transactions away from hierarchies may also create (or, rather, strengthen) a "culture of poverty" (fatalism) and a "culture of criticism" (egalitarianism). This is not to say that such policies should not be pursued, but to say that those who believe that those policies will bring about a world peopled only with individualists will be disappointed.

Dismantling hierarchy in the direction of individualism entails change in two separate directions: one (from right to left across the grid-group diagram) away from collectivized patterns of relationships and toward individualized ones; the other (from top to bottom) away from differentiated statuses and toward equalized ones.

The first of these changes will increase fatalism. Creating a more individualized social context, in which group relationships are absent or little developed, forces individuals to rely on their own resources. Some—the energetic, the skillful, the adventurous, the lucky—will be able to set themselves up at the center of personal networks and prosper. Others—those less energetic, less skillful, less adventurous, less lucky—will find themselves always out at the peripheries of other people's networks. The push toward "privatization," we predict, will have not only the intended effect of strengthening individualism but also the unintended consequence of increasing fatalism.

The second change—reduction of social prescriptions—will strengthen the egalitarian way of life. Individualists may not be overly concerned with the increase in fatalism that their policies are creating—far from threatening their way of life, fatalism is necessary to sustain it—but an increase in the strength of egalitarianism is another matter altogether. Given freer rein to criticize authority, egalitarians will not hesitate to attack the inequalities generated by competitive individualism. By destabilizing hierarchy, individualists are simultaneously letting loose the forces that can undermine their own way of life.[7]

CHANGE IS ESSENTIAL TO STABILITY

The question of why ways of life wax and wane, like the question of why nations rise and fall, has absorbed most, if not all, of the great social theorists. Yet our knowledge of social change remains fragmentary at best, as is evidenced by social science's poor track record in predicting change.[8] That so many have yielded so little is comforting to us as we survey what we have learned about change.

Theories of culture, it is often said, are peculiarly unable to account for change because they work from the assumption of continuity.[9] Indeed, so close is the association between the expectation of continuity and the concept of culture that change itself often is regarded as evidence against a culturalist theory. Our conception of ways of life rejects this static view of culture as being transmitted unquestioned from generation to generation. Ways of life, to be sure, have an impressive array of ways of reinforcing commitment by directing attention away from discomforting facts. But surprises—the cumulative mismatches between expectation and result—we have argued, can and do dislodge individuals from a way of life. If they are to ensure the continued allegiance of individuals, ways of life must deliver at least some of what they promise.

We would go a step further and suggest that change is essential to the stability of a way of life. Individualism, for instance, in order to maintain itself, must push some individuals up-grid into the fatalist category. The movement of individuals between the different ways of life is not some additional complication that the basic theoretical framework has somehow to cope with; it is essential to the framework's very existence. Stability without change is like trying to balance oneself on a bicycle without turning the pedals. Just as turning the pedals of a bike is essential to stabilizing the rider, so change is essential to the maintenance of cultural patterns.[10]

Having explained why people are tipped from one way of life to another, we are presented with another puzzle: How is it, as this tipping proceeds, that one way of life does not eventually win out over all the others? What stops everyone from moving to a single way of life? That this does not occur is plain enough: The variety in ways of life is all around us. But how are we to explain this fact? This is the question we pose and answer in Chapter 5.

NOTES

1. The mythic and the actual worlds are never completely separate realms. People act in the world on the basis of how they believe it to be, and in acting, they profoundly change that world. In other words, the world does not sit there; it changes, and much of that change is *endogenous,* namely, change that is generated by interactions among the purveyors of rival myths who seek to support the ways of life within which they are ensconced.

2. The theory of surprise is well summarized in W. C. Clark and R. E. Munn, eds., *Sustainable Development of the Biosphere* (Cambridge: Cambridge University Press, 1986).

3. The hermit's withdrawal from all this engagement means that in this chapter and in Chapter 5 we can largely ignore his myth.

4. Michael Thompson and Paul Tayler, "The Surprise Game: An Exploration of Constrained Relativism," Warwick Papers in Management, no. 1, Institute for Management Research and Development (Coventry: University of Warwick, 1986).

5. F. A. Hayek, *Individualism and Economic Order* (Chicago: University of Chicago Press, 1948); Israel M. Kirzner, *Competition and Entrepreneurship* (Chicago: University of Chicago Press, 1973).

6. Allowing for the fifth context—the hermit's—filling up and emptying as individuals use it as a transitional state in going from one of the four states to another, it tells us even less.

7. This argument parallels in certain respects that made by Joseph A. Schumpeter in *Capitalism, Socialism, and Democracy* (New York: Harper, 1942).

8. See Raymond Boudon, "Why Theories of Social Change Fail: Some Methodological Thoughts," *Public Opinion Quarterly* 47, 2 (Summer 1983): 143–60; and Seymour Martin Lipset, "The Limits of Social Science," *Public Opinion,* October-November 1981, 2–9.

9. See, for example, Ronald Rogowski, *Rational Legitimacy* (Princeton: Princeton University Press, 1974).

10. On "pattern-maintaining change," see Harry Eckstein, "Culturalist Theory of Political Change," *American Political Science Review* 82, 3 (September 1988): 789–804, quote on 793–94.

CHAPTER 5

Instability of the Parts, Coherence of the Whole

Look up at a flock of starlings and you will see that though the flock can remain directly overhead for minutes on end, its shape undergoes constant change. Its shape *has* to change. The flock itself can avoid moving away only if the individual starlings are continually changing their positions within it. Contrast this with migrating birds—geese or pelicans, for instance—which assume an aerodynamically optimal V-formation that remains roughly fixed throughout their flight. What geese and pelicans cannot do, having chosen this unchanging pattern, is remain directly overhead the way starlings do.

Human beings, in our view, are organized much like a flock of starlings. This conception of human life conflicts with that offered by most social science theories, which implicitly treat mankind as more analogous to geese or pelicans. We prefer the starling analogy because it suggests that change is (1) ubiquitous and endogenous, (2) necessary to stability, and (3) neither unilinear nor unidirectional. The relative strengths of the rival ways of life, we maintain, are constantly ebbing and flowing, but no one way of life ever wins. Far from rushing off, gooselike, along some predetermined flight path, whether capitalism or communism, ruin or salvation, human life, like the flock of starlings, stays intact while changing shape.

TRAVELING HOPEFULLY, NEVER ARRIVING

For starlings, as for humans, change is pervasive. In contrast to a skein of geese, whose fixed formation changes only with some environmental disturbance (gunshot from hunters, for instance), change is built into the starling flock. If the starlings stopped moving, the flock would fall to the ground; if they got themselves into a fixed formation, the flock would not remain overhead. They could, of course, arrange them-

selves into a fixed sequence and fly round and round in circles, but
this would mean that the flock would have an empty center, like a
doughnut, and that some starlings would be flying flat out all the time
while others would be trying desperately not to stall. Starlings, being
sensible birds, reject this doughnut option in favor of a much less
stressful pattern of movement between the four quadrants that define
their airspace.[1] It is worthwhile pausing here to ask what this option
entails. The dynamics of this pattern of movement are by no means
obvious; they are remarkably different from those that enable geese
and pelicans to go from point A to point B, and, most important for
social scientists, these dynamics have much in common with the erratic
patterns of movement between the four ways of life that constitute the
human equivalent of the starlings' flock: society.[2]

At this stage in the development of our theory we have shown:

1. There are five, and just five, ways of life that are viable.
2. Each of these ways of life is viable only if all the others are
   present.
3. These essential mutualities can be sorted out into two linked
   hypercycles: a primary hypercycle in which each of the four
   engaged ways of life does something vital for the others that they
   cannot do for themselves, and a secondary hypercycle in which
   the hermit is able to withdraw from all the intense transactional
   activity generated by the primary hypercycle.
4. Each way of life is dynamically stabilized, that is, the movement
   of individuals in and out is a necessary condition for its persistence through time.
5. (If we consider just the primary hypercycle) these movements in
   and out can follow any of the twelve transitions that are logically
   possible.
6. It is the cumulative mismatches between promise and performance
   that, from time to time, dislodge an individual from his or her
   way of life.

These, we can now say, are the specifications for the *total system*. The
question we are asking in this chapter is, What does this total system
look like?

The first part of our answer is that the system looks nothing like
the dualistic schemes that have long dominated social science thinking.
The second part of our answer is that a system built upon these
specifications is likely to be extraordinarily inaccessible. J.B.S. Haldane
(who was reputed to know more science than any other person) was
of the opinion that the world is not only queerer than we imagine it

to be but queerer than we could ever imagine it to be; current developments in the theory of chaos (strange attractors, fractals, random walks between reflecting and absorbing boundaries, and so on) strongly suggest he was right. One of our aims in developing cultural theory is to modernize social science by detaching it from the overdeterministic and unqueer assumptions in which it is at present trapped. To this end, having specified our total system, we will now try to explore it a little by taking just its primary hypercycle—the four engaged ways of life—and asking ourselves what sorts of properties it must have if it is the dynamic homologue of the starlings' flock.

Since there is no Generalissimo Starling to tell each bird when to move and where to move to, individual starlings must be responding to some easily read signals that are built into their relationships with their fellows. Overcrowding is such a signal. The birds want to be together—that ensures they remain a flock—but if they end up too close together, their ability to keep flying will become impaired. If each individual bird follows the rule "Stay in your quadrant until it become too crowded, then move to one of the other quadrants," the flock itself will remain both airborne and overhead. The four quadrants of the airspace, when combined with this simple rule, provide the constraints that must be at work if the micro level, the individual starlings, is to aggregate into a flock at the macro level. The starlings are the flock and the flock is the starlings if, and only if, these conditions are met.

Initially, the urge to be together results in the starlings flying quite strongly in one direction, causing the flock to bulge in that quadrant of their airspace and to grow smaller in the other three. Before they can all end up in that quadrant, however, the countervailing force comes into play as some of the starlings fly away from this by now overcrowded quadrant into one or more of the others, which, as a consequence of the initial surge, have become less crowded and therefore more attractive. If the starlings lived in a two-dimensional world, these endless reversals of opportunity that come with overcrowding of first one quadrant and then another would lead to a straight back and forth oscillation between the initial direction of movement and its reverse. But the starlings' three-dimensional world is more loosely constrained.

As one quadrant becomes overcrowded, an individual starling is able to leave through any one of three exits. Not all of them will leave, nor will those who do leave all leave by the same exit, nor is it likely that all three sets of leavers will distribute themselves equally among the three exits. In consequence one of the other quadrants, we cannot say which, will eventually become overcrowded, speeding its leavers in their constrained but indeterminate ways. And so on and on.

This, we can now see, is the homologue of the total system that is specified by cultural theory (and that we have already explored to some extent in our discussion of surprise). Always in disequilibrium, always on the move, never exactly repeating itself, always having a definite shape, yet never staying the same shape, the system itself is indestructible (unless, of course, all its constituents, the starlings or the people, are wiped out). Yet, for all its indestructibility, no single shape (or regime, as we might say, in the human case) has material permanence. It is only the competing destinations—the inextinguishable cultural biases for the four ways of life—that persist.

THE MAKING AND BREAKING OF ALLIANCES

Though the dynamics—staying with the quadrant you are in until it becomes uncomfortable enough for you to leave it for one of the others—are exactly the same as you go from starlings and their airspaces to humans and their ways of life, the mechanisms that do the tipping are not. The universal decision rule for the individual human has nothing to do with overcrowding. Rather, it has to do with making sense of his or her predicament: with zeroing in, with others, on a set of values and beliefs that will guide and justify actions that in their turn will, by their perceived results, confirm the validity of those values and beliefs.[3] The universal decision rule, by itself, will ensure that an individual is attracted to a way of life, but it will never do anything to tip that individual out of it. For this to happen, something must interfere with the self-reinforcing feedback loop, so that eventually some other set of values begins to make more sense. That something, as we have already argued, is surprise.

Cultural theory's impossibility theorem states that there are just five cultural biases that can provide this sort of feedback loop, and the theory's requisite variety condition states that none of these five can ever become permanently uninhabited. It is, therefore, this requisite variety condition—the fact that each way of life, though it competes with the rest, ultimately needs them—that ensures that the whole remains a whole. In contrast to the starlings, who are so cohesive that were it not for the fact that each of them needs some airspace to fly in, they would all end up as a point mass, humans form themselves into cohesive clumps that, were it not for the fact that each of those clumps needs the others to make itself cohesive, would go their own sweet ways: five separate flocks, each one winging its way toward its chosen destination. Starlings move ever closer together until a countervailing force cuts in and pushes them apart; humans gather themselves into clumps—ways of life—which then fly apart until a countervailing force cuts in and says, "This far and no farther." Both, however, lurch back and forth between contradictory forces, both have four quadrants, and both have to keep their individuals on the move between those quadrants if their total system is to remain in existence. Both total systems, in other words, are characterized by *permanent dynamic imbalance.*

Since starlings are tipped from one quadrant to another when they get too close together and humans are tipped from one way of life to another when those ways of life get too far apart, the mechanisms by which their two systems actually achieve their permanent dynamic imbalance are very different. Because it is the surprises—the cumulative failures of a way of life to deliver on its promises—that tip individuals out of their way of life, the easiest way of understanding what is happening in the human system (that is, at the macro level) is to look at these individual departures from the point of view, as it were, of the way of life that suffers them. What can those who are still loyal to a way of life do to strengthen it, to increase the number of recruits and decrease the number of leavers? The answer, at its broadest, is to form alliances with other ways of life when they happen to be advantageous and sever them when they become disadvantageous.

Because there is no way of life whose supporters can see in all directions at once, excluding adherents of rival biases inevitably generates nasty and destructive surprises. By rejecting the insight and vision of competing biases, the dominant way is bound to miss opportunities, to make promises that cannot be fulfilled, and to stumble into undetected pitfalls. As one way stumbles, the path is cleared for hitherto excluded ways to say, "I told you so," and to show how they could have foreseen the dead ends, avoided the mistakes, and capitalized on the missed opportunities.

Undiluted individualism, for instance, degenerates into lawless violence. This was a lesson of "bleeding Kansas," in which the absence of authoritative rules defining voter qualifications and establishing who had jurisdiction over disputed ballots, as well as the absence of an authority empowered to settle land disputes, placed the locals in a virtual state of nature[4] in which competing claims could be settled only by resorting to intimidation and murder.[5] Without some modicum of hierarchy to make rules and to enforce contracts, unmitigated self-regulation leads to chaos.

Where egalitarians have achieved a hegemonic position within a nation, as during the Cultural Revolution in China or under the Khmer Rouge in Cambodia, their rule has been nightmarish but short-lived. Without other biases to temper their zeal and to expose the limitations of their assumptions, the egalitarian blind spots have proved debilitating. Believing that man's potential for goodness was being thwarted by corrupt institutions, Mao's Red Guard attempted to destroy all existing institutions in its marauding path. Instead of a new and more just society, however, the result was economic breakdown. The outcome was so at odds with the promise that it enabled rival (i.e., hierarchical and individualist) ways of life to attract adherents and gain political power.

What about hierarchy? Here it might seem is a way of life that could survive on its own. What need could it possibly have for egalitarian gadflies or competitive individualists? One answer is suggested by the experience of the contemporary Soviet Union. The social relations of the Soviet Union are strongly hierarchical, often despotic. Fatalism, according to most accounts, is widespread among the population. The political sphere is regarded as "a threatening, hostile, and alien sector" to be avoided as much as possible.[6] Individualism (not to mention egalitarianism) has been driven underground. Many of the Soviet Union's difficulties, we would suggest, particularly low economic growth and massive coercion, stem from the hegemonic position of hierarchy. The lack of vibrant egalitarian or individualist ways of life allows hierarchy's deficiencies to go unremedied. Authority unchallenged becomes stagnant, corrupt, and unresponsive. Mistakes are more often covered up and repeated than learned from. Innovation is quashed, not rewarded.

The incapacities of the three active ways of life (hierarchy, egalitarianism, and individualism) prompt them to reach out for cultural allies who can compensate for their weaknesses. Thus, adherents of each way of life try to undermine the other ways and simultaneously rely on these competitors to compensate for their way's deficiencies. It is this ambivalence (being both attracted to and repelled by rival ways of life) that generates the "switching mechanisms," which continually forge, break apart, and re-form alliances.[7]

The alliance of individualism and hierarchy may be called, in current parlance, "the establishment." From this mixed-motive coalition individualists gain stability in property relationships and defense against outsiders, while hierarchy receives the enhanced economic growth to pay off its promises to future generations. Hierarchy also receives enhanced capacity for innovation, which its structure militates against, all without fundamental challenge to its division of labor. This alliance is facilitated by a similar disposition toward long-term risk. Adherents of both ways of life tend to play down long-range risk because their sights are on immediate dangers (growth in the individualists' case, cohesion in the hierarchists' case) and because they expect their innovation (in the case of individualists) or their expertise (in the case of hierarchists) to be able to counter distant dangers.

An alliance can help make up for the defects of a single way of life, but it can never provide a lasting solution. Allies remain competitors; antagonism is always there just beneath the surface. Individualists, although pleased to have their contracts enforced and foreign adversaries deterred, always fear, with good reason, that hierarchists may intervene to restrict competition when competition is having what hierarchists deem are disruptive effects. Hierarchy cannot quite let economic losers fend for themselves, for this violates norms of noblesse oblige. Although hierarchists get increased flexibility from joining with individualists, they are also aware of the danger that the excitement of life with the high rollers may lure their adherents into high-payoff ventures that will undermine their ordered life.

Despite their disagreements with each other, hierarchists and individualists often opt for an establishment alliance instead of joining with egalitarians. Individualists, for instance, may put up with the disabilities of hierarchy rather than submitting to the egalitarian demand for redistributing wealth. Similarly, hierarchists may prefer the defects of bidding and bargaining to being undermined from below by egalitarians, who reject differences in rank.

An alliance with fatalism comports well with the egalitarian cosmology that tells its members that the establishment is coercive and inegalitarian. But this alliance also tends to keep egalitarians on the fringes of society, away from the levers of power, because fatalists are not readily persuaded that action is desirable. The egalitarian attraction toward fatalists is rarely, if ever, reciprocated by fatalists, who prefer (if that is the right word) to suffer in silence.

Frustrated by this unrequited love, egalitarians who wish to rule and not just criticize (the "Realos" as opposed to the "Fundis" in the current parlance of the German Greens) may seek out an alliance with one of the other active ways of life. An alliance with hierarchy promises to make it easier for egalitarians to reach decisions. The hierarchists' belief in the sacrifice of the parts for the whole and in the obligation that those on top have to help those below makes it possible for egalitarians to call on hierarchical supporters to enact an egalitarian agenda. The egalitarian hope is to use hierarchical means to achieve redistributive ends, à la Swedish Social Democracy. In order to do this, however, egalitarians must moderate their suspicion of authority. Hierarchists may opt for this social democratic alliance as a way of bringing dissidence under control but will remain fearful that the alliance with egalitarianism may erode the differences between statuses that they cherish. So, too, egalitarians worry that coercive hierarchical means may pervert voluntary egalitarian ends.

An alternative route for egalitarians is to try to make up for their deficiencies by reaching out to individualists. This alliance enables both partners to live a life of only minimal intervention by authority. For egalitarians the cost is a sacrifice in the achievement of equality, while individualists may find that egalitarian jeremiads about self-help cramp their style. This alliance was evident in the Jacksonian era of U.S. history, in which both sides believed that inequality was largely an artificial product of government intervention and that equality of opportunity would thereby increase equality of condition. Where inequality is seen as an inevitable by-product of bidding and bargaining, however, as in the contemporary United States, this alliance is unlikely to remain viable.

Egalitarians are deterred from allying with either individualism or hierarchy for reasons that have to do with both the nature of egalitarianism and egalitarianism's relation to the other active ways of life. Egalitarianism constitutes, if we may use the vocabulary of the Middle East, a "rejectionist front." Allowing no internal differentiation (for that would lead to inequality), egalitarians put all their moral weight on the boundary separating their voluntary collective way of life from the coercive life on the outside. Reliance on a single, impermeable boundary separating members from nonmembers often makes egalitarians more comfortable opposing than allying with the two other active ways of life (hence their affinity with fatalists).

Another inhibiting factor in the formation of an alliance between egalitarianism and either of the other two active ways of life is that egalitarianism shares a dimension of sociality with both hierarchy (positive group) and individualism (negative grid). Individualism (negative group, negative grid) and hierarchy (positive group, positive grid), by contrast, are cultural opposites. The claim that opposites attract and likes repel has a paradoxical ring to it, but the paradox is easily resolved. Precisely because they are so different, opposites have less cause to fear that an alliance will result in one way of life taking over the other. Cultural likes, by contrast, must always be wary that each may be transformed into the image of its ally. Just as political parties compete most fiercely against those ideologically closest to them (because they appeal to similar voters), so cultural likes reserve a special enmity for those just enough alike to be potentially seductive.

Having run through the alliances and shown how, though each of them is possible, they are all ambivalent, we now face the critical question: How is it that the interactions of a pair of allies start off binding them together and end up driving them apart? The answer has to do with the irreversibility (what economists call the "sunk costs") of some of the decisions the allies take in cementing their alliance.

Though an alliance has fewer blind spots than does each way of life on its own (a potential advantage that provides the incentive to form an alliance), it is not without weaknesses, and these weaknesses eventually catch up with it. Blind spots plus investments become time bombs that eventually blow the alliance apart. That is why policies of a decade ago are often so obviously wrong that we cannot understand how they could have been adopted with such enthusiasm and confidence. British energy policy provides a nice example.

Throughout the 1960s and early 1970s this policy was largely shaped by an "energy orthodoxy," in which individualists and hierarchists were allied (by their conviction that energy growth was both possible and desirable) and from which egalitarians were excluded (by their conviction that energy growth was not socially or environmentally sustainable).[8] The blind spots of this orthodoxy, combined with an increasingly turbulent environment (Organization of Petroleum Exporting Countries [OPEC], the revolution in Iran, et cetera), made it difficult for the alliance to deliver on its promises. At the same time, egalitarians' criticisms and predictions, which once seemed far-fetched, even irresponsible, were now given greater credence (for instance, the Central Electricity Generating Board's [CEGB's] projections of future demand, after innumerable revisions, lined up closely with projections made in the 1960s by egalitarians). Those who believed this energy orthodoxy, and the alliance between the individualistic and hierarchical ways of life on which it rested, to be the natural state of things were (and still are) astounded by the "unholy alliance" of radical (individualistic) conservatives and dyed-in-the-wool Greens that suddenly began springing up around them.

The energy orthodoxy placed many time bombs as it busied itself with its investment decisions. For example, the fact that combined heat and power schemes (in which the high-grade heat from the power station generates electricity and the low-grade heat is used for district heating and hot water) are economically viable in the United States but not in Britain is the direct consequence of the highly centralized control that was exercised by the British CEGB. The British National Grid (the creation of the CEGB and without counterpart in the United States) has allowed production to be concentrated in a few large power stations remote from the centers of consumption. Electricity can flow along this grid but hot water cannot. Now that combined heat and power is increasingly being perceived to be a good thing, the overly hierarchical outfit that has ensured that British consumers cannot have it is clearly in trouble.

The time bombs do not just blow the old alliance apart, they create the conditions for the new one to form. The time-lagged effects of the sunk costs associated with their shared decisions explain how it was that the two old pals fell out, one of them making friends with their former enemy, thereby putting his former pal out in the cold. This, we hardly need point out, is a process that has no end.

In its early years as a nation, the United States, to take another instance, was dominated by an alliance of egalitarian and individualistic biases. Lacking a strong hierarchical presence, the nation was often slow to perceive external dangers and to mobilize the resources necessary to defend itself against invasion. Knowing that the threat of invasion is often used by those who wish to justify greater authority, individualists and egalitarians continually played down the threat from abroad. Great Britain, they insisted, was a dying hierarchy, "tottering under the weight of a King, a Court, a nobility, a priesthood, armies, navies, debts, and all the complicated machinery of oppression."[9] When they guessed wrong, as in the War of 1812, the nation suffered humiliating defeats.

The nation's embarrassing setbacks during the War of 1812, including the burning of the Capitol, discredited the dominant alliance of individualism and egalitarianism. Hierarchical spokesmen for authority, who prior to the war were on the fringes of the policy debate, now found their arguments were more persuasive to others. Following the war, it was the hierarchists' policy preferences (reliance on a regular army rather than a civic-minded militia, federally sponsored "internal improvements" such as roads and canals, a national bank, higher salaries for public officials), long blocked by the dominant coalition, that were enacted into law. Egalitarian warnings of usurpation, which before had resonated with individualists, now fell on deaf ears as individualists began to see a need for making peace with proponents of hierarchy.[10]

Is it possible to create an alliance that would incorporate all three active ways of life? Could such an alliance terminate the endless process of shifting coalitions by which a former ally is jilted in favor of a former foe? Such alliances, we contend, are both rare and extremely short-lived. Wartime furnishes instances of adherents of rival ways putting aside their differences for the purpose of defeating a common adversary. Such truces, however, are extremely fragile and are usually jettisoned soon after (and often even before) the common threat is removed. Prime Minister Winston Churchill's defeat in Britain after World War II is but a case in point.

An instructive example of a failed effort to fuse the three ways of life is provided by the Era of Good Feelings in U.S. history, a period that has long puzzled historians. The bitter conflicts that characterized the period extending from the Revolution to the War of 1812 created a desire among many politicians, as well as citizens, for a respite from the uninterrupted battle of principles of the past four decades. President James Monroe assumed office in 1816, vowing to make the Republican party a home for all persuasions, hierarchical Federalists as well as individualist and egalitarian Republicans. Rather than producing the hoped-for harmony, however, the effort to create a coalition of all three active ways quickly degenerated into a politics of unprecedented vituperation and ill will. The Monroe cabinet, because it included representatives of all three ways of life, was unable to come to agreement on important issues of the day. Monroe's presidency became, in Secretary of State John Quincy Adams's words, an administration "at war with itself." The fractiousness and paralysis of Monroe's second term prompted prominent politicians, including Martin Van Buren and Andrew Jackson, to advocate (and bring about) a return to the parties of old that had countenanced no more than two ways of life within an alliance. The formless confusion and ill will engendered by the short-lived Era of Good Feelings is evidence that a tricultural alliance cannot be sustained for more than fleeting moments.[11]

The discrediting of the Old Republicans after the War of 1812, the eclipse of the energy orthodoxy in Britain, the collapse of the Cultural Revolution in China, and the current reform movement in the Soviet Union all illustrate the same sociocultural dynamic: Every bias (or combinations of biases) encounters situations it did not predict, cannot explain, and is ill equipped to cope with. What is anomalous from one perspective, however, is predictable and solvable from another. As one bias (or alliance of biases) becomes discredited, other previously excluded biases are bolstered. The newly strengthened way (or alliance of ways) of life, however, must also be biased, ensuring that it too will suffer if its rivals are repressed or weaken of their own accord. The inevitability of bias, together with the distinctive ambivalences that characterize the relationships between ways of life, thus ensure that although the biases are permanent, no alliance of biases can be. All that is permanent is bias. This is why those who are forever forecasting cultural convergence leading to "the end of history" are always being (and, we contend, always will be) disappointed.[12]

FATALISM'S FUNCTIONS

So far we have emphasized what the active ways of life get from allying with one another. We have not yet, however, said much about the fatalists. What need, one might wonder, could anyone have for fatalists? Fatalists, we suggest, are the cultural equivalent of compost: a rich, generalized, and unstructured resource, formed from the detritus of the active biases, and upon which these active biases, each in its distinctive way, can then draw for their own sustenance. It is through this recycling process that fatalists assume their position in the primary hypercycle.[13]

Fatalists, therefore, are an essential component of the total system, even though (indeed, precisely because) they do not feature in the policy debates that so exercise the three active ways of life. This three-cornered policy arena, we have shown, sets up an endless sequence of alliances that succeed one another in a quite predictable way. In other words, there is nothing queer about it. But the fact that this sequence cannot get going (and then stay running) if there is not a "reservoir" outside it, to take up the excess and at other times to make good the shortfall, suggests that things are not nearly so simple and predictable as they seem. The addition of the hermits, who can be seen as forming a reservoir that performs the same sort of function for the entire primary hypercycle—the three active ways of life and their reservoir of fatalists—makes the total system queerer still. The total system, in other words, may well be queerer than we can ever imagine. All we can do is concede that this may be so and imagine what we can. Here we will stretch our imaginations only as far as the fatalists.

Fatalists comprise those expelled by hierarchy because they do not conform to group norms, or ejected from individualism because they are unable to come up with the entry fee, or excluded from egalitarianism because they cannot muster sufficient commitment. Movement out of fatalism is likely to be involuntary because, once established there, people lose independent initiative: Masters command and slaves learn servility. Slave revolts are few and far between. Fatalists develop a self-reinforcing cultural bias that rationalizes their resignation. The likelihood, therefore, is that when fatalists do change, it is because they have been propelled out by the active ways of life. Unlike the followers of the active ways of life, fatalists rarely contribute to their own dislodgement.

Hierarchies define themselves as all-encompassing, yet they maintain themselves by casting into outer darkness those who do not fit in. The bottom of a hierarchy, in consequence, is always a gray and contradictory area: the "outcastes" of the Hindu caste system, for instance, or the "social rubbish" that eighteenth-century Britain dumped upon its far-flung colonies, or the "nonconforming users" that are such a bane to city planners. Since the presence of something on the outside of a hierarchy is an affront to it, hierarchists are always on the lookout for ways in which this unnatural stuff might be reincorporated (or, more chillingly, in the case of hierarchies that cannot increase their internal differentiation, for ways in which it might be eliminated—final solutions). Distinguishing the "deserving poor"—those who can be persuaded to present themselves with their needs nicely matched to the resources the hierarchy is prepared to bestow on them—is one way. Sending recruiting sergeants and press gangs to gather up the "scum of the earth" and turn them into disciplined soldiers and sailors, who can then be relied upon to keep the furthest outposts of the empire in order, is another.

Individualists, in insisting that the best of all possible worlds is one in which each sovereign individual bids and bargains with every other, are dismayed to find in their midst many who seem to have no stomach for all this. Bankrupts are supposed to buckle-to and rejoin the competitive fray. That it might sometimes be the individualist's exuberant commitment to that fray that is preventing the losers from rejoining it is not something that the followers of this way of life can comfortably entertain. Their great moral principle—equality of opportunity—is violated if losers are permanently disqualified. But if everyone were actively bidding and bargaining, the incentive for any one person to join the struggle would diminish. Only so many can lead the pack at once. The presence of fatalists makes competition more rewarding, but this presence must not be massive. Competition does require competitors. It requires exactly what fatalists lack (or, more accurately, what they see no point in acquiring or using): organizational skills and sufficient trust to make bargains. Too many fatalists spoil the individualist broth. Excluding some individuals from a game that is supposed to be open to all threatens to undermine the way of life to which individualists are committed. The excluded must be lured back by lowering the entry fee to the point where a little bit of good luck will be enough to get a fatalist across the threshold and into the game once more. But there will always be an entry fee, and there will always be some people on the wrong side of the threshold.

Fatalists are God's gift to egalitarians. Without fatalists, egalitarians would lack ammunition with which to attack the establishment—the hierarchists and individualists. The more fatalists, therefore, the better. Hence egalitarians consistently exaggerate the ranks of the homeless, the disaffected, and the alienated as a means to discredit established authority (just as the other active ways of life will downplay the size of these groups in order to bolster existing authority). Powerless and exploited, fatalists, in egalitarian eyes, are prime candidates for missionary work. Since fatalists are the meek who, one day, will inherit the earth, the egalitarians' task is to "empower" them so that the glorious day is not postponed indefinitely. Although egalitarians deplore apathy, it is the presence of such an apathetic population that fuels the outraged fervor by which they stabilize themselves.

Each relationship with fatalists is ambivalent: Disdain for their way of life is mixed with a dependence on those people being the way they are. Apathy is anathema to the egalitarian way of life, which requires everyone to participate in (nearly) every decision; yet the apathy of others, by testifying to the oppression of the system, justifies their actions. Individualists deplore those too lazy to work, but wherever there are "big men" (those at the center of personal networks) there must also be "rubbish men" (those at the peripheries of other people's networks). Hierarchists, though they are critical of the fatalists' lack of overt support for the system, find it useful to have a quiescent mass that will not question the decisions of experts.

WHY PLURALISM IS ESSENTIAL

"What a wonderful place the world would be," cry the devotees of each way of life, "if only everyone were like us." We can now see the fallacy in this frequently expressed lament: It is only the presence in the world of people who are different from them that enables adherents of each way of life to be the way they are.

Many plans for social reconstruction remain utopian because they fail to take into account the ineradicability of bias and the relations of dependence that exist between the rival ways of life. "Ecotopia"—a world inhabited entirely by egalitarians—is one such instance of a unicultural utopia. Another example is Ayn Rand's "Galt's Gulch," a world consisting solely of individualists.[14] Plato's Republic, which would exclude individualists and egalitarians entirely, provides yet another example.[15] All of these worlds can be imagined, desired, or detested, but not lived in, because they fail to recognize that adherents of each way of life need the rival ways, either to ally with, define themselves in opposition against, or exploit.

Aristotle was onto a profound truth about the human condition when he concluded that a balance of political cultures was the key to good government. Our theory of sociocultural viability contributes by telling us why this is so. A nation in which ways of life are nicely balanced (or, at least, "never entirely excluded") is less prone to being surprised and will have a wider repertoire to draw from in responding to novel situations. It will still blunder, of course, but it will blunder less than its more monolithic competitors. The more ways of seeing that are included, the less there is that will go unseen. Those regimes that have largely excluded a particular cultural bias lose the wisdom attached to that bias, and thus inevitably pile up trouble for themselves. If this reasoning is valid, it implies that those political systems that promote a diversity of ways of life are likely to do better than those that repress the requisite variety. Governments need not let a thousand flowers bloom, but they may do well not to nip any of the five cultural biases in the bud.

This variety, we show in Part 2, has been largely neglected by the greatest social science theorists of the nineteenth and twentieth centuries. Though the differences between Marx and Weber, Durkheim and Spencer, are otherwise large, these theorists were all unable to go beyond the goose model of human life: flip-flop between individualism and hierarchy. This neglect, we contend, has weakened their explanations of social viability and impoverished their theories of social change.

CULTURAL THEORY RESTATED

The basic assumption of cultural theory is, as the saying goes, that life is with people: What matters most to people is how they would like to relate to other people and how they would like others to relate to them. Whereas most theories in the social sciences tell us how individuals or groups go about getting what they want from government or markets, cultural theory seeks to explain why they want what they want as well as how they go about getting it. Thus its focus on preference formation, not just degrees of preference realization, distinguishes cultural theory from public choice theories that begin with the unstated postulate: Assume objectives.

The causal mechanism driving cultural theory's predictions of "who will want what, when, and why," to redirect Harold Lasswell's famous dictum beginning "who gets what," is that *as people organize so they will behave.* By social organization, cultural theory comprehends what it considers to be the five viable ways of life. (Why these and only these five are viable we will turn to next.) It is the combination of the two discriminants: group ("the experience of a bounded social unit") and grid (the pervasiveness of "rules which relate one person to another on an ego-centered basis")[16] that leads people who organize themselves in one of the viable ways to seek the objectives they do. Because hierarchists (strong group, strong grid) desire a highly stratified society, a typical proposition would go, they value process (who has the right to act) as much as purpose (say, building roads). Preaudits are a favorite hierarchical mechanism. Individualists (weak group, weak grid) prefer postaudits; because they wish to substitute self-regulation, they wish to be judged by results, their "bottom line," not by following rules made by others. Egalitarians (strong group, weak grid) have a different objective in mind. It is not just building bridges, say, but constructing them so as to increase equality of conditions that matters. Therefore they seek social audits. Fatalists (strong group, weak grid) do not audit others but are instead audited by others.

Given that human life is social life and that people's preferences vary with their way of life, this understanding leads to cultural theory's rationality postulate: Rational people support their way of life. It follows that what is rational depends on the way of life these actions are undertaken to support. Hence there cannot be any one set of actions rational for everyone any more than there could be only a single way of life.

But why must there be at least five but no more than five ways of life? And why must these be the ones we say they are: hierarchy, egalitarianism, individualism, fatalism, and autonomy?

The basic hypothesis in cultural theory (it is called the *impossibility theorem*) is that viable ways of life—distinctive patterns of values and beliefs supporting distinctive patterns of social relations—will be strictly limited by the number of patterns that can be formed from social relationships. Cultural theory is concerned, first, with understanding how many patterns there can be and, second, with interpreting the contentions within any society in terms of the never-ending struggle in which each of these patterns strives to extend itself by chewing bits off the other patterns (the failure of a market, for instance, is also the success of something else).

Cultural theory, in other words, sees each way of life in dynamic contradistinction to the others. Including some people inevitably entails excluding other people. Those who are individualized are not all in-dividualized in the same way. Those individuals who are successful in building extensive personal networks, for instance, will inevitably be preventing those who find themselves toward the peripheries of these networks from doing the same. Nor are those who are collectivized all collectivized in the same way. Those groups that manage to arrange themselves into networks of groups (by establishing ranked and ordered relationship with one another) will inevitably diverge from those groups that (having opted to maximize transactions by ensuring that every member is personally related to every other member) define themselves by their fervent rejection of established inequality.

Cultural theory argues that there are three experienceable patterns of social relationships: ego-focused networks, egalitarian-bounded groups, and hierarchically nested groups, each of which, in maximizing its constituents' transactions, forms itself into a dynamic equilibrium. In addition, there are two other experienceable positions: involuntary ex-clusion from all these organized patterns (the fatalist's experience) and deliberate withdrawal (the hermit's experience). In the latter case, social transactions are minimized, thereby distancing the hermit from all the transaction-maximizing forms of involvement. The fatalist's transactions, as a consequence of his involuntary exclusion, are neither maximized nor minimized; they are imposed on him by the other organized ways of life.[17]

Cultural theory's overall picture is of a fivefold, self-organizing system in which transactions are being maximized (or, in the hermit's case, minimized) without at the same time destroying the cognitive means by which those who are busy organizing themselves this way or that are able to experience, and hence promote, their different ways of organizing. Groups and networks (separately or in combination), in providing both concentrated and patterned relationships, form the foci (the multiple equilibria, if you like) for all this self-organization. But it is not the grand patterns that organize the people, even though the people do end up organized into those grand patterns. If anything, it is the other way round. In seeking to make sense of their lives, people inevitably organize themselves into patterns that enable them to do this. Cultural theory's aim is to explain those patterns and the processes by which they are sustained.

NOTES

1. Why four? The tetrahedron—the "quantum of the universe," as Buckminster Fuller called it—is the simplest geometric form capable of structural integrity in three dimensions (B. Fuller, *Synergetics, Explanations in the Geometry of Thinking* [London: Macmillan, 1975]). If you take its center of gravity and draw lines from there to each of its four apices you will obtain the blueprint for the device (made of four nails welded together at their heads) that striking miners in Virginia scatter on the road to immobilize coal trucks. They could weld more than four nails together, but fewer than four would not work.

2. Though we will have something to say about him presently, we are ignoring the hermit at this stage to keep the argument as simple as possible.

3. The full argument for this feedback loop is set out, in terms of transaction theory, in Michael Thompson, *Rubbish Theory: The Creation and Destruction of Value* (Oxford: Oxford University Press, 1979).

4. More properly, biologists now tell us that nature is seldom if ever like that, viz., a Hobbesian war of all against all.

5. Richard Ellis and Aaron Wildavsky, *Dilemmas of Presidential Leadership: From Washington Through Lincoln* (New Brunswick, N.J.: Transaction Publishers, 1989), 161.

6. Kenneth Jowitt, "An Organizational Approach to the Study of Political Culture in Marxist-Leninist Systems," *American Political Science Review* 68 (1974): 1171–91, quote on 1179.

7. An "alliance" differs from a "regime" in that regime refers to the relative strengths of the ways of life that exist within a given entity, while alliance refers to how those ways of life relate to each other. To describe a regime one would want a snapshot of the distribution of people along the grid and group axes; to describe an alliance one would have to know about how adherents of one way of life got along with adherents of rival ways of life. So, for instance, in mapping "the mid-nineteenth-century American regime," one would ask what proportion of people were individualists, egalitarians, fatalists, and hierarchists. One would probably find that individualists were most numerous, followed at some distance back by egalitarians, hierarchists, and fatalists, in roughly that order. To ascertain the alliances that existed within this regime, however, one would need to look at how adherents of different ways of life related to each other. One would then find that the Whig party was an alliance of hierarchists and individualists (i.e., hierarchists and individualists who were Whigs cooperated with each other), and that the Jacksonian party was a coalition of individualists and egalitarians (i.e., egalitarians and individualists who were Jacksonians sought to support each other).

8. The way in which the cultural biases are inextricably caught up in (and actually make possible) the process of technological change, of which this is only one small example, is set out in Michiel Schwarz and Michael Thompson, *Divided We Stand: Redefining Politics, Technology and Social Choice* (Hemel Hempstead: Harvester-Wheatsheaf, 1990).

9. William Branch Giles, quoted in Drew R. McCoy, *The Elusive Republic: Political Economy in Jeffersonian America* (Chapel Hill: University of North Carolina Press, 1980), 141. Also see Ellis and Wildavsky, *Dilemmas of Presidential Leadership,* 50, 76–80.

10. Ellis and Wildavsky, *Dilemmas of Presidential Leadership,* 80–82, 94.

11. Ibid., chap. 5.

12. For a recent example of this type of convergence argument, see Francis Fukuyama, "The End of History?" *The National Interest,* no. 16 (Summer 1989): 3–18.

13. We are indebted to C. S. Holling for this formulation.

14. Ayn Rand, *Atlas Shrugged* (New York: Random House, 1957).

15. See Karl Popper, *The Open Society and Its Enemies* (Princeton: Princeton University Press, 1962).

16. These root definitions of group and grid are from Mary Douglas, *Natural Symbols: Explorations in Cosmology* (London: Barrie and Rockliff, 1970), viii.

17. The process by which relationships can be built up into patterns can be expressed mathematically in terms of a "transaction matrix," which, it can be proved, has only four (or five if you count the fatalists' "nonsolution") solutions. These solutions have been shown to match the ways of life in Douglas's fourfold typology and to be "truly distinct types that cannot be transformed into each other unless the principal conditions are altered" (M.E.A. Schmutzer and W. Bandler, "Hi and Low—In and Out: Approaches to Social Status," *Journal of Cybernetics* 10 (1980): 283–99; and M.E.A. Schmutzer, personal communication, 1989.

THE MASTERS

Introduction to Part Two: The Indispensability of Functional Explanation

The viability of a way of life, we have argued in Part 1, depends on its generating practices, values, and beliefs that in turn legitimize its pattern of social relations. We have, moreover, identified five viable ways of matching social relations with cultural biases and shown how, for all their ineradicable antagonisms, these ways of life ultimately depend on one another. In Part 2, we ask how our theory of viability (both its typology and its mode of explanation) compares with those offered by the past greats of sociological theory.

COMPARING TYPOLOGIES OF VIABLE WAYS OF LIFE

By comparing our typology of viable ways of life with the more familiar typologies offered by past masters, we hope to make our own more intelligible to the reader. We share Bernard Barber's concern that "one tendency in new schools is to pay more attention to the development of ideas than to communicating them as effectively as possible to others [and defining] . . . for others how they are a continuation of older developments."[1] Our objective is to show that despite its unconventional language of "grid" and "group," our typology refers to many of the same types of social relations that concerned Montesquieu, Spencer, Marx, Durkheim, and Weber.

We wish not only to demonstrate the parallels between our typology and those employed by the past masters but also to argue for the superiority of our typology. On logical grounds, we contend, our types are superior because they are derived from common social dimensions (both the grid and group dimensions measure social restrictions upon individual autonomy), and together these two dimensions give us a mutually exclusive and jointly exhaustive set of categories. None of the masters (Durkheim is only a partial exception) can make a similar claim. Max Weber's famous threefold categorization—tradition, legal-rational, and charisma—for instance, is formed from completely different sorts of dimensions: Tradition is a historical criterion, legal-rational refers to a mode of rationality, and charisma refers to the qualities of a leader. A lack of symmetry, we show, also weakened Talcott Parsons's typologies.

In addition to being symmetrical and systematic, our categorization of ways of life also offers a more variegated conception of social life than that offered by the misleading tradition/modern dichotomy that has formed the basis for so much sociological theorizing. Such typologies as Durkheim's distinction between mechanical and organic solidarity assume that integration (group) and regulation (grid) both decline with the advance of technology. Although it may be that the trend toward increased technological complexity has been accompanied by a general decline in prescriptions and group-boundedness, conflating the grid and group dimensions results in overlooking two types—egalitarianism (positive group, negative grid) and fatalism (negative group, positive grid)—that resemble neither modern individualism nor traditional hierarchy. Moreover, the tradition/modernity dichotomy cannot account for the widespread occurrence of competitive individualism in technologically primitive areas, and the important role of hierarchy in technologically advanced areas.

Our survey of past masters reveals that although social forms closely resembling egalitarianism and fatalism are observed and remarked upon, these two ways of life are not systematically integrated into the original typology. They remain anomalies and as such are regularly pushed aside, pigeonholed, or ignored. Perhaps the greatest strength of the grid-group typology is that the egalitarian and fatalist ways of life are derived from dimensions that can also produce the more familiar categories of hierarchy and individualism. Including these two neglected ways of life, we suggest, adds significantly to necessary diversity without sacrificing manageability.

CULTURAL-FUNCTIONAL EXPLANATION

Our theory of sociocultural viability adopts the logic of functional explanation, which, following Arthur Stinchcombe, we define as an explanation "in which the consequences of some behavior or social arrangement are essential elements of the causes of that behavior."[2] Egalitarians, we contend, blame "the system," endow leaders with charisma, and highlight the risks of new technologies because (although they need not be aware of it) these patterns of behavior sustain their social relations. Similarly, in claiming that individualists adhere to a cornucopian view of nature, promote self-blame, and downplay the risks of technological innovation, or that members of a hierarchy blame deviants for failure and build up leadership, we are making a functional argument that behavior can be explained in terms of the contribution it makes to maintaining a way of life.[3]

Functional explanations are vulnerable to the charge of positing an illegitimate teleology. Illegitimate teleology exists "when it is presumed that social processes and structures come into existence and operate to meet end states or goals, without being able to document the causal sequences whereby end states create and regulate these structures and processes involved in their attainment."[4] To get from the system-maintaining consequence of a behavior back to the cause of that behavior (in the absence of human intention) seems to require a "group mind," i.e., endowing institutions with human qualities of intention and purpose. Not so, we argue. One of our goals in Part 2 is to show that our cultural theory can demonstrate not only how a behavioral pattern sustains a social system but also how that system-maintaining consequence, in turn, sustains the behavioral pattern, all without anything resembling a group mind.

Attempting to answer the question of how patterns of behavior (and the social relations within which these behavioral patterns are embedded) are reproduced has consistently led social scientists to a functional mode of explanation. Yet despite its distinguished place in the history of sociological inquiry, sociologists today regard the "f" word with the same trepidation that American politicians currently regard the "t" (for tax) word. Functional analysis has become, according to one observer, "an embarrassment in contemporary theoretical sociology."[5] It is routinely dismissed as static, conservative, tautological, irrelevant, and worse.

Believing functional analysis to be largely vacuous, some critics have attempted to account for its dominance within sociology and anthropology in terms of the West's "colonial commitments,"[6] or "the middle class's need for an ideological justification of its own social legitimacy."[7] The delicious irony here is that these explanations of functionalism's intellectual hegemony are in fact functional in character: Adherence to functionalism is explained by the consequence this mode of analysis has for a particular social group, in these cases the middle class or colonial elites. No matter how hard sociologists try (and they have tried extremely hard), they cannot get functional analysis to stay buried. Marxists, for example, who have been among the most persistent critics of functionalism, now find that Marx's explanations (as well as their own) follow a functional logic—e.g., institutional arrangements or patterns of belief are explained by their consequences for the capitalist economy.[8] Functional explanations continue to be employed—even if the label itself is now shunned—because, we argue, such a mode of analysis is necessary to explain how forms of social life cohere.

To say that functional explanation is essential to account adequately for social stability is not to suggest that there is not much to criticize in the past practice of functional analysis. Far from it. Few developments would be more detrimental to sociology, in our opinion, than a return to the functionalism championed by Malinowski or Parsons. Among our aims in Part 2 is to demonstrate that (1) functional explanation in the social sciences is not inherently flawed but flawed only in its past practice; and (2) that our cultural-functional explanations can avoid the pitfalls that befell earlier practitioners of functionalism.

The reader looking for a comprehensive history of functional analysis will likely be disappointed by our analytic survey. Our interest in Part 2 is not in establishing the effect that one theorist had on another (the "who to whom" sequence), or in covering every theorist who employed, explicitly or implicitly, the concept of function. Rather our journey through the classics is intended to find (and pursue) promising but neglected theoretical leads, as well as to identify those dead ends that produced the disillusionment with functionalism that prevails today.

Perhaps the most debilitating error made by past practitioners of functional explanation was to look for functions that went with entire societies. The assumption that behavior that is functional for some individuals and groups within a society is necessarily functional for all left functional analysis wide open to the criticism that it neglected conflict. Our theory, by tying functions to ways of life, explicitly addresses the question of conflict. The question of who benefits from a pattern of behavior, which went unasked by those who attached functions to "society," is explicitly confronted by cultural-functional analysis because it allows that behavior, which is functional for one way of life, will often undermine other ways of life.[9]

Among the many criticisms of functionalism is that it produced many definitions and concepts but few propositions. Rational choice theories, it has been argued, are preferable because they can "explain a wide variety of empirical facts in terms of a small number of theoretical assumptions."[10] Our cultural-functional theory shows that the paucity of propositions generated by functionalist approaches is not inherent in a functional mode of explanation. Like rational choice models, cultural theory generates a large number of explanations and predictions from a few simple theoretical assumptions.

Another charge commonly leveled against functional explanation is that it commits one to an ideologically conservative perspective—that by showing a behavior's purpose one is therefore predisposed against changing it. Though past functionalists may have often pursued a conservative agenda, our contention is that functional explanation per se is ideologically neutral. To suggest, for instance, that a belief in an evil outside world helps to sustain an egalitarian mode of social relations is to say nothing about whether we think these beliefs are valid, let alone that the social relations they uphold are desirable.

Our theory improves upon traditional functional explanations in another important way. Dating back to Comte, functionalists have sought functional requisites that are valid for all social systems. What interested Comte, Radcliffe-Brown, and Parsons is what *all* social systems must do to survive. The result of this search was a banal list of (largely definitional) functions that every system must perform. It is not very illuminating to say, as Parsons does, that a "functional imperative" of every society is that it be integrated, i.e., have a means for regulating internal conflicts. If, moreover, one attempts to turn this largely definitional statement into a testable hypothesis—for example, in order to cohere, relations between individuals must be well defined—then it becomes demonstrably false. Both egalitarianism and individualism sustain themselves in the absence of formal mechanisms of social control. Cultural-functional analysis pursues what we believe is the more fruitful tack of asking how types of social relations vary and how these different modes of social relations vary in the resources they can employ to resolve internal conflicts.

Having identified errors in the past use (and abuse) of functional explanation, we conclude Part 2 by showing that cultural-functional explanation, by attaching functions to types of ways of life, can meet the criteria for a successful functional explanation. Those readers who desire evidence on the empirical, as opposed to logical, validity of our theory must await Part 3.

NOTES

1. Bernard Barber, "Structural-Functional Analysis: Some Problems and Misunderstandings," *American Sociological Review,* April 1956, 129–35, quote on 129. This tendency can be seen in its most extreme form in Comte's adherence to what he called the "principle of cerebral hygiene." Comte, explains Merton, "washed his mind clean of everything but his own ideas by . . . not reading anything remotely germane to his subject" (Robert Merton, "On the History and Systematics of Sociological Theory," in *Social Theory and Social Structure* [New York: Free Press, 1968], 34).

2. Arthur L. Stinchcombe, *Constructing Social Theories* (New York: Harcourt, Brace & World, 1968), 80.

3. If an *explanation* of a behavior, belief, or institution is not being offered, there seems little justification for using the term "function" rather than simply "effect" or "unintended consequence." In arguing that certain activities have the *function* of maintaining a pattern of social relations (rather than the *effect* or *consequence* of maintaining a pattern of social relations), there is an implied claim not only that the activity maintains the social relations but also that the activity can be explained by its consequences for those social relations. When political scientist Donald Matthews, for instance, reports that senatorial "folkways" such as "apprenticeship," "reciprocity," or "courtesy" are "functional to the Senate social system" (*U.S. Senators and Their World* [New York: Vintage, 1960], 116), he is offering not just a description of how the folkways affect the Senate but also an explanation of the existence of those folkways. That is, he seeks the explanation for behavioral norms in terms of their stabilizing consequences for the system.

4. Jonathan H. Turner and Alexandra Maryanski, *Functionalism* (Menlo Park, Calif.: Benjamin/Cummings, 1979), 123.

5. Wilbert E. Moore, "Functionalism," in Tom Bottomore and Robert A. Nisbet, eds., *A History of Sociological Analysis* (New York: Basic Books, 1978), 321.

6. See, e.g., Jeremy Boissevain, *Friends of Friends: Networks, Manipulators and Coalitions* (Oxford: Basil Blackwell, 1974), 19.

7. Alvin W. Gouldner, *The Coming Crisis of Western Sociology* (New York: Basic Books, 1970), 126.

8. G. A. Cohen, *Karl Marx's Theory of History: A Defense* (Oxford: Clarendon, 1978).

9. We do not mean to suggest that all functional analysts have ignored this point. Over thirty years ago, Peter M. Blau cautioned that "the same social condition may be experienced as adjustment or as maladjustment, depending on the value-orientation of participants." Blau observed, for instance, that monopolistic practices could be functional in cultures that abhorred conflict and yet be dysfunctional in those "cultures in which some types of competitive conflict are defined as socially desirable" (*The Dynamics of Bureacracy: A Study of Interpersonal Relations in Two Government Agencies,* rev. ed. [Chicago: University of Chicago Press, 1963], 11).

10. John C. Harsanyi, "Rational-Choice Models of Political Behavior vs. Functionalist and Conformist Theories," *World Politics,* July 1969, 513–38, quote on 515.

CHAPTER 6

Montesquieu, Comte, and Spencer

We begin our survey with the eighteenth-century theorist Baron de Montesquieu (1689–1755). In doing so, we are not claiming that he was the first functionalist; one can undoubtedly find functional formulations going all the way back to the Greeks and beyond. Montesquieu is important for us because he attempts to attach functions to *types* of social organization. His brand of functional analysis is radically different from that offered by Auguste Comte (1798–1857) and Herbert Spencer (1820–1903), both of whom tried to find what *all* social systems must do to maintain themselves. Whereas modern "structural-functionalism" took its cue from Comte and Spencer, we take ours from Montesquieu.

MONTESQUIEU

Montesquieu is commonly hailed as a founding father of social science.[1] He is praised (and rightly so) for introducing the scientific method into the study of human societies—by which is normally meant empirical observation and an attention to constructing lawlike generalizations about human conduct. Less often appreciated is the distinctly functional cast of his analysis.

In part Montesquieu's functionalist orientation has been neglected because functional analysis in the social sciences is commonly assumed to have been borrowed from the biological sciences. Yet Montesquieu's functionalist formulations, when couched in scientific metaphors, are expressed in language derived from physics, not biology: "The relation of laws to this principle strengthens the several springs of government and this principle derives thence, in its turn, a new degree of vigor. And thus it is in mechanics, that action is always followed by reaction."[2]

This suggests that whereas the use of the word "function" may be derived from biology, the concept is not.

Although never employing the term, Montesquieu uses the concept of function in much the same manner as we do today. "When a law appears strange and one cannot see that the Legislator had an interest in making it in such a manner," Montesquieu reasons, "one must assume that it is more rational than it appears and that it is based upon sufficient reason."[3] Translated into the language of modern functionalism (and into a hypothesis rather than an axiom), this passage would read: Practices that seem at first glance to serve no purpose must be scrutinized for latent (i.e., unintended and unrecognized) functions. Throughout *The Spirit of the Laws,* Montesquieu analyzes the ways in which "things in appearance the most indifferent" serve (function) to sustain "the fundamental constitution" of a social order.[4]

A particularly striking illustration of Montesquieu's functionalism is his analysis of Chinese social relations. It is worth quoting at length:

> The [Chinese] empire is formed on the plan of a government of a family. If you diminish the paternal authority, or even if you retrench the ceremonies which express your respect for it, you weaken the reverence due to magistrates, who are considered as fathers; nor would the magistrates have the same care of the people, whom they ought to look upon as their children; and that tender relation which subsists between the prince and his subjects would insensibly be lost. Retrench but one of these habits and you overturn the state. It is a thing in itself very indifferent whether the daughter-in-law rises every morning to pay such and such duties to her mother-in-law; but if we consider that these exterior habits incessantly revive an idea necessary to be imprinted on all minds— an idea that forms the ruling spirit of the empire—we shall see that it is necessary that such or such a particular action be performed.[5]

This passage contains the essence (and the best) of the functionalist approach. Societies, from Montesquieu's perspective, are not random collections of artifacts and customs. "Every particular law is connected with another law, or depends on some other of a more general extent."[6] Each practice or belief is integrally related to the viability of the whole. Even behavior as seemingly inconsequential as a daughter-in-law paying homage to her mother-in-law is seen as contributing to the maintenance of the entire Chinese social system by inculcating the deference that sustains hierarchical social relations.

Montesquieu is not arguing that deference is a functional requisite for *all* societies. Rather he is suggesting that different *types* of society require different beliefs and practices to remain viable. It is to this typology of societies that we now turn.

Montesquieu distinguishes three types of government: republican, monarchical, and despotic. Sociologists and anthropologists have largely neglected this typology in the belief that it is essentially a restatement of classical political thought dating back to Aristotle.[7] To be sure, Aristotle had divided up governments into democracy, oligarchy, and monarchy (and their respective deviations: polity, aristocracy, and tyranny). But similarities in language disguise a revolution in thinking. For Aristotle and the classical tradition, different political structures could be superimposed on the same mode of social organization. But Montesquieu's classification of governments was also a typology of social relations. Each political form, in the words of Raymond Aron, "is also seen as a certain type of society."[8]

Montesquieu set himself the task of explaining how each of these ways of life sustains itself. Each mode of sociopolitical organization, he argues, has a distinct ethos (or cultural bias) that is necessary to maintain its institutions: honor in a monarchy, virtue in a republic, and fear in a despotic government. Having identified these three principles, Montesquieu demonstrates how laws in each type of society, ranging from education to punishment to the condition of women, serve to shore up that particular type. (Montesquieu leaves unanswered the question of whether these functions are intended and/or recognized by the actors themselves.) The viability of each of Montesquieu's three types of society thus depends on a consistency between institutions, values, and practices or, to use Montesquieu's language, between its nature, principle, and laws. Put another way, social relations and cultural biases cannot be mixed and matched.

Acutely conscious of the fragility of society that results from the interdependence of parts and whole, Montesquieu prefaces *The Spirit of the Laws* with the warning that "to propose alterations [in a society] belongs only to those who are so happy as to be born with genius capable of penetrating the entire constitution of a state."[9] That is, only those capable of perceiving the latent functions of practices should attempt to modify them. Because each part is inextricably tied to the whole, removing or adjusting any one part may irreparably damage the entire structure of social relations.

Like many later functionalists concerned with explaining (and preserving) social stability, Montesquieu stresses the integrative function of religion. What distinguishes Montesquieu's analysis from other functional approaches to religion is his attention to relating the functions of religious beliefs to different types of society. "The most true and holy doctrines may be attended with the very worst consequences, when they are not connected with the principles of society; and on the contrary, doctrines the most false may be attended with excellent consequences, when contrived so as to be connected with these principles."[10] To be functional, religion, like laws, must correspond to a matching mode of social relations. For instance, Montesquieu suggests that Protestantism, "a religion which has no visible head," sustains the republican mode of government, while Catholicism shores up monarchical government.[11] This typology of ways of organizing social life, by showing which religions are integrative (and disintegrative) for which ways of life, thus elevates Montesquieu's analysis above the platitude that religion serves an integrative function.

The animating principle of a monarchy is honor, by which Montesquieu means "the sense of what each man owes to his rank and station."[12] Dowries in this hierarchical way of life, Montesquieu suggests, "must be considerable . . . in order to enable husbands to support their rank." Education too "is obliged to conform" to the principle of honor: It must teach "that when we are raised to a post or preferment, we should never do or permit anything which may seem to imply that we look upon ourselves as inferior to the rank we hold." Montesquieu also points out that laws "which preserve the estates of families undivided are extremely useful" in monarchies, for they prevent a flattening of the social order and maintain the stratification of social power, privilege, and responsibility.[13]

Virtue is "the spring which sets the republican government in motion." Montesquieu defines virtue as love of the collectivity and equality.[14] Education in a republic, Montesquieu contends, must inculcate "self-renunciation," for otherwise the pursuit of self-interest will tear apart the community by generating inequality. Preservation of this egalitarian/collective way of life, Montesquieu writes, also makes it "absolutely necessary there should be regulation in respect to women's dowries, donations, successions, testamentary settlements, and all other forms of contracting."[15] Only by closely regulating individual freedom to dispose of one's property can this egalitarian mode of social relations be maintained.

In a despotism, where fear is the master principle, there are none of the reciprocal restraints that characterize power in the monarchical order. Although his functional analysis of this way of life is much less developed than that of the other two modes of social relations, Montesquieu nonetheless offers insight into how despotism reinforces and reproduces its social relations. For example, the custom in despotic countries of giving presents when seeking help serves to shore up the arbitrary power of the superior by showing that "a superior is under no obligation to an inferior."[16]

One of the chief virtues of Montesquieu's classification of social relations is that it is not premised upon the primitive/modern dichotomy. In this respect, Montesquieu's work stands in marked contrast to that of most social science theorists, who have been concerned with isolating those qualities that distinguish modern, industrial societies from premodern, technologically primitive societies. We follow Montesquieu's lead because only by going beyond the primitive/modern dichotomy can we distinguish what we see as the critical variations in social relations between and within technologically advanced societies.

No doubt Montesquieu's typology is incomplete and uneven. For instance, fear—which, in contrast to honor and virtue, is nowhere explicitly defined—is a consequence that might be produced in all ways of life, albeit for different reasons. Moreover, the underlying dimensions from which the categories are derived are not spelled out. And if there are underlying dimensions to the typology, should there not be a fourth way of life lurking somewhere?[17] Our aim is not to disregard the advances in understanding social organization that have taken place since 1750 but rather to applaud Montesquieu's general approach or, as he might say, the "spirit" of his enterprise.

AUGUSTE COMTE

Comte had high praise for *The Spirit of the Laws.* "The great strength of this memorable work," Comte observed, lay "in its tendency to regard political phenomena as subject to invariable laws, like all other phenomena."[18] Like Montesquieu, Comte posited the interdependence of the parts within a social system. In Comte's words, "each of the numerous social elements . . . is always conceived as relative to all the others, to which it is bound in fundamental solidarity." Because "social phenomena are closely interconnected," Comte argued, "every isolated study of social elements is from the very nature of social science quite irrational, and will remain sterile."[19] So far Comte is in complete agreement with Montesquieu.

Having reached this point, however, Comte was determined to avoid the pitfalls into which he believed Montesquieu had stumbled. The fatal flaw of *The Spirit of the Laws,* Comte believed (not without cause), was that it deteriorated into demonstrating the unique interdependencies of every society. The execution of the work, Comte lamented, fell far short of Montesquieu's stated intention. "We find no reference," he complained, "of social phenomena to the laws whose existence was announced at the outset." Instead the work was buried under an avalanche of facts relating to the varied institutions and manners of individual countries. Comte chided Montesquieu not only for failing to develop a theory of the limits of social variation but also for falling "back, like all others, upon the primitive type[s] offered by Aristotle's treatise."[20]

Having dismissed Montesquieu's typology of ways of life—which had in fact been Montesquieu's effort to limit social variability—as nothing more than a restatement of "primitive" Aristotelian categories, Comte (like so many after him) could find no resting point between infinity—the unique interdependencies of each society—and unity—reifying "society" as if it were everywhere the same. Anxious to avoid the "not in my tribe" theory-invalidating syndrome, Comte swung to the opposite extreme of searching for "the primary laws of society necessarily common to all times, and to all places."[21] Lacking a typology, Comte was unable to specify the conditions under which his lawlike statements would hold. Consequently he ran into the sociologist's dilemma described by the American anthropologist, Alfred Kroeber: "By the time he finds a formula that no one can cite exceptions to, it has become so essentially logical, so remote from phenomena, that no one knows precisely what to do with it."[22] This is exactly what happened later to functional analysis, which, in chasing after Comte's elusive vision of formulating lawlike functional relationships that hold for all societies, often ended up with banalities.[23] Resuscitating functionalism, we contend, requires embedding functional relationships in a *constrained diversity,* i.e., tying functions to types of social relations.

Comte divided sociology into social statics and social dynamics. Statics is the study of "the conditions of existence of a society," whereas dynamics entails an examination of "the laws of its movement."[24] In other words, social statics addresses the question of what makes social life possible, and social dynamics speaks to the question of how societies change. Comte's developmental theory—the three stages of human development (from theological to metaphysical to scientific)-is well known and need not concern us here. What interests us instead is his theory of social viability.

The most important functional requisite, Comte argued, is value consensus among the members of a society. Competing ways of thinking within a nation, Comte believed, would lead to the breakdown of that society. He attributed "the great political moral crises that societies are now undergoing" to the lack of "necessary agreement on first principles."[25] The view that society is possible only if members of a society share a system of values was to become an important postulate of later functional theorizing.

The difficulty with this thesis, as critics of functionalism have often pointed out, is that it does not fit well with the facts. For many (if not all) societies continue to persist, even thrive, in the face of fundamentally divergent values and beliefs. The source of this error, we would suggest, is in adopting society as the unit of analysis. Dissensus is normal, indeed essential to societies, because societies are composed of competing ways of life. Shared values exist, not at the societal level, but rather at the level of ways of life.

The error in attaching functions to a generic "society" rather than to ways of life can be seen in Comte's functional analysis of religion. According to Comte, religion functions to fulfill the "two great ends of human existence," i.e., "to regulate and combine" members of a social unit. Through "*regulating* each personal life no less than in *combining* different individual lives," Comte argues, religion establishes the requisite conditions for social order.[26] This formulation assumes that the only viable way of life is one in which individual behavior is highly prescribed and the individual is a member of a tightly bounded group. In the absence of these two conditions, Comte would have us believe that social life cannot be sustained. Rather than accept this assumption, we argue that this highly prescribed and collectivized way of life (which we, along with many others, call hierarchical) is only one among four ways of life (or five, if we keep the hermit on our social map)—all derived from these two dimensions of "combining" (group) and "regulating" (grid)—that are viable.

That the social order Comte has in mind is hierarchical becomes evident in his elaboration of the functions of religion. "Every government," Comte goes on to argue, "supposes a religion to consecrate and regulate commandment and obedience."[27] Comte, Raymond Aron explains, believed that religion "must sanctify the temporal power in order to convince men of the need for obedience, because social life is impossible unless there are men who command and others who obey. But spiritual power must not only regulate, rally, and sanctify; it must also mitigate and limit temporal power."[28] Comte is correct in arguing that religion so conceived would function to sustain a hierarchical way of life. What he fails to see is that such a religion would *subvert* other ways of life. Because it places limits on authority, it would undermine a fatalist way of life, which is sustained by arbitrariness and capriciousness. By the same token, adherents of egalitarian and individualist ways of life, where prescription of behavior is minimal, would not tolerate the relations of subordination upon which Comte's vision of religion is based.

Raymond Aron has aptly characterized Comte "as, first and foremost, the sociologist of human and social unity."[29] Comte's conception of sociology leads us down a path that arrives eventually at the doorstep of Parsonian functionalism. Having seen the result, most sociologists agree that it was a wrong turn. But instead of criticizing a particular version of functionalism that sought universal functions or needs, sociologists have tended to retreat from functional analysis altogether. Our claim is that by pursuing the less traveled road of constrained diversity—a path blazed by Montesquieu—functional analysis can be made a useful, indeed essential, tool.

HERBERT SPENCER

Few social scientists count themselves in Herbert Spencer's debt; fewer still have ever read him. Yet Spencer's formulations were instrumental in shaping the channel through which the mainstream of structural-functional sociology subsequently flowed.[30] Particularly influential was Spencer's conception of development as a process of structural differentiation and functional specialization.[31]

Spencer was the first systematically to apply the concepts of *structure* and *function,* terms that had long been in use among physiologists and anatomists, to the study of social life. "There can be no true conception of a structure," Spencer wrote, "without a true conception of its function." Societies, he suggested, were analogous to biological organisms since, in the course of their growth, "progressive differentiation of structures is accompanied by progressive differentiation of functions." In "undeveloped" societies "all parts of a society have like natures and activities" and thus perform the same functions for the whole, while in "developed" societies each differentiated structure serves a distinctive function in sustaining the social entity.[32]

His magnum opus, *The Principles of Sociology,* is devoted, in large part, to analyzing how different institutional structures—kinship, political, religious, professional, economic—function to maintain society. "Family organizations," for instance, "have first to be judged by the degrees in which they help to preserve the social aggregate they occur in." In the same manner, Spencer sets out to show how religious institutions "maintain and strengthen social bonds, and so conserve the social aggregate."[33] Spencer's functional proclivity is nicely illustrated by a story related by Francis Galton, a pioneer in the use of fingerprints as a means of identification: "I spoke of the failure to discover the origins of these patterns [on the fingers], and how the fingers of unborn children had been dissected to ascertain their earliest stages, and so forth. Spencer remarked that this was beginning in the wrong way; that I ought to consider the purpose the ridges had to fulfill, and to work backwards."[34] Spencer expressed the same sentiments in his academic writings, arguing that "to understand how an organization originated and developed, it is requisite to understand the need subserved at the outset and afterwards."[35]

Spencer's analysis prefigures the quest in postwar American sociology for the functional requisites of all societies.[36] "There are certain general conditions," Spencer argues, "which, in every society, must be fulfilled to a considerable extent before it can hold together, and which must be fulfilled completely before social life can be complete."[37] These "social requirements" include procreation ("maintenance of the race"), production ("social sustenance"), exchange ("social distribution"), communication ("internuncial function"), and the control of individual behavior ("social regulation").[38]

Spencer continued Comte's search for the universal functional requisites of society because he believed, as Comte did, that whereas history may explain the peculiar tenets of this or that religion, sociology's task was to explain the universality of religion. By erecting a rigid line between "special facts due to special circumstances" and "general facts displayed by societies in general,"[39] Spencer, like Comte, foreclosed the possibility of a more modest functional analysis geared to different types of societies.

The claim that Herbert Spencer, popularizer and propagator of evolution, was a pioneer of functionalism may seem peculiar to those accustomed to a strict separation between functional and evolutionary modes of analysis. Evolution, after all, is occupied with the development of social relations, while functional analysis is concerned with relationships between patterns of behavior at a single point in time. In Britain functional anthropology emerged in opposition to the nineteenth-century evolutionary doctrines of Lewis Morgan and E. B. Tylor that attempted to establish the historical origins and propagation of customs and practices. But history and functionalism are not so distinct as this dichotomy between diachronic and synchronic analysis would have us believe, for a functional explanation must specify how the consequences of a behavioral pattern account for the persistence of that pattern *over time*.[40] Spencer's evolutionism tries to provide just such a feedback mechanism.

Evolutionary and functional modes of analysis had coexisted uneasily in Comte's work. His "Law of Three Stages," the core of his social dynamics, bore little relation to the functional analysis of his social statics. Social change—through the theological, metaphysical, and scientific stages—is explained by Comte in terms of the unfolding of immanences. "Our Evolution," he wrote, "can be nothing but the development of our nature."[41] Social development, Comte continued, was produced by those "properties which, latent at first, can come into play only in that advanced state of social life for which they are exclusively destined."[42]

Spencer explicitly dissented from Comte's view of change as immanent in the social entity. "Evolution is commonly conceived to imply in everything an *intrinsic* tendency to become something higher. This is an erroneous conception of it. . . . [The] tendency to progress from homogeneity to heterogeneity [of structure] is not intrinsic but extrinsic."[43] Social development, in Spencer's view, was a product of interaction with the environment. By abandoning the doctrine of change as immanent in the social entity and embracing the principle of selection, Spencer opened the way to linking functionalism with evolution. Evolution in the direction of greater differentiation takes place, Spencer argues, not because of any inherent tendency toward perfection, but because the more differentiated social entities are, on the whole, better adapted to the environment than homogeneous social structures. "Survival of the fittest" thus provides a feedback loop explaining how social relations maintain themselves.

Rather than just produce a list of functional needs that must be met by institutional structures, Spencer attempts to establish how a given structure provides a selective advantage in an environment characterized by competition between societies.[44] Consider, for example, Spencer's discussion of kinship. His contention is not only that families meet the functional requisite of procreation and socialization. It is that by meeting these functional needs organized kinship structures bestowed a selective advantage on social entities possessing such relationships. "The struggle for existence between societies," Spencer argues, means that as "the rearing of more numerous and stronger offspring must have been favored by more regular sexual relations, there must, on the average, have been a tendency for the societies most characterized by promiscuity to disappear before those less characterized by it."[45] The validity of Spencer's substantive point aside, the logic of Spencer's formulation does, at least, provide a selection mechanism that shows how the consequence of a pattern of social behavior might become a cause of its maintenance.

What is worth preserving in Spencer's sociology and what should be jettisoned? Jonathan Turner has suggested that "to appreciate the power of Spencer's analysis, we should minimize his more functional statements."[46] Our task, he contends, should be "to salvage substantive theoretical ideas from their functional trappings."[47] There is certainly something to the view that, head-to-head, technologically advanced societies have competitive advantages over primitive ones, though the record is not yet complete. Technology does matter. But then we would be at a serious disadvantage in analyzing technologically advanced societies. We prefer a different route: pursuing Spencer's conception of functional adaptation by applying it to competition between ways of life rather than between societies, while relegating to the past his idea that what is important—or adaptive—in social relations is the "advance from the simple to the complex, through a process of successive differentiations."[48] A necessary step on the road to functionalism's redemption, we contend, is uncoupling it from the primitive/modern dichotomy upon which Spencer fastened it.

Spencer's own work, to be fair, is not concerned solely with the process of increasing differentiation. Most notable in this respect is his typology of "militant" and "industrial" societies.[49] Spencer's unfortunate use of the label "industrial" has led many commentators to assume, erroneously in our view, that this typology is a restatement of the familiar primitive/modern dichotomy. This was not Spencer's view; he explicitly states that these two types of social organization can be found at every stage of the evolutionary process. Societies, Spencer argues, cycle in and out of these two phases according to the level of hostility between societies.

What Spencer intended to denote by the term "industrial" were social relations characterized by self-regulation or, to use his words, "voluntary co-operation." In contrast, militant societies are those in which a central authority regulates the affairs of individuals. Spencer regarded "the contrast between their traits as among the most important with which Sociology has to deal."[50] And indeed this typology covers the two modes of social organization most familiar to social scientists— hierarchy and individualism (though it leaves out two less familiar, but equally important, forms—fatalism and egalitarianism).

This typology points us in the right direction, but unfortunately in Spencer it too often takes a backseat to his evolutionary scheme of increasing differentiation. The analysis is suggestive: Where war between societies is prevalent, Spencer hypothesizes, "societies in which there is little subordination disappear, and leave outstanding those in which subordination is great."[51] But that analysis is not developed. With a few, intriguing exceptions—for example, ceremonial institutions in militant societies function as mechanisms of social control by symbolizing the authority of hierarchy, while during industrial phases, ceremony is transformed into a concern with politeness as a means of facilitating interaction among strangers[52]—Spencer fails to integrate his typology into his discussion of the functions of institutions.

Although his militant/industrial typology is sometimes illuminating, Spencer does not significantly help us in our effort to attach functions to types of ways of life. His main contribution to functional analysis lies instead in his attempts to identify feedback loops that can explain the maintenance of a social organization in terms of its consequences. Functional explanations, we learn from Spencer, must show how the consequences of a mode of social relations contribute to the persistence of those relations.

Another salutary aspect of Spencer's theory is its attention to the way in which types of social organization cycle in and out rather than simply following a unidirectional path of change. Spencer's cycles are not mechanical, alternating between ways of life at regular predestined intervals. Rather, the process of cyclical change is driven by environmental changes. It is this environmental contingency that gives Spencer's cyclical formulation a surprisingly (surprising because cyclical theories date back to antiquity) modern ring.

THE BIOLOGICAL PARALLEL

Spencer's cyclical ideas parallel in some respects the recent work of modern theoretical biologists, who have increasingly become dissatisfied with the orthodox unilinear account in which an initially disparate assemblage of weeds and other opportunist species (they call them "r-strategists") progressively transforms itself into a mature and highly ordered "climax community" (of "k-strategists," each of which plays its specialized part) and then stays like that.[53] There is, these biologists have come to realize, more to ecosystem dynamics than r- and k-strategists. The parallel with our argument for there being more to social life than markets and hierarchies makes it worth pausing to explain these biological dynamics before going on to show what might have happened in the development of social theory if only Spencer's cycles had been united with Montesquieu's more variegated conception of ways of life. If that had happened, our theory of sociocultural viability would have been in place, in all its essentials, almost a century ago. Although we personally have reason to be pleased that this did not happen, we cannot help but feel that much intellectual energy has been expended over the past hundred or so years in forcing social theory up a number of blind and largely unrewarding alleys.

The orthodox pattern of development begins with a new niche, where the r-strategists do well because the environment is new and unpredictable and they are able (thanks to their opportunism, their lack of specialization, and their rapid growth rates) to learn about that environment by exploiting it. As they engage in this trial-and-error process, they inevitably knock their environment into shape, making it more predictable than it was to start with and creating conditions less favorable to themselves and more favorable to the k-strategists, who (thanks to their specialization and low growth rates) are more efficient at harvesting food in crowded but orderly environments. As the k-strategists steadily displace the r-strategists, the environment becomes more and more ordered and the increasingly connected whole (special-ization going hand-in-hand with interdependence) moves toward the climax community that has traditionally been seen as the final stage of ecosystem evolution. This is not, however, Holling tells us, the end of the road.

Holling argues that "the increasing strength of connectance between variables in the maturing ecosystem eventually leads to an abrupt change. In a sense, key structural parts of the system become 'accidents waiting to happen.'"[54] This thesis, that as the system becomes more complex and more connected, it reaches a threshold beyond which it becomes highly unstable, has been described mathematically[55] and is now largely accepted by biologists. This sudden implosion of the sta-bility region destroys the complex pattern of relationships that consti-tuted the climax community and ushers in a new system state that Holling (aware of the parallel with Schumpeter's theory of economic transitions) calls "creative destruction." Nor is this the end of the evolutionary road.

The destruction is creative because it releases, through decomposi-tion, all the nutrients and energy that until then were stored within all the differentiations of the climax community. Everywhere the ecosystem is suddenly awash with capital—compost—and conditions are ripe for the emergence of some other kind of strategists: those who can mobilize and retain these riches before they disappear (by soil leaching, for instance) down the drain. Since all the heavyweight specialists of the climax community have been destroyed by the unexpected implosion of their stability pocket, it is the meek, small-scale collaborators—the unspecialized, the simple, and the uncompetitive—who, for a brief and not very visible span, inherit the earth and set about rebuilding its fences.

Once enough of these fences are in place, the stage is set for the next phase, in which more thrusting and entrepreneurial species (the r-strategists) can begin to profit by tapping the energy potentials that now exist between the insides and outsides of these newly erected, but as yet unrelated, fences. Like cinema-goers who have entered a contin-uous program, we are now back where we came in. There is, we realize, no end to the road, and we can now see how it is that the r-strategists and the k-strategists are able (thanks to the existence of two other, less visible, ways of biological life) to cycle, not back and forth, as Spencer thought, but round and round between the four engaged ways of life: individualism (r-strategists), hierarchy (k-strategists), fatalism (compost), and egalitarianism (small-scale, cooperative fence builders).

This cycle, of course, is highly idealized, giving us a regular sequence in which each way of life has its day to such an extent that all the others, for the moment, disappear. The reality, we expect, will be much more patchy and uneven, with the ways of life gaining here and retrenching there rather than succeeding one another in strict rotation. Even so, it is the differing capabilities and constraints of each way of life that provide the basis for the permanent dynamic imbalance on which our theory of sociocultural viability rests. Though Spencer, we feel sure, would have been attracted by this parallel between biological and social life, most nineteenth- and twentieth-century social theorists (including most of the time, Spencer) have rejected cycles, even oscillations, and have plumped instead for unidirectional transitions: progress, modernization, rationalization, and the like. When cycles and oscillations do force their way in, they create enormous conceptual problems for existing social theories.

CYCLING IN AND OUT IN HIGHLAND BURMA

One well-known intrusion of cycles is Leach's description of the political system of the Kachins (in highland Burma), in which "two quite contradictory ideal modes of life" coexist. Kachin communities, he insists, "oscillate" between *gumsa* (the hierarchically feudal Shan system) and *gumlao* (a seemingly anarchic form of organization that stresses equality of opportunity).[56] Less well known, but in much the same vein, is Meggitt's description of the political organization of the Mae-Enga people in the New Guinea Highlands.[57] Meggitt discerns a cyclical pattern generated by the interaction of the "big men" system (equivalent to the Kachins' *gumlao*) and the segmentary lineage framework (a hierarchically ordered genealogy that can be equated with *gumsa*). Within the history of each clan (not of the whole society—no genealogies extend that far) there is, Meggitt insists, a fairly predictable alternation in the style of operation of the Big Men: expansive optimism giving way to defensive pessimism, and periods of peace alternating with outbreaks of war.[58]

Leach's analysis, honed to a sharp polemical edge, caused a tremendous brouhaha when it was published; to this day, the conceptual dilemmas it raised for the linearists and for those who saw functions as going with entire societies have not been resolved.[59] Since there is nothing at all contentious about the two forms of organization Leach and Meggitt have described—they are the familiar hierarchies and markets—the cause of all the consternation must lie not in their existence but in their coexistence and, worse still, in their apparent oscillation.

Our cultural theory, however, has no difficulty with the coexistence of and the apparent oscillation between these two ways of life. It would have difficulty with the reverse: the progressive and irreversible demise of one and the triumph of the other. Moreover, our theory of socio-cultural viability enriches the analyses of Leach and Meggitt by showing how their cycles have to include two more ways of life before they can appear to oscillate. In the New Guinea Highlands, where we know from extensive ethnographic research that if there are Big Men, there will always be some "rubbish men," the fatalists are certainly there. That egalitarians are also present would seem to be confirmed by the millenarian movements—*cargo cults*—that are such a dramatic feature of the region.

In highland Burma, alas, we will never know. Leach's fieldwork was terminated by the outbreak of World War II; his fieldwork notes were lost; and Kachin society is now very different from what it once was. What does survive, however, is Leach's succinct account of the per-manent dynamic imbalances that drive the system.

> The two types are, in their practical application, always interrelated. Both systems are in a sense structurally defective. A *gumsa* political state tends to develop features which lead to rebellion resulting, for a time, in a *gumlao* order. But a *gumlao* community . . . usually lacks the means to hold its component lineages together in a status of equality. It will then either disintegrate altogether through fission, or else status differences between lineage groups will bring the system back into the *gumsa* pat-tern.[60]

Rather than recoiling in horror from such a pulsating and pluralistic spectacle (which, by and large, is what modern social scientists have done), Montesquieu and Spencer (or, more precisely, the nonevolution-ary Spencer) teach us to accept this nonlinear state of affairs and get on with the task of deducing and describing the other two ways of life that have to be present if the system is to cycle in the way it does.

NOTES

1. "It is Montesquieu," Durkheim wrote, "who first laid down the funda-mental principles of social science" (Emile Durkheim, *Montesquieu and Rous-seau: Forerunners of Sociology* [Ann Arbor: University of Michigan, 1960], 61). The first essay in *The Founding Fathers of Social Science,* ed. Timothy Raison (London: Scolar, 1979), is devoted to Montesquieu.

2. Baron de Montesquieu, *The Spirit of the Laws,* trans. Thomas Nugent, two volumes in one (New York: Hafner, 1949), 40. All page references are to this edition.

3. Cited in David Wallace Carrithers, "Introduction," in *The Spirit of Laws* (Berkeley: University of California Press, 1977), 22.

4. Montesquieu, *The Spirit of the Laws,* vol. 1, 303.

5. Ibid., vol. 1, 303–04.

6. Ibid., vol. 1, lxvii.

7. Some notable exceptions are Emile Durkheim, *Montesquieu and Rousseau: Forerunners of Sociology* (Ann Arbor: University of Michigan, 1960), 24–35; Raymond Aron, *Main Currents in Sociological Thought,* vol. 1 (Garden City, N.Y.: Anchor, 1968), and E. E. Evans-Pritchard, *A History of Anthropological Thought* (New York: Basic Books, 1981).

8. Aron, *Main Currents,* vol. 1, 22.

9. Montesquieu, *The Spirit of the Laws,* vol. 1, lxviii. Elsewhere Montesquieu contrasts arithmetic, in which the subtraction of one figure produces a calculable effect, to politics, "where one can never predict the result of the change that one makes" (Carrithers, "Introduction," 31).

10. Montesquieu, *The Spirit of the Laws,* vol. 2, 38–39.

11. Ibid., vol. 2, 30–31.

12. Aron, *Main Currents,* vol. 1, 23.

13. Montesquieu, *The Spirit of the Laws,* vol. 1, 107, 32, 53.

14. Ibid., vol. 1, lxxi. Thus "virtue" is not, as Montesquieu is at pains to point out in an "explanatory note," a synonym for morality: "My ideas are new, and therefore I have been obliged to find new words or to give new acceptations to old terms, in order to convey my meaning. They, who are unacquainted with this particular, have made me say the most strange absurdities, such as would be shocking in any part of the world, because in all countries and governments morality is requisite" (ibid.).

15. Ibid., vol. 1, 34, 43.

16. Ibid., vol. 1, 65.

17. Durkheim thought he detected a fourth type of society in Montesquieu's reference to barbaric and savage peoples, who lack, in contrast to monarchies and republics, "a clearly defined sovereign power" (Durkheim, *Montesquieu and Rousseau,* 35).

18. Auguste Comte, *The Positive Philosophy of Auguste Comte,* trans. and condensed by Harriet Martineau, vol. 2 (London: Kegan Paul, 1893), 47. Comte had in mind Montesquieu's declaration that "man, as a physical being, is like other bodies governed by invariable laws" (Montesquieu, *The Spirit of the Laws,* 3).

19. Auguste Comte, *The Essential Comte: Selected from Cours de Philosophie Positive,* ed. Stanislav Andreski (New York: Barnes & Noble, 1974), 149, 158–59.

20. Comte, *Positive Philosophy,* vol. 2, 48.

21. Auguste Comte, *Auguste Comte and Positivism: The Essential Writings,* ed. Gertrud Lenzer (New York: Harper & Row, 1975), 392.

22. Evans-Pritchard, *History of Anthropological Thought,* 202.

23. In a review of "the structural-functional approach" of Parsons and Marion Levy, Barrington Moore, Jr., comments that while "there are perhaps a few illuminating statements that can be made about *any* kind of human behavior . . . most of them are likely to be banal" ("The New Scholasticism

and the Study of Politics," in N. J. Demerath III and Richard Peterson, eds., *System, Change, and Conflict* [New York: Free Press, 1967], 333–45, quote on 337; emphasis in original).

24. Comte, *The Essential Comte*, 147.

25. Ibid., 83. Also see Aron, *Main Currents*, vol. 1, 81, 95–96.

26. Comte, *Comte and Positivism*, 394. Emphasis in original.

27. Quoted in Lewis A. Coser, *Masters of Sociological Thought: Ideas in Historical and Social Context* (New York: Harcourt Brace Jovanovich, 1977), 11.

28. Aron, *Main Currents*, vol. 1, 112.

29. Ibid., 73.

30. Howard Becker writes: "'From Spencer to Durkheim to British and British-influenced functional anthropology to structural-functional sociology in the United States'. . . may not be a drastic distortion of the actual 'who to whom' sequence" ("Anthropology and Sociology," in John Gillin, ed., *For a Science of Social Man* [New York: Macmillan, 1954], 102–59, quote on 132). Also see Stanislav Andreski, "Introductory Essay," in *Herbert Spencer: Structure, Function and Evolution*, ed. Andreski (London: Michael Joseph, 1971), 7–32, quote on 21.

31. See Andrew C. Janos, *Politics and Paradigms: Changing Theories of Change in Social Science* (Stanford: Stanford University Press, 1986).

32. Herbert Spencer, *The Principles of Sociology* (New York: Appleton, 1896), vol. 3, 3; vol. 1, 450, 593–94.

33. Ibid., vol. 1, 160; vol. 3, 102.

34. Quoted in Robert L. Carniero, "Introduction," in *The Evolution of Society: Selections from Herbert Spencer's Principles of Sociology* (Chicago: University of Chicago Press, 1967), xxix.

35. Spencer, *Principles of Sociology*, vol. 3, 3.

36. See, e.g., D. F. Aberle et al., "The Functional Prerequisites of a Society," *Ethics*, January 1950, 100–11; Marion J. Levy, Jr., *The Structure of Society* (Princeton: Princeton University Press, 1952); and Gabriel A. Almond and James S. Coleman, *The Politics of Developing Areas* (Princeton: Princeton University Press, 1960).

37. Herbert Spencer, *The Study of Sociology* (New York: Appleton, 1875), 347.

38. Robert G. Perrin, "Herbert Spencer's Four Theories of Social Evolution," *American Journal of Sociology*, May 1976, 1339–59, quote on 1345.

39. Spencer, quoted in ibid., 1347–48.

40. Arthur Stinchcombe suggests that in fact "a functional causal structure generally *implies* a historicist structure" (*Constructing Social Theories* [New York: Harcourt, Brace & World, 1968], 104; emphasis in original).

41. Quoted in Robert L. Carniero, "Classical Evolution," in Raoul Naroll and Frada Naroll, eds., *Main Currents in Cultural Anthropology* (Englewood Cliffs, N.J.: Prentice-Hall, 1973), 57–121, quote on 70.

42. Comte, *Positive Philosophy*, vol. 2, 124.

43. Spencer, *Principles of Sociology*, vol. 1, 95, emphasis in original. Spencer quoted in Perrin, "Spencer's Four Theories," 1353.

44. Jonathan H. Turner, *Herbert Spencer: A Renewed Appreciation* (Beverly Hills, Calif.: Sage, 1985), 108. Andreski, "Introductory Essay," 24.

45. Spencer, *Principles of Sociology,* vol. 1, 653.

46. Jonathan H. Turner and Leonard Beeghley, *The Emergence of Sociological Theory* (Homewood, Ill.: Dorsey, 1981), 84.

47. Turner, *Herbert Spencer,* 61.

48. Herbert Spencer, "Progress: Its Law and Cause," in J.D.Y. Peel, ed., *Herbert Spencer: On Social Evolution* (Chicago: University of Chicago Press, 1972), 45.

49. Spencer, *Principles of Sociology,* vol. 1, 556–75.

50. Ibid., vol. 1, 574.

51. Ibid., vol. 1, 595. A classic example is Poland's complete disappearance as a nation-state in 1795. Poland's *liberum veto,* by which a single negative vote could dissolve the parliament, made it impossible for the nation to mobilize the collective resources necessary to defend itself against the highly authoritarian societies that surrounded it, particularly Prussia and Russia. However the thesis that hierarchically oriented societies fare better in wars than nonhierarchical societies seems to work less well in the twentieth century (think of the two world wars or the Soviet invasion of Afghanistan).

52. Turner and Beeghley, *Emergence of Sociological Theory,* 93–94.

53. C. S. Holling, "The Resilience of Terrestrial Ecosystems," in W. Clark and R. Munn, eds., *Sustainable Development of the Biosphere* (Cambridge: Cambridge University Press, 1986).

54. C. S. Holling, "Resilience of Ecosystems: Local Surprise and Global Change" (Unpublished working paper, International Institute for Applied Systems Analysis, 1984); and Holling, "The Resilience of Terrestrial Ecosystems."

55. R. May, "Will a Large Complex System be Stable?" *Nature* 238 (1972): 413–14.

56. E. R. Leach, *Political Systems of Highland Burma* (Boston: Beacon Press, 1954), 8.

57. M. J. Meggitt, "The Pattern of Leadership among the Mae-Enga of New Guinea," *Anthropological Forum* 2, 1 (1967).

58. The cyclical (not oscillating) path by which this might actually happen, and its commonalities with the theory of the trade cycle in economics, are set out in Chapter 9 of Michael Thompson, *Rubbish Theory: The Creation and Destruction of Value* (Oxford: Oxford University Press, 1979). Though the cyclical path, the two states Meggitt has described and the threshold between them, is clearly visible in this treatment, the remaining two ways of life (which, of course, must be there if the cycle is to turn round on itself) are not clearly identified. It is this omission that our cultural theory remedies.

59. For a survey of these, see D. Kent McCallum, "Structural Dynamics in Political Anthropology: Some Conceptual Dilemmas," *Social Research* 37, 3 (1970): 399–401.

60. Leach, *Political Systems of Highland Burma,* 203–04. That the system cycles round and round rather than oscillating back and forth (and that there have to be four types and not just two) is revealed by some confusions in

Leach's account of the "switching mechanisms." His transition from individualism to hierarchy (by the *gumlao* order's inability to maintain equality of opportunity and the subsequent emergence of status differences between lineage groups) is correctly identified, but he runs into difficulties when he tries to reverse the direction of change. He sees the total system failure of the hierarchy (the *gumsa* order) as leading straight to individualism without any intervening fatalist stage, and he wrongly identifies fatalism as one of two possible outcomes of the failure of individualism (the other being the correctly identified transition to hierarchy). Had he gotten from hierarchy to fatalism, Leach would then have had to identify a further transitional stage—the emergence of unrelated egalitarian groups—before he could have completed the cycle and returned to individualism.

CHAPTER 7

Durkheim

How do people know what they know? Why, as all have access to the same nature, physical and human, don't they come to the same conclusions? Or, if each individual is different, why don't they come to wholly different conclusions? A sociology of perception must explain both why the world resembles neither an epistemological Tower of Babel in which communication between individuals is impossible nor a homogenized blend in which communication is no longer necessary.

Our ideas about how the world works, Durkheim (1858–1917) argued, are derived from our social relations.[1] As he formulated the proposition in *Primitive Classification,* "the classification of men reproduces [the] classification of things."[2] Neither individual experience nor innate reason, Durkheim insisted, could generate such basic notions as time, space, and causality. Only by recognizing the social origins of thought, he reasoned, could one account for both the shared nature of categories and their variation across different places and times.[3]

Individuals, according to Durkheim, internalize the social order for a purpose, which may be hidden from them but which the sociologist can see. That purpose, or function, is to sustain a way of life. "Society could not abandon the categories to the free choice of the individual without abandoning itself."[4] The consequence of internalizing beliefs about what is sacred and profane, what constitutes a criminal action, or what ideas make sense, is the protection of a particular social order. Social relations generate ways of perceiving the world that contribute to the maintenance of those relations.

This does not mean that society eradicates individuality. Durkheim explicitly rejects such a notion. "We do not mean to assert," he explains, "that social beliefs and behaviors insinuate themselves in invariant fashion in individuals. . . . There is no social uniformity which does not admit a whole range of individual gradations." What Durkheim insisted upon was that "the range of possible and tolerated variation is . . . always and everywhere more or less restricted," and that "sooner or later there is . . . a limit beyond which we cannot go."[5]

Durkheim held that the roles and norms that constitute social institutions are both inside the individuals who have internalized them and outside those individuals in that, once established, these norms exercise an independent influence on their creators. It is this realm of "social facts," by which Durkheim signified the consequences of interpersonal relations, that he believed should be the special province of the social scientist.[6]

Durkheim resolutely refused to separate the knower from what he claimed to know, the thinker from what was thought. In Durkheim's imagination there is no philosophical mind-body problem. Minds and bodies, thoughts and thinkers, are always connected. However, it was not only or mainly the mind of the individual but that mind as it was connected to others through the joint products of their interactions, the collective representations available to all, that interested him.[7] These collective representations, Durkheim explained, are "the result of an immense co-operation; . . . to make them, a multitude of minds have associated, united and combined their ideas and sentiments."[8]

Put this way, with the sociology of knowledge out in front, our debt to Durkheim is obvious and immense. This intellectual debt creates both problems and opportunities. The opportunities lie in trying to extend his thought. The problems come in confronting again the criticisms with which he had to contend, from the creation of a fictitious group mind to ideological bias. So be it. We shall try to meet these challenges by reanalyzing his work according to certain precepts.

YOUNG EMILE AND MASTER DURKHEIM

Durkheim has left us a large and variegated body of work, susceptible to more than one interpretation. In touch with a profound core idea—rooting perception in social life—Durkheim, like other great thinkers, equivocated, trying out somewhat different formulations, moving this way and that so as to keep his sense of responsibility to the ideas to which he devoted his life. It cannot be unequivocally stated about any single interpretation, therefore, including our own, that that interpretation alone retains his only meaning.

In this spirit, we shall henceforth refer to Young Emile as the creative but conflicted child of his time who wanted it all—his core theory, his science, and his policies. We shall reserve the designation Master Durkheim for the rigorous scholar solely concerned with fidelity to an epistemology of social construction. Plain old Durkheim is used for the continuities that kept Young Emile and Master Durkheim interested in the relationship between knowledge and society.

For all the revolution in thinking that he created, Young Emile inevitably shared many of the biases of his contemporaries. Chief among these was the conception of "individualism," a term coined, Koenrad Swart tells us, "to designate the disintegration of society, which many conservatives believed had resulted from the French Revolution and the doctrine of the individual rights of man."[9] Whereas Samuel Smiles's book *Self-Help* bespoke the English understanding of individualism as freedom, Durkheim followed the French development of the term *self-help* that stressed the atomization and exploitation of the poor caused by the destruction of collective bonds.[10]

Young Emile was a committed socialist (he was a close friend of, and had considerable influence upon, Jean Jaurès, the great socialist leader) and an aspiring sociologist. Like any man with several mistresses, he fervently believed he could serve all of them, viz., that the infusion of science into sociology would improve the prospects of social reform. Although he did not hold with Marx's economic determinism, neither did Young Emile approve of the gross inequalities and weakening of the social bond, both of which were developments he attributed to capitalism. One consequence of Emile's skepticism toward capitalism was that, although his theory would lead him to conceive of individualism as a social form of its own, he alternated between that conception and one in which individualism is an abnormally weak form of community. The unrestrained individual, to Young Emile, is an abomination, a social monster. License was not liberty but rather cause of a "diseased state."

Durkheim vacillated between the everyday view of individualism as antisocial and his theories that told him that even individualism must be a social product. This tension has been captured by Robert Nisbet, who observes

an apparent contradiction in Durkheim's concept of individualism. At times individualism is made to appear as nonsociety, as the mode of behavior or thought that ensues when man is divorced from society. It is, in this view, the very opposite of the social. But there is another view of the matter, one that arises from his sweeping insistence that everything above the level of physiology derives from society. And in this second view individualism becomes, along with the collective conscience itself, something social in origin.[11]

We agree with Nisbet's judgment that "it is the second view that is more consistently Durkheimian—that is, consistent not only with his premises but also with the full body of his work."[12] Young Emile may have had the word count, but Master Durkheim kept faith with the original premises.

THE ELEMENTARY FORMS OF THE RELIGIOUS LIFE

Scholars often write papers in ways that falsify the true history of their ideas. The accepted mode of presentation—problem, hypotheses, evidence, conclusions—does violence to the trials and errors, not to say accidents, along the way to what they later rationalize as a linear march to theory treated as if it were there from the beginning.[13] The same is often true of the order in which books appear during a lifetime. While it is tempting to take each work as part of a steady progression of ideas, building upon and advancing what had gone before, historical and theoretical time often differ. It is not so much that ideas may change, which they do, but also that chance and hindsight play their part. Books may get written because of the availability of data, financial resources, collaborators, or challenges that lead a scholar to alter a theoretical timetable. Equally important is a theorist's sense of how the ideas hang together, of their appropriate sequence and emphasis.[14] That the "last shall be first" has special applicability to Durkheim's corpus, for in his last book, *The Elementary Forms of the Religious Life,* he sought to go back to bedrock by returning to the core proposition—that the social controls individual thought and behavior—with which he began and which, to the very end, he tried to understand.

If *Suicide* could be likened to a battleship, with all guns blazing, ready to boldly claim possession of a new land, *The Elementary Forms* might be likened to a submarine cruising barely above the bottom, surfacing only briefly to let loose with a well-aimed shaft, submerging well before any fire can be returned. For the final volume of a leading academic figure, with pretensions (and the capacity) to found a new discipline, *The Elementary Forms* reads oddly. Whereas one might have expected summary statements of dogma, the reader is instead freighted down with fact upon fact. The subject, instead of being a topic of the times, is situated in a remote spot (Australia) and is as little known (aboriginal religion) as possible. No big target, no big splash. Durkheim evidently hoped that by layering his theory in fact, his radical ideas would not seem so outlandish.

In *The Elementary Forms* Durkheim sets out to demonstrate how members of society exercise control over one another through religious beliefs and rituals. The "distinctive trait" of religion, he argues, is the "division of the world into two . . . radically opposed . . . domains, the one containing all that is sacred, the other all that is profane."

Sacred things, Durkheim explains, "are those which the interdictions protect and isolate." The domain of sacred things is not limited to "personal beings which are called gods or spirits," but may include "a rock, a tree, a spring, a pebble, a piece of wood, a house [or, dare we add, a snail darter or a dolphin], in a word, anything can be sacred."[15] What is to be considered sacred is grounded in social relations, not in the nature of things.

When Durkheim says that "god is only a figurative expression of society" or that "the sacred is nothing more nor less than society transfigured and personified,"[16] he is not uttering metaphysical cant but arguing that members of society come together to create, in Mary Douglas's words, "a host of imaginary powers, all dangerous, to watch over their agreed morality and to punish defectors."[17] By setting aside those things that are sacred from those that are profane, society teaches its members what can be questioned, interrogated, and probed, and what must be left unexamined. One can see that Durkheim's theory of the sacred, put in this way, as Douglas points out, "is a theory about how knowledge of the universe is socially constructed."[18]

As a contribution to the sociology of knowledge, *The Elementary Forms* improves upon *Primitive Classification* (an essay Durkheim wrote with his cousin and collaborator Marcel Mauss) by bringing functions into the picture. In *Primitive Classification,* Durkheim argued that categories of thought reflected (or were "modeled" on) the social organization. For instance, the sevenfold classification of space among the Zuni was held to be a product of a sevenfold division of the Zuni camp. Or the fact that certain Australian tribes lived in camps organized in circles is said to "reproduce" a conception of space as an immense circle.[19]

The analysis of religion in *The Elementary Forms* is explicitly functional in orientation. The function of religion, Durkheim argues, is to "strengthen the bonds attaching the individual to the society of which he is a member." Although the forms of religious practice and belief may vary, they "fulfill the same functions everywhere," namely, integrating the individual into the social group. Thus Durkheim concludes there is no "essential difference . . . between an assembly of Christians celebrating the principal dates of the life of Christ, or of Jews remembering the exodus from Egypt or the promulgation of the Decalogue," for all enable "the group [to] periodically renew the sentiments which it has of itself and of its unity."[20]

Young Emile's claim that religious ritual serves a positive function by integrating the individual into the group seems to assume that integration is a prerequisite for social viability. This assumption, we believe, is unwarranted because it ignores the considerable evidence, even among remote and technologically primitive peoples, of ways of life thriving in the absence of much in the way of integrative rituals.[21] If the assumption is false, and religious rituals do, as Durkheim argues, increase an individual's sense of belonging to a group, then it follows that one man's cohesion is another man's subversion. In other words, to increase an individual's sense of belonging to a group would subvert the individualist way of life, which is premised on freeing individuals from the control of groups. Ritual, we suggest, is functional for egalitarianism and hierarchy, but dysfunctional for individualism.

Emile maintains further that commemorative rites are universal because they fulfill the essential function of "attach[ing] the present to the past."[22] But is it functional for all modes of social organization to remember their ancestors to the same degree and in the same way? Master Durkheim would argue that ancestor cults, while supportive in a hierarchical context, where "remembrance of things past" in an unbroken line of succession helps legitimate inequalities in status, would be subversive in the context of individualistic social relations, where the demands of precedent would restrict the freedom to transact, or in egalitarian contexts, where the "dead hand" of the past might impose the inequalities of a less-enlightened age.[23] Hermits, as we have seen, dismantle the past systematically (by, for instance, not mentioning the names of the dead) in order to stabilize themselves in their autonomous way of life.

If Young Emile sometimes seems to forget that one social type's function is another's dysfunction, Master Durkheim well understood this point. Because "a social fact can be construed as normal or abnormal only relatively to a given social species," the Master explained in *The Rules of Sociological Method,* sociology must be "devoted to the constitution and classification of these species." The concept of social species, continued the Master, furnishes "a middle ground" between the view that each society is unique (thereby making "all generalizations . . . well-nigh impossible") and the opposing view that all humanity is everywhere the same. Identifying types of social species combines "both the unity that all truly scientific research demands and the diversity that is given in the facts, since the species is the same for all the individual units that make it up and since, on the other hand, the species differ among themselves."[24] We agree.

THE DIVISION OF LABOR IN SOCIETY

Durkheim's first published book, *The Division of Labor in Society,* identifies two distinct social species or types. The first type is that of the preindustrial, undifferentiated society, in which social cohesion is based upon a common set of beliefs and sentiments (he terms this "mechanical solidarity"). The second social type is that of industrial, differentiated society. Durkheim poses the question: How does modern society cohere in the absence of the consensus that binds primitive social systems? His answer was that the division of labor, conceived as occupational specialization, functions to fill "the role that was formerly filled by the common conscience."[25] This form of cohesion he terms "organic solidarity."

Much of *The Division of Labor* constitutes a dialogue with Herbert Spencer. Durkheim devotes the final chapter of Part 1 to distinguishing his conception of organic solidarity from the "contractual solidarity" of Spencer's industrial society. The social type described by Spencer under the rubric of industrial society is not, Emile tells us, a viable way of life. In this type,

> Society does not have to intervene to assure the harmony which is self-established. Spencer says that each man can maintain himself through his work, can exchange his produce for the goods of another, can lend assistance and receive payment, can enter into some association for pursuing private enterprise, small or large, without obeying the direction of society in its totality. The sphere of social action would thus grow narrower and narrower, for it would have no other object than that of keeping individuals from disturbing and harming one another. . . . Under these conditions, the only remaining link between men would be that of an absolutely free exchange.[26]

This contractual solidarity, in Emile's view, was equivalent to no social solidarity at all. For exchange, he argued, brings men "only in superficial contact; they do not interpenetrate, nor do they adhere strongly to one another."[27] Such a society, built on bidding and bargaining, could produce only "transient relations and passing associations" and must therefore degenerate into an anarchic war of all against all.[28]

If Emile were arguing only that exchange alone is insufficient to sustain a modern nation-state, there would be little reason to quarrel. Laws of contract must, of course, be enforced for exchange to continue. To the extent that Spencer neglected this necessary pluralism, Durkheim provides a useful corrective. But Emile goes further than merely pointing out the dependence of exchange relations on other modes of social relations. In our judgment he often (though not always) underestimates the social viability of an individualist life of minimal prescriptions and low group involvement.

At other times and in other places, Young Emile gives way to Master Durkheim, who sees clearly that individualism is no less a social product than other modes of organizing human existence. "Individualism," he explains unequivocally in an essay entitled "Individualism and the Intellectuals," "itself is a social product, like all moralities and all religions. The individual derives from society even the moral beliefs which deify him."[29]

The tension between Master Durkheim, the thoroughgoing social constructionist, and Young Emile, who limited his radical theories to premodern man, is evident from his analysis of crime and punishment in *The Division of Labor*. Durkheim argues that in mechanical societies based on likeness, criminal acts as well as punishment of those transgressions serve a latent function of drawing people together in a common posture of outrage and reminding them of the interests and values they share. Durkheim points to "what happens, particularly in a small town, when some moral scandal has just been committed. They stop each other in the street, they visit each other, they seek to come together to talk of the event and to wax indignant in common."[30] Punishment "does not serve, or else only serves quite secondarily, in correcting the culpable or in intimidating possible followers."[31] Instead its "true function" is "to maintain social cohesion intact by maintaining the conscience commune in all its vitality."[32]

But in modern industrial society, in which cohesion does not depend on a common set of symbols and beliefs, there is apparently no need for crime or punishment. Durkheim's contention that punishment gives way to restitution as society passes from the mechanical to the organic stage of development has often been criticized as empirically untenable.[33] This substantive defect of Young Emile's theory should not obscure the theoretical potential of Master Durkheim's approach to crime and punishment. Criminality, the Master argues, does not inhere in the action itself, but rather is socially constructed: "We must not say that an action shocks the common conscience because it is criminal, but rather that it is criminal because it shocks the common conscience." What confers the quality of crime upon acts "is not the intrinsic quality of a given act but that definition which the collective conscience lends them."[34] Rather than search for the criminal mind, Master Durkheim teaches us to explore the social "mind" that does the classifying, branding, and punishing.

The Master's insight that criminality is socially conferred seems more promising than Emile's formulation that "crime is functional" (a formulation that seems susceptible to charges of function-mongering). Rather than ask what the function of crime is, we prefer to ask about the function of defining certain acts as criminal. Following Master

Durkheim's research program, we believe, entails showing how criminality (and deviance more generally) is socially conferred, and how these social constructions support particular modes of social relations.[35]

For egalitarian animal liberation groups, for instance, inflicting pain upon animals is criminal, just as for radical vegetarians, "meat is murder." The desire to reduce distinctions between animals and human beings stems from and in turn justifies the egalitarian way of life. After all, if one concedes that it is illegitimate to discriminate between animals and people, one can hardly justify discriminating between people.

For Emile, only in undifferentiated, mechanical societies does society impose upon individuals practices and beliefs that contribute to that society's viability. For Master Durkheim, however, social control over the individual is present in every society; it is, in the language of his last work, the "elementary form" of social life. As the Master pushes the mechanical conscience collective down to form the "social substratum" (*substrat social*) upon which viability in all social systems rests, so too does he pluralize the organic so that there become several different viable types of modern life. This more variegated typology of ways of life is most in evidence in his sociological classic, *Suicide.*

SUICIDE

The subject of suicide, a seemingly "individual action affecting the individual only," provided Durkheim with a dramatic vehicle for demonstrating the social origins of individual action. Demonstrating that different social entities have different suicide rates allowed Durkheim to challenge the validity of commonsense explanations that focus on the individual's psychological disposition.[36] Variations in suicide rates among and within modern "organic" societies, moreover, prompted Durkheim to develop a classification of social types that would enable him to distinguish among different types of modern social structures. The act of abandoning life,[37] Durkheim argued in *Suicide,* varies according to four types (he called them "currents") of social environment: egoism, altruism, anomie, and fatalism.[38]

In egoistic suicide, it is "excessive individuation" that leads people to commit suicide. "The bond attaching man to life relaxes," Durkheim explains, "because the ties uniting him with others are slackened or broken."[39] Altruistic suicide is the opposite of egoistic suicide. Rather than inadequate integration into the group, altruistic suicide results when "social integration is too strong," i.e., the individual is "completely absorbed in the group." In such a social environment, in which "the ego is not its own property," the individual cannot resist the collectivity's demand for sacrifice.[40]

Anomic suicide differs from egoistic and altruistic suicide, Durkheim explains, "in its dependence, not on the way in which individuals are attached to society, but on how it [society] regulates them." Although both egoism and anomie are characterized by "society's insufficient presence in individuals," egoistic suicide results from the fact that this form of life "is deficient in truly collective activity," while anomic suicide occurs when "man's activity lacks regulation."[41] The opposite of anomic suicide is fatalistic suicide. In contrast to the lack of social prescriptions that produces anomic suicide, this fourth form of suicide derives from "excessive regulation." It is the suicide of the powerless and is found among "persons with futures pitilessly blocked and passions violently choked by oppressive disciplines."[42]

In terms of the categorization employed, *Suicide* represents a significant advance over *The Division of Labor.* This is not because four is necessarily better than two types but rather because in *Suicide* Durkheim distinguishes the dimensions of group integration and individual regulation that are conflated in the dichotomy of mechanical and organic solidarity. These two dimensions, we should point out, are essentially identical with Mary Douglas's group and grid dimensions.[43] The difference between Durkheim's and Douglas's categories is that Durkheim fails to ask how these two dimensions interact. It is not enough to say, for example, that a person is weakly integrated into a group; one also has to ask whether that person is strongly or weakly tied to a prescriptive grid; the former leads to fatalism, and the latter produces individualism.

Durkheim's failure to distinguish consistently between these two dimensions of regulation and integration has led a number of commentators to conclude that egoism (weak integration) is indistinguishable from anomie (weak regulation) or, at a minimum, that lack of social regulation is but one property of egoism.[44] This confusion, we now see, is due to the fact that he did not discern that the combination of weak regulation and strong integration generates a distinctive social type, which we, following Mary Douglas, term *egalitarianism.*

Instead, anomie seems to be often described as the antithesis of social life. Rather than make anomie a social type in which the norm is minimal regulation of personal behavior, Emile inclines toward a definition of anomie as normlessness. Anomie, Emile writes, is produced by a crisis or abrupt transition that makes society "momentarily incapable of exercising . . . [its] influence."[45] If anomie is to be defined as normlessness, then it seems that it is a condition that could afflict all social types. The question then becomes, given a social type (whether hierarchic, individualist, egalitarian, mechanical, organic, or some other), are those members who have not internalized the cultural norms more likely to commit suicide than those within that social type that have internalized the norms?

Emile's treatment of anomie and especially egoism frequently betrays his tendency to regard modern capitalism as antisocial and even pathological. In the preface to *Suicide,* Emile suggests that the book not only speaks to "the causes of the general contemporary maladjustment being undergone by European societies" but suggests "remedies which may relieve it."[46] Emile associates high levels of egoism with a "weakening of the social fabric," "society's . . . disintegration," "a collective asthenia," and so on.[47] The "enormous" increase in the number of suicides over the past century was clear evidence to Emile of a "pathological phenomenon" that was "becoming daily a greater menace."[48] If the diagnosis is inadequate integration and regulation, the remedy is a call for occupational organizations that could provide the regulation and particularly the integration necessary for society to function.[49]

It is instructive to contrast Emile's discussion of anomie and egoism with his analysis of altruism. Never is there any suggestion that altruism, even in its extreme form, is in any way pathological. Although highly integrated societies generate high suicide rates, Durkheim argues that these suicides are functional for the social order. Altruistic suicide, Durkheim explains, is "imposed by society for social ends." It is obligatory for Hindu women to kill themselves upon their husbands' death or for personal followers to end their lives when their chief dies, Durkheim argues, because "if another possibility were to be admitted social subordination would be inadequate."[50] That is, these obligatory suicides serve to demonstrate (and hence to sustain) not only the part's subservience to the whole but also the hierarch's superiority over the lowerarchs. One wonders, however, why these acts are not classified as executions rather than suicides.[51]

The question of what counts as a suicide suggests a most interesting (and most Durkheimian) line of criticism, a line that has been developed by Jack Douglas in *The Social Meanings of Suicide.* Contra Emile, Douglas argues that variation in suicide rates is due to differences in reporting procedures rather than the incidence of suicide itself.[52] This line of criticism, as Douglas himself recognizes, is consistent with an important strand of the Master himself. Indeed, it is precisely with this type of question that Durkheim's social constructionist approach is at its most powerful. What people count as suicide, Master Durkheim teaches us, will vary by social environment. The boundary between suicide, sacrifice, martyrdom, and even murder, Master Durkheim would say, is socially constructed, not just out there ready to be plucked like whole fruit from a tree.

Consider, for instance, the homeless man who hurls himself off a bridge. Upon reading the story in the next day's newspaper, the egalitarian cries out, "Murderers!" The coercive and inegalitarian "system," he believes, has driven this poor, innocent creature to his undeserved and unwanted death. Reading the same paper, the individualist skips over the story with barely a thought, except perhaps to express regret at the personal tragedy it represents.

In the highly prescribed hierarchy of India, a woman who kills herself upon her husband's death will be classified as a suicide (or perhaps a sacrifice). But to adherents of an individualist or egalitarian culture, this sort of death is likely to be viewed as an execution. How the death is classified, moreover, is of critical importance for the maintenance of the practice. As long as it is seen as suicide (or sacrifice), it can be accepted; to interpret it as a coercive execution, however, is to question its very legitimacy.

Jack Douglas offers the example of the competing meanings that were attached to Marilyn Monroe's death.[53] For the individualist Ayn Rand, Monroe was driven to her death by egalitarian envy of her success; in Rand's view, her death can be seen quite literally as an egalitarian murder. For Norman Mailer, Monroe's death was due to her failure to become the "greatest actress who ever lived," and was thus confirmation of the destruction of the individual that a highly competitive society breeds. People's cultural biases, Master Durkheim would say, serve as filters through which events are sifted in order to support their ways of life.

Viewing the problem of suicide in this way returns functions unambiguously to the center of the stage. People, we predict, will classify suicide and attach meanings to suicide in ways that will defend their way of life. The social construction of suicide can be explained by the contribution it makes in shoring up one way of life and destabilizing others.[54]

THE MASTER, NOT THE WHIPPERSNAPPER

Surveying Durkheim's work, going from *The Elementary Forms* through *The Division of Labor* and *Suicide,* at least four conclusions can be drawn. First, it is valid to speak of Durkheim as having pursued a single line of inquiry. From beginning to end he is concerned with elucidating the social construction of reality. Second, functional explanation was intimately tied up with Durkheim's program of social constructionism.[55] By uncovering the functions (usually, in Durkheim's view, hidden from the view of the participants[56]) served by a practice or belief, Durkheim believed that one could find the social sources of individual thought and action.

Third, between *The Division of Labor* and *Suicide* there is a growth in the richness and variety of social types. The theoretical potential of the implicit fourfold typology employed in *Suicide,* however, was not picked up until Mary Douglas's work in the 1970s. Instead, Durkheim worked primarily within the confines of the dichotomy between primitive (or "mechanical") and modern (or "organic") societies. It was (unfortunately, in our view) this twofold categorization that informed the work of most social scientists who modeled themselves upon Durkheim. The result was not only to neglect egalitarianism and fatalism as social types but also to overlook the prevalence of individualism in so-called primitive societies.

Throughout his work (but particularly in *The Division of Labor* and *Suicide*) there is a constant tension between Young Emile, who looks upon individualism as a pathological and antisocial phenomenon, and Master Durkheim, who treats individualism as a social construction like any other way of life. Young Emile may have the advantage in quantity but Master Durkheim, we think, has the qualitative edge. Both are there; neither is "wrong" or "ridiculous" as an interpretation of Durkheim. Our sympathies, as Part 1 makes all too evident, are with the master, not the whippersnapper.

NOTES

1. Durkheim set apart "scientifically elaborated and criticized concepts" from social constraint. Of course, he could and did say that there were very few scientific concepts. Nevertheless, as Bloor wisely observes: "It represents a concession of principle. It . . . debars the sociology of knowledge from the knowledge that we take most seriously" (David Bloor, "Durkheim and Mauss Revisited: Classification and the Sociology of Knowledge," *Studies in the History and Philosophy of Science* 13, 4 [December 1982]: 267–97; quote on 292–93). Also see Mary Douglas, *Implicit Meanings: Essays in Anthropology* (London: Routledge and Kegan Paul, 1975), xi–xii. Ever since, his intellectual heirs have been quarreling about whether he really meant it and whether it was a warranted concession. See, for example, Thomas F. Gieryn, "Durkheim's Sociology of Scientific Knowledge," *Journal of the History of the Behavioral Sciences,* April 1982, 107–29, esp. 108–10.

2. Emile Durkheim and Marcel Mauss, *Primitive Classification,* trans. R. Needham (Chicago: University of Chicago Press, 1963), 11; first published in 1903.

3. Emile Durkheim, *The Elementary Forms of the Religious Life: Study in Religious Sociology,* trans. Joseph Ward Swain (New York: Free Press, 1965), 21–33; first published in 1912.

4. Ibid., 30.

5. Emile Durkheim, "The Realm of Sociology as a Science," trans. Everett K. Wilson, *Social Forces,* June 1981, 1054–70; quote on 1065.

6. Emile Durkheim, *The Rules of the Sociological Method,* trans. Sarah A. Solovay and John H. Mueller, ed. George E.G. Catlin (Chicago: University of Chicago Press, 1938), first published in 1895. Durkheim, "Realm of Sociology," esp. 1061–62.

7. Paul Bohannan, "Conscience Collective and Culture," in Kurt H. Wolff, ed., *Emile Durkheim, 1858–1917* (Columbus: Ohio State University Press, 1960), 77–96, esp. 79–80.

8. Durkheim, *The Elementary Forms,* 29.

9. Koenrad W. Swart, "'Individualism' in the Mid-Nineteenth Century (1826–1860)," *Journal of the History of Ideas* 23, 1 (Jan.-March 1962): 77–90; quote on 78.

10. Ibid., 80–84.

11. Robert A. Nisbet, *Emile Durkheim* (Englewood Cliffs, N.J.: Prentice-Hall, 1965), 57.

12. Ibid., 58.

13. See Aaron Wildavsky, "Rationality in Writing: Linear and Curvilinear," *Journal of Public Policy* 1, pt. 1 (February 1981): 124–40; also in Wildavsky, *Craftways* (New Brunswick, N.J.: Transaction Publishers, 1989), 9–24.

14. For a recent instance, noteworthy for its candor, see Mary Douglas's preface to her *How Institutions Think* (Syracuse: Syracuse University Press, 1986), in which she admits that "this is the first book I should have written after writing on African field work" (ix).

15. Durkheim, *The Elementary Forms,* 52–53, 56.

16. Ibid., 258, 388.

17. Douglas, *Implicit Meanings,* xiv.

18. Ibid.

19. Durkheim and Mauss, *Primitive Classification.*

20. Durkheim, *The Elementary Forms,* 257–58, 17, 475, 420. Durkheim was not, of course, the first to analyze religious phenomena from a functional perspective. We have already seen that Montesquieu, Comte, and Spencer all adopted an essentially functional approach in accounting for religion's persistence. And Durkheim's thinking on this subject was directly influenced by William Robertson Smith's *The Religion of the Semites* (published in 1889, over twenty years before *The Elementary Forms*), which presented the thesis that "religion did not exist for the saving of souls but for the preservation and welfare of society." (Cited in Mary Douglas, *Purity and Danger* [London: Routledge and Kegan Paul, 1966], 19. Also see E. E. Evans-Pritchard, *Theories of Primitive Religion* [London: Oxford University Press, 1965], chap. 3.) Taking note of Durkheim's intellectual debts in no way belittles the originality of his formulation. We would do well to remember Alfred North Whitehead's aphor-

ism that "everything of importance has been said before by somebody who did not discover it."

21. Consider, for instance, Colin M. Turnbull's account of the pygmies of the Ituri forest in *The Forest People* (New York: Simon and Schuster, 1961) and *Wayward Servants: The Two Worlds of the African Pygmies* (Garden City, N.Y.: Natural History Press, 1965).

22. Durkheim, *The Elementary Forms,* 423.

23. Our point, it bears stressing, is not that nonhierarchical ways of life do not use the past but that they use the past in different ways. Egalitarians, for instance, may keep alive their sense of outrage by reminding each other of past persecutions and martyrs.

24. Durkheim, *The Rules of Sociological Method,* 76–77. Master Durkheim criticized Comte for having "failed to appreciate the existence of social species." Comte erred, the Master observed, in that he "thought he could represent the progress of all human societies as identical with that of a single people" (77).

25. Emile Durkheim, *The Division of Labor in Society* (New York: Free Press, 1933), 49, 173; first published in 1893.

26. Ibid., 200–01. Durkheim also criticizes Spencer and others of a "utilitarian" persuasion for advancing an illegitimate teleology in explaining the growth of the division of labor. The benefits accruing from the division of labor, Durkheim argues, cannot explain its proliferation, for it assumes actors had that end in mind (ibid., 165–66, 233–55); Durkheim's confusion about Spencer is reproduced in Raymond Boudon, *The Logic of Social Action* (London: Routledge and Kegan Paul, 1979), 153. However valid this is as a criticism of utilitarian thought in general, it is not a fair criticism of Spencer. Spencer explicitly repudiates the view that "advantages or disadvantages of this or that arrangement furnished motives for establishing or maintaining" the arrangement. "Conditions and not intentions determine," argued Spencer (*The Principles of Sociology,* vol. 2 [New York: Appleton, 1896], 395). For Spencer, it is environments and not individuals that do the selecting.

27. Here we have used the translation in Steven Lukes, *Emile Durkheim: His Life and Work* (Stanford: Stanford University Press, 1985), 145.

28. Durkheim, *The Division of Labor,* 204. Steven Lukes shares Durkheim's bias, arguing that "the assumption that . . . a vast system of bargaining and exchange . . . would be a system as opposed to chaos was merely Spencer's inheritance from Adam Smith and the Manchester School" (Lukes, *Emile Durkheim,* 143).

29. Emile Durkheim, "Individualism and the Intellectuals," trans. S. Lukes and J. Lukes, with note, *Political Studies* 17 (March 1969): 14–30, quote on 28.

30. Durkheim, *The Division of Labor,* 102–03. Similarly, George Herbert Mead argued that "the criminal . . . is responsible for a sense of solidarity, aroused among those whose attitude would otherwise be centered upon interests quite divergent from each other. . . . That attitude of hostility toward the lawbreaker has the unique advantage of uniting all members of the community" ("The Psychology of Punitive Justice," *American Journal of Sociology* 23 [1918]: 577–602; quote on 591).

31. Durkheim, *The Division of Labor,* 108.

32. Translation of passage from *The Division of Labor* is from Lukes, *Emile Durkheim,* 161.

33. According to T. Anthony Jones, Durkheim subsequently recognized his mistake ("Durkheim, Deviance, and Development: Opportunities Lost and Regained," *Social Forces,* June 1981, 1009–24, especially 1012, 1014).

34. Durkheim, *The Division of Labor,* 81; and *Rules of Sociological Method,* 70.

35. Examples of this approach (which currently goes under the heading of "labeling theory") include Howard S. Becker, *Outsiders: Studies in the Sociology of Deviance* (New York: Free Press, 1963); Kai T. Erikson, *Wayward Puritans: A Study in the Sociology of Deviance* (New York: Wiley, 1966); and E. M. Schur, *Labeling Deviant Behavior: Its Sociological Implications* (New York: Harper and Row, 1971).

36. Jack D. Douglas, *The Social Meanings of Suicide* (Princeton: Princeton University Press, 1967), 16; Emile Durkheim, *Suicide: A Study in Sociology* (Glencoe, Ill.: Free Press, 1951), 46; first published in 1897. In addition to demonstrating the inadequacy of individual psychology as an explanation for suicide, Durkheim was also concerned with disproving explanations of suicide based upon the objective physical environment: "One man kills himself in the midst of affluence," he observed, "another in the lap of poverty. . . . There is nothing which cannot serve as an occasion for Suicide" (*Suicide,* 298, 300).

37. Durkheim defined suicide as "all cases of death resulting directly or indirectly from a positive or negative act of the victim himself, which he knows will produce this result" (*Suicide,* 44). By adopting a definition requiring only that the individual know the consequences of his action (or inaction) will be death, Durkheim thereby cut himself off from the common understanding of suicide requiring that the individual desire to kill himself. The consequences of Durkheim's definition for his theory are discussed in Whitney Pope, *Durkheim's Suicide: A Classic Analyzed* (Chicago: University of Chicago Press, 1976), 10–11.

38. In arguing that social currents ("states of the varying social environments") cause variation in suicide rates, Durkheim asserted that the four main types of social environment are found in all societies, albeit in different degrees. When these currents are in equilibrium, suicide is lower; when one force gains greatly at the expense of the others, society's well-being diminishes and the form of suicide grows that corresponds to the most extreme social environment. As Jack Douglas asserts: "Durkheim's idea that a balance of egoism, altruism, and anomie is the critical determinant of the suicide rate of a society is used here for the sake of being consistent with the theory presented in *Suicide.* Since, however, Durkheim and almost everyone else has overlooked this point, nothing much will be made of it here" (*The Social Meanings of Suicide,* 40).

39. Durkheim, *Suicide,* 217, 281; also see 214–15.

40. Ibid., 217, 221.

41. Ibid., 258.

42. Ibid., 276n.

43. A similar congruence is pointed out in David Ostrander, "One- and Two-Dimensional Models of the Distribution of Beliefs," in Mary Douglas, ed., *Essays on the Sociology of Perception* (London: Routledge and Kegan Paul, 1982), 17–18.

44. Barclay D. Johnson, "Durkheim's One Cause of Suicide," *American Sociological Review* 30 (1965): 875–86, esp. 883–84. Also see Andrew F. Henry and James F. Short, Jr., *Suicide and Homicide* (Glencoe, Ill.: Free Press, 1954), 74. One can find a number of places in *Suicide* where Emile seems to collapse anomie (regulation) and egoism (group integration). See, for example, p. 382, where he writes that anomie "springs from the lack of collective forces at certain points in society; that is, of groups established for the regulation of social life."

45. Durkheim, *Suicide,* 252.

46. Ibid., 37.

47. Ibid., 281, 214.

48. Ibid., 370.

49. Ibid., 381–82; Lukes, *Emile Durkheim,* 225.

50. Durkheim, *Suicide,* 220.

51. The same question is raised by Raymond Firth in "Suicide and Risk-Taking in Tikopia Society," in Anthony Giddens, ed., *The Sociology of Suicide: A Selection of Readings* (London: Frank Cass, 1971), 212.

52. J. Douglas, *Social Meanings of Suicide.* Also see J. M. Atkinson, *Discovering Suicide* (London: Macmillan, 1978); Atkinson, "Societal Reactions to Suicide: the Role of Coroners' Definitions," in S. Cohen, ed., *Images of Deviance* (Harmondsworth: Penguin, 1971), 165–91; and Lincoln H. Day, "Durkheim on Religion and Suicide—A Demographic Critique," *Sociology* 21, 3 (August 1987): 449–61.

53. J. Douglas, *Social Meanings of Suicide,* 218–20.

54. Where is the evidence? The layman (i.e., all of us outside our specialties) is confronted by a bewildering series of reports in which, from year to year, it is said that Durkheim has been refuted, has triumphed again, or is someplace in between. Interested readers might consult James R. Marshall and Robert W. Hodge, "Political Integration and the Effect of War on Suicide: United States, 1933–76," *Social Forces* 58, 3 (March 1981): 771–78; Steven F. Messner, "Societal Development, Social Equality and Homicide: A Cross-National Test of a Durkheimian Model," *Social Forces* 61, 1 (September 1982): 225–40; K. D. Breault and Karen Barkey, "Comparative Analysis of Durkheim's Theory of Egoistic Suicide," *Sociological Quarterly* 23 (1982): 321–31; K. D. Breault, "Suicide in America: A Test of Durkheim's Theory of Religious and Family Integration, 1933–1980," *American Journal of Sociology* 92, 3 (November 1986): 628–56; and Day, "Durkheim on Religion and Suicide."

55. That the concept of function lay at the heart of Durkheim's conception of social science is evident from his inaugural lecture at the University of Bordeaux, in which he suggested that "it is to the study of functions that we must above all apply ourselves." Functional analysis was central to social science, Durkheim explained, because only then could one "determine the

conditions for the conservation of societies," which, for him, "was the object of sociology" (Lukes, *Emile Durkheim,* 138–39).

56. See, for example, in *The Elementary Forms* where Durkheim writes that "the reasons with which the faithful justify [their behavior] may be, and generally are, erroneous; but the true reasons do not cease to exist, and it is the duty of science to discover them" (15).

CHAPTER 8

Marx

Throughout this section we have addressed two questions to these masters of social thought: Did they use functional explanation, and did they go beyond the same two types of analytic categories—hierarchy and individualism? The question of functional explanation is easily disposed of, despite the fact that Marxists have been among the most vocal critics of functionalism. Among their chief complaints is that functional analysis fails to account for change and is biased toward preserving the status quo. Yet, looking past the labels, one finds that no school of thought more frequently draws upon functional explanation, i.e., explanations in which action or belief is explained by its consequences. Even their put-downs of functionalism are frequently functional in character—witness, for instance, Michael Burawoy's recent claim that "structural functionalism provided an intellectual framework for celebrating the virtues of American society."[1]

The question of analytic categories, however, is more difficult. For one thing, Marx had no formal typology; for another, Marx's theory is evolutionary in that capitalism gives way to communism. He felt it necessary, therefore, to show that another type existed before capitalism. In this way he would be consistent in arguing that just as a primitive, egalitarian society gave way to feudalistic hierarchy, which in turn was superseded by individualistic markets, so would capitalism be overtaken by communism.

After a quick foray into Marx's functional explanation, we shall undertake a search for his use of different ways of life. We begin with Marx's theory of historical materialism, *material* in that the political economy most productive at a given time triumphs over other modes of organizing production and *historical* in that this technological or productive superiority changes over time, except, of course, until communism demonstrates its superiority.

MARX'S HISTORICAL MATERIALISM

The case that functional explanation is inherent in the theories of Karl Marx (1818–1883) has been argued most persuasively by G. A.

Cohen in *Karl Marx's Theory of History*.[2] Cohen contends that Marx's theory of historical materialism, as outlined by Marx in his famous 1859 "Preface" to *A Contribution to the Critique of Political Economy*,[3] entails two types of functional explanations: (1) the forces of production (the means of production: tools, machinery, raw materials, and so on; and labor: skills, technical knowledge, and so on) explain the relations of production (the distribution of economic power); and (2) economic power relations explain the legal, governmental, and ideological superstructure. These are functional explanations, Cohen reasons, "because I cannot otherwise reconcile them with two further Marxian theses, namely that (3) the economic structure [relations of production] of a society promotes the development of its productive forces, and (4) the superstructure of a society stabilizes its economic structure."[4]

Statements (3) and (4) assert that the economic power relations are functional (have positive consequences) for the development of the productive forces and that the superstructure is functional for the stability of economic relations (which Marx terms the "base"). Cohen recognizes that "these claims do not by themselves entail that economic structures and superstructures are *explained* by the stated functions: A may be functional for B even though it is false that A exists *because* it is functional for B."[5] But when combined with statements (1) and (2), which argue for the explanatory primacy of productive forces over economic relations, and of economic relations over the superstructure, it becomes necessary to interpret Marx as presenting, not just a functional statement of the effect of A on B, but a functional *explanation* of A in terms of its effect on B. More specifically, the prevailing mode of economic relations (the base) is explained by the needs of the productive forces. Similarly, the legal, governmental, and ideological superstructure is explained by the needs of the economic base.

Cohen concedes that so far, "Marxists have not done much to establish that [their functional explanations] are true."[6] Yet historical materialism, on the face of it, is plausible enough to warrant study: Productive forces do develop, social relations are related to economic power, and ideology justifies them both. Best is the Scottish verdict: not proven. Rather than rummaging history for examples that are bound to be inconclusive, we prefer to see what a comparison with our cultural theory can tell us about functional relationships in historical materialism.

From our perspective, assigning primacy to technological-material forces is misleading. All four ways of life, we have argued, are compatible with any level of technological development. Some, of course, do better at certain stages of technological development than do others. Our point is that the four ways of life are what actually make technological development possible.[7] Technologies come and go, but the viable ways of life are always with us. Social relations, in our view, together with the cultural biases that justify those relations, deserve explanatory primacy, for it is ways of life that give meaning to technologies. "Meaning" cannot be inherent in things. The human controls the nonhuman, not the reverse.

Marx's second functional thesis connecting economic power relations to the political and ideological superstructure is more closely akin to our theory of social viability. We agree with Marx that "in the social production of their life, men enter into definite relations that are indispensable and independent of their will."[8] That such relations functionally explain much of individual behavior and belief is a central claim of our theory. Where we differ is that Marx appears to limit social relations to an individual's relationship to the means of production. The remainder of this section is devoted to Marx's second thesis concerning the relationship between the economic base and the political and ideological superstructure on the grounds that (1) it provides greater scope for a dialogue between Marxian theory and our cultural theory, and (2) most observers, Marxist and non-Marxist alike, regard the functional relationship between the economic base and the political and ideological superstructure as the more fundamental Marxian thesis.

MYSTIFICATION IN MARXIAN AND CULTURAL THEORY

No teacher teaches what Robert Merton terms "manifest functions"; no one begins by saying that the world of experience is exactly what it looks like. This is not done for fear of the obvious retort, "Why, then, do I need you, Herr Professor?" Instead, social scientists specialize in latent functions: "The world might look like this," we say confidently, "but it's really something else again; stick with me and I'll show you how to distinguish appearances from realities." In this respect, Marx is not unlike the rest of us.

Things are never as they seem in class societies, Marx tells us, because exploitation must be disguised for the social order to be sustained. Since rulers do not like to think of themselves as exploiters, benefiting unjustly from the labor of others, and the exploited must be kept ignorant of their subjection, lest they revolt, the truth must be kept from both rulers and ruled alike. For instance, the capitalist system of wage labor, by which workers are paid by the hour, conceals "every trace of the division of the working day into necessary labour and surplus-labour."[9] Workers are thus fooled into believing they are being adequately compensated for their work (just as employers are deluded into believing that they are offering just compensation), while in reality a surplus product is being extracted from workers by capitalists.

In Volume 3 of *Capital,* Marx voiced his belief that "all science would be superfluous if the manifest form and the essence of things directly coincided."[10] Implicit in this statement, as G. A. Cohen has shown in a lovely appendix called "Karl Marx and the Withering Away of Social Science,"[11] is the belief that social science would cease to be necessary in a socialist society, because socialism, unlike capitalism, would not be based on deception. Instead, socialist planning, through a popularly conceived and implemented plan, would tell everyone what is happening and why. Socialist society would abolish all institutions, which, according to Marx, represent "fixation of social activity, consolidation of what we ourselves produce into an objective power above us, growing out of our control, thwarting our expectations, bringing to naught our calculations."[12]

Among the many things radically altered by the socialist revolution would thus be the replacement of latent with manifest functions. With self-realization replacing institutional constraint, individual behavior in Marx's future society could be explained solely in terms of what individuals said they wanted. Having liberated people from necessity, socialism would then free them from those social institutions that shape human behavior (to use Marx's phrase) "behind the back" of the individual.[13] Born good, mankind would no longer be corrupted by evil institutions.

The difference between Marx and us on this point, as on others, lies in how thoroughly the standpoint of mystification is pursued. To Marx, mystification is limited to exploitative systems such as capitalism and feudalism (roughly akin, respectively, to individualism and hierarchy). In our view, mystification applies to all ways of life. There are no privileged ways of life. *Fetishism,* defined by Marx as a "social relation between men that assumes, in their eyes, the fantastic form of a relation between things,"[14] is a characteristic of all ways of life, except that its content differs according to its cultural bias. That a hierarchy invests a royal seal with special powers or that egalitarians appeal to "the balance of nature" to stop unwanted development does not make an adherent of these ways of life any more or less mystical than the entrepreneur who claims to foresee better than others which way the stock market will turn. If a way of life is to appear plausible either to adherents or to potential converts, it must make what is socially constructed appear part of the natural order. What is needed then is a theory that reveals how all ways of organizing social life, not just the ones we don't like, reproduce themselves.

MARX'S CLAIM TO A PRIVILEGED POSITION

Marx's claim for a transcendent way of life is closely linked to an argument for a privileged position for Marxist theory. George Lukacs, among others, reasons that Marxism is privileged because it is the theory of the proletariat, the only class that acts in the interest of humanity rather than in its own narrow class interest. For Marx, rival theories advanced by bourgeois social scientists are regarded more as ideologies to be demystified than as competing views of social reality. More specifically, a theory is to be explained by its function in legitimating ruling class domination. Were the Marxist view generalized to all ways of life, we would think better of it.

If it is possible to find a stance above the struggle, a perspective free of bias, such as the one Marx claims for his theory, then we should of course seek these lofty heights. Who would peer "through a glass darkly" when he might see with crystal clarity? If, however, as we think, only partial views are possible, the best mankind can do is seek to understand each source of bias, criticizing it from the perspective of the other biases. The hermit's cave, which is most definitely not the station from which those who call themselves critical theorists survey their fellow humans, is only a partial exception to this stricture. The hermit cleaves to a way of life that has its own distinctive bias: away from all coercive social involvement. Since to criticize the followers of the engaged ways of life would be to coerce them (or, at any rate, to provide justifications for interfering in their lives), the hermit must withdraw through cool contemplation. If he opts for hot-headed rejection, he will end up somewhere else: among the egalitarians.

Does our essential pluralism run up against the usual objections to relativistic statements, namely, if I claim your truth is partial, mine must be also. Are all socially grounded theories, cultural as well as Marxian, false? Socially grounded, yes; false, not necessarily. Mary Douglas calls her seminal essay "Cultural Bias," signifying that all perception is biased, not necessarily that it is untrue. Each of the cultural biases may be correct under different circumstances. The nonexistence of a privileged position means not that we cannot get closer to the truth but rather that each bias must be critically evaluated. We can expose the weaknesses of each way of life, but we cannot create a godlike way of life without weaknesses.

Marx sometimes assumes that demonstrating the function a theory serves for a class absolves him from the responsibility of ascertaining the validity of the theory. If, as Marx states in *The German Ideology,* "the ruling ideas are nothing more than the ideal expression of the dominant material relationships,"[15] then it is easy to see why a search for the hidden agenda motivating an idea becomes a substitute for gauging the truth of that idea. So, for instance, Marx dismisses Kant as the "whitewashing spokesman" of the German bourgeoisie, and ridicules Jeremy Bentham as "that insipid, pedantic, leather-tongued oracle of the ordinary bourgeois intelligence."[16]

We would do well, as Jon Elster and G. A. Cohen have both suggested, to divorce the origins of a theory from its subsequent diffusion and acceptance. Elster proposes "to understand [Marx] more charitably as explaining not the actual emergence of the views of Malthus or Kant, but their subsequent diffusion and acceptance."[17] Similarly Cohen, who is even more charitable, senses "traces in Marx of a Darwinian mechanism, a notion that thought-systems are produced in comparative independence from social constraint, but persist and gain social life following a filtration process which selects those well adapted for ideological service."[18] Distinguishing persistence from emergence would allow Marxists to avoid the tendency to treat intellectuals as class lackeys, while still grounding ideology in social relations.

This "filter model" of ideology based on search and subsequent selection constitutes, as Cohen argues, an elaboration of a functional explanation. Intellectuals producing ideas do not (or need not) intend to produce the beneficial consequences for the ruling class. But members of the ruling class, who are constantly on the lookout for ways to justify their dominance, both to themselves and others, select out those ideas they think will legitimate their rule. Thus although beneficial consequences need play no role in the *emergence* of an idea, they do explain why some ideas spread while others seem to fall on deaf ears.

The assumption of ruling class hegemony tends to undercut Marx's attempt to construct a sociology of knowledge. According to Marx, "the class which has the means of material production at its disposal, has control at the same time over the means of mental production, so that thereby, generally speaking, the ideas of those who lack the means of mental production are subject to it."[19] But if the object of a sociology of knowledge is to find what ideas go with which set of social relations and ideological justifications, Marx impedes the project by positing (or, more precisely, to the extent that he posits) that a single set of ideas— those ideas of the ruling class—will be diffused throughout the entire society. Cultural theory, we argue in the next section, improves on Marx's conceptualization by increasing the variety of cultural biases that can exist within a society.

BEYOND INDIVIDUALIST HEGEMONY

Marx's strength as a theorist is his attention to how individualism as a way of life coheres by working "behind the back" of individuals to form preferences; his weakness, which we have seen he shares with many others, is a lack of variety in his conceptualization of social relations. Like many other thinkers of his time, Marx consigns hierarchy to history. He downgrades fatalism into a social existence lacking in its own sustaining mechanisms while egalitarianism, projected far into the future, or located, as we shall see, deep in the past, is postulated but not analyzed. Why should not egalitarianism, like hierarchy and individualism before it, have its own internal dynamics and contradictions?

Fascination with the question of how the capitalist system reproduces itself, a good question about any system, leads Marx to the functionalist position that behavior can be explained by its beneficial consequences for the capitalist class. But his exaggerated view of individualism's hegemony leads him (and his followers) to view almost every type of behavior as explainable in terms of its benefit for capitalism. Neglected is the possibility that some behavior patterns may be better explained in terms of the beneficial consequences for adherents of competing ways of life.

Take, for instance, the apathy of the masses. Marx observed that a fatalistic attitude on the part of the oppressed is a great asset to the capitalist class. Here as elsewhere, Marx does not treat this as an accidental consequence. In Marx's view, the fatalistic attitudes of the exploited can be *explained* by the benefits such attitudes bring to the exploiter. But might not fatalistic attitudes, we ask, be as well or better explained by the benefits that accrue to the exploited?

In a critique of Marx's thesis, Jon Elster puts forward an alternative explanation that highlights the possible beneficial psychic consequences that accrue to those who adhere to fatalistic ideas. Following Paul Veyne, Elster suggests that fatalistic attitudes reduce cognitive dissonance for fatalists by teaching them not to want what they couldn't get anyway.[20] The explanation for fatalistic attitudes is thus to be sought not (or, at least, not only) in its function for individualism but in its consequences for members of a fatalistic way of life.

Elster is correct in singling out Marx's explanation for apathy as an unsuccessful functional explanation, for Marx fails to specify how the benefits of fatalistic attitudes for individualism cause *fatalists* to adhere to these beliefs. But if Elster's explanation is superior to Marx's, it is not, as Elster claims, because Marx's explanation is functional in form and Elster's is not. For Elster's psychologically based explanation—adherence to fatalistic beliefs is explained by the function those beliefs serve for the psychic well-being of those in fatalist social relations—is no less functional in character than that offered by Marx. The difference is that Elster provides an individual-level mechanism that explains how the consequences of fatalistic beliefs become their cause. Marx's theory is deficient, not because it is functional in character, but because it does not recognize that fatalism is a way of life, which, like individualism, shapes the preferences of its members.

The inadequacy of positing capitalist hegemony is also illustrated by Marx's attempt to explain why capitalists, particularly in England, did not directly control the state apparatus. Abdication in favor of the aristocracy, Marx explained, served the long-term interest of English capitalists because the political struggle between rulers and ruled blurred the lines of economic struggle between exploiters and exploited.[21] Couched in terms of an unintended effect of losing a power struggle, this statement would be unobjectionable. But as a latent functional explanation for capitalist "abdication," it becomes problematic, for, as Elster has pointed out, such an indirect strategy requires that the action be deliberately sought by capitalists.[22]

Marx's tendency to explain even apparent setbacks in terms of their beneficial consequences for capitalism is due in large part, we believe, to his teleological view of history. Because the outcome is predetermined and capitalism has to triumph in order to fulfill its "world-historical" role, albeit only for a time, there is a strong tendency in Marx (and Marxism) to discount behavior that may benefit competing ways of life. It is his teleological view of history and not the use of functional explanation per se, we believe, that makes Marx particularly vulnerable to the charges of illegitimate teleology leveled by Elster. Because it posits no known goal or certain direction to history, our cultural theory provides what we believe is a more solid grounding on which to revitalize functional explanation. In contrast to Marxism, which often seems to posit that, like Lola, whatever capital needs, capital gets, our theory recognizes that there is nothing guaranteeing that a way of life will maintain or expand itself in any specific time or place.

Seen from a cultural-functional viewpoint, which allows for the weakness of individualism and for cooperation between ways of life, the "abdication" of the English bourgeoisie described by Marx is understandable. The individualists' reluctance to exercise state power need not reflect either the needs of capital or the capitalists' innate craftiness. Instead such behavior can be explained by the individualists' acceptance of a coalition with hierarchy in which state authority was limited and egalitarianism was resisted. As G.D.H. Cole explains, capitalists were satisfied with aristocratic rule "provided that the government did not govern too much, and protected their property against levellers from below."[23] Had the terms of the alliance been broken— e.g., had the government tried to increase regulation of economic behavior substantially—individualists might have been provoked to break away.

Marx's dichotomy between exploiter and exploitee has the virtue of emphasizing conflict, but the twofold defect of slighting cooperation and granting functions to only one group, the exploiter. Ways of life, we believe, do not inhabit a zero-sum universe. Cultural cooperation may benefit both members of an alliance. Individualism, for instance, may profit from an alliance with hierarchy by providing the central authority necessary to repel foreign aggression, and hierarchy may gain the economic growth that it might not otherwise achieve. Cooperation, of course, does not mean an absence of manipulation (exploitation, if you prefer). But exploitation, we wish to emphasize, is not the monopoly of a single way of life. Adherents of each way of life enter into manipulative relationships with rivals. Only hermits neither manipulate nor are manipulated, but they would not be able to take up, and reproduce, their distinctive way of life if there was not always a manipulative system in the four engaged ways of life for them to withdraw from.

If all members of this manipulative system were to abandon their preferred ways of life and rush headlong toward the hermit's way of life, that way of life would become unlivable before any of them got there. Fortunately, most adherents of the engaged ways of life, most of the time, find the hermit's way of life repulsive. The hermit's way of life, we should stress, is not free from bias. Its bias, in contrast to the other four ways of life, is against manipulation, both its exercise and its acceptance. This, we will now show, is certainly not the bias that sustains communism.

IS COMMUNISM A NEW WAY OF LIFE?

The transition from feudalism to capitalism described by Marx is readily recognizable as the transition from (technologically primitive) hierarchy to (technologically developed) individualism. This same development is described in the theories of all the great nineteenth-century social thinkers. What is new in Marx is the introduction of communism as a form of social organization, in both the very distant past and the very distant future. The question arises whether communism represents something new under the sun. Has Marx at last uncovered a way of life that cannot be subsumed under one of our five ways?

Marx never described this future life of communism at any length, perhaps because this would have detracted from revolutionary activity, making it easier for opponents to attack and proponents to disagree, or just because there was not time. We can gain some clues, however, as to what this communist future was to look like, through Marx's description of its mirror image, primitive communism.

Maurice Bloch's fine book *Marxism and Anthropology* documents Marx's efforts to find in primitive societies models of alternative ways (i.e., alternative to feudalistic hierarchy and competitive capitalism) of organizing social life. Marx and Engels wanted, Bloch informs us, "examples and cases to show that the institutions of capitalism are historically specific and therefore changeable; in order to demonstrate this, they looked for examples of institutions which were as different from those of capitalism as possible."[24] Was not Victorian England celebrated for its sexual monogamy, family life, and private property? Why, then, Marx would find peoples purporting to be promiscuous, sharing sex, and holding property in common. Was not the capitalist market impersonal? Marx would emphasize kinship ties with all sorts of reciprocal moral obligations. If men were dominant under capitalism, he would find groups in which women were equal to or better than men. Thus Marx (and Engels, too, who was active in this endeavor[25]) created the vision of an undifferentiated society without marriage, the family, sex roles, and private property. In this primitive world as portrayed by Marx, Bloch explains, "there was no exploitation, there was no inequality of any kind even between men and women."[26]

From this description, technologically primitive peoples would appear to have lived an egalitarian way of life (certainly it is not individualistic, fatalistic, or hierarchical).[27] This finding opened up the possibility that human beings could again live an egalitarian life, only this time, with advanced technology, it would be even better.

Many scholars insist that Marx was not really an egalitarian because he opposed equality of condition, which he regarded as rhetoric redolent of bourgeois sentimentality. Worse, "he views it in practice," as Allen Woods concludes, "as a pretext for class oppression."[28] By this, Marx signifies that the ideas of the oppressing capitalist class, equality in civil society and equal opportunity to acquire property, are essentially inegalitarian. Only the abolition of classes would bring genuine equality. Whether Marx opposed equality of condition per se or just bourgeois versions of equality cannot be determined by the available evidence.

Sameness, it is insisted, moreover, was not Marx's goal. Rather Marx scholars say that he envisioned a society in which people could fully realize their potential. Communism would give each according to his needs without necessarily giving each the same.

This objection misses the defining characteristics of the egalitarian way of life. The central feature of egalitarianism, as we have conceptualized that way of life, is not equality of material conditions but equality of power relations. No one, in an egalitarian way of life, has the right to tell another what to do or what to be. In this sense of the term, Marx is every bit an egalitarian and communism is a typically egalitarian vision.

Communism, as Marx conceived it, was to be a life without differentiation. In *The German Ideology,* he expressed his vision of communist society as one "where nobody has one exclusive sphere of activity." Instead communist man can "do one thing today and another tomorrow, to hunt in the morning, fish in the afternoon, rear cattle in the evening, criticize after dinner, just as I have a mind, without ever becoming hunter, fisherman, shepherd or critic."[29] In this future society, no human being will have the authority to tell another what to do.

Communist society, in Marx's view, is to be characterized not only by an absence of authority but also, as the word "communist" suggests, by a strong sense of community. Each individual will participate in the running of common affairs. In contrast to the self-seeking, competitive individualism of capitalism, communist society is to be characterized by cooperation and spontaneous coordination among individuals. Combining these two features—strong communitarianism and the absence of authority—shows communist society as envisaged by Marx to closely resemble the high group–low grid way of life that we label egalitarianism.

If, as we have argued, communism is an egalitarian way of life, we would expect it to confront certain predictable organizational difficulties in trying to rule a society rather than only to criticize established authorities. Egalitarian ways of life, our cultural theory tells us, face two defining organizational problems: (1) they are unable to command members to contribute to group purposes, and (2) they require that every group decision be consented to by each member. The "free-rider problem" means that egalitarian ways of life have a difficult time obtaining resources from group members to achieve their aims, and the requirement of consensus among the members results in frequent paralysis, indecision, and schism.

There are two alternative routes out of these egalitarian dilemmas. One is to replace collective action with self-regulation. Without a collectivity there can be no free riders, nor any need for consensus. This individualism is unacceptable to Marxists, however, for not only does this take them back to the very free-market capitalism from which they wish to escape, but for those who wish to make a revolution, rather than standing back and waiting for it to occur, collective action is precisely what is called for.

Hierarchy, as Lenin saw, is a solution to both egalitarian dilemmas. Members of a hierarchy cannot ride for free because their participation, including their financial contribution, can be commanded. And hierarchy makes decisionmaking, and hence group action, possible by tying authority to position.[30] Lenin's genius was to see that while anti-authority principles were well-suited to discrediting existing authority, they were inadequate to the task of creating and carrying out a revolution. An effective revolutionary group, Lenin argued, would have to be structured in a hierarchical fashion.[31] The hierarchical Communist party was thus a means to defeat existing authority.

As a theorist, Marx's major deficiency is that he never gave the same searching scrutiny to the biases of egalitarianism that he gave to those of individualism, hierarchy, and fatalism. Had he analyzed the conditions and behaviors that an egalitarian way of life needs to sustain itself with only half the insight he brought to bear on the question of individualism's viability, he might have seen the flaw in his future communist utopia. Had he, and his followers, understood the dynamics of the egalitarian way of life, they would have seen that its coherence depends on being out of power and that its adherents certainly could not rule alone. Marx's failure to see that egalitarianism is not a privileged position, that it, like every other way of life, has limitations had not only theoretical but practical consequences.

That means become ends is less surprising when viewed from a cultural perspective in which the adage "As you organize, so shall you behave" holds. Out of power, Soviet Communist party leaders could espouse egalitarian rhetoric without being committed to it. In power, they acted out the implications of their hierarchical internal structure. The one exception we know of is the Cultural Revolution in China where, as the hierarchical Communist party faltered, Mao Zedong became a charismatic leader of an egalitarian faction (see Chapter 12 for a cultural analysis) in order to reverse the very state of affairs—early egalitarian rhetoric out of power, hierarchy in power—we have claimed is built in to the organization of communist parties when they assume power. The organizational dilemma explains the disparity between the egalitarian communism described by Marx and the authoritarian communism experienced by the Soviet and other peoples.

NOTES

1. Michael Burawoy, "Introduction: The Resurgence of Marxism in American Sociology," *American Journal of Sociology,* 1982, S1.

2. G. A. Cohen, *Karl Marx's Theory of History: A Defense* (Princeton: Princeton University Press, 1978). Also see Robert K. Merton, *Social Theory and Social Structure* (Glencoe, Ill.: Free Press, 1957), 39–42; and Arthur L.

Stinchcombe, *Constructing Social Theories* (New York: Harcourt, Brace & World), 93–98.

3. The relevant passage from Marx reads: "In the social production of their life, men enter into definite relations that are indispensable and independent of their will, relations of production which correspond to a definite stage of development of their material productive forces. The sum total of these relations of production constitutes the economic structure of society, the real foundation, on which rises a legal and political superstructure and to which correspond definite forms of social consciousness" (Karl Marx, "Preface" to *A Contribution to the Critique of Political Economy,* in Robert C. Tucker, ed., *The Marx-Engels Reader,* [New York: Norton, 1978], 4).

4. G. A. Cohen, "Functional Explanation, Consequence Explanation, and Marxism," *Inquiry* 25 (1982), 27–56, quote on 32.

5. Ibid., 33.

6. Ibid., 54. A step in the right direction is offered by Paul Wetherly in "Marxist Functionalism: Some 'Problems' Considered," paper presented at the PSA Conference, Plymouth Polytechnic, April 12–14, 1988.

7. For the cultural theory of technology (and its policy implications), see Michiel Schwarz and Michael Thompson, *Divided We Stand: Redefining Politics, Technology and Social Choice* (Hemel Hempstead: Harvester-Wheatsheaf, 1990).

8. Marx, "Preface" to *A Contribution to the Critique of Political Economy,* 4.

9. Karl Marx, *Capital* (New York: International Publishers, 1967), 1:539.

10. Cohen, *Marx's Theory of History,* 326.

11. Ibid., 326–44, esp. 336–38. The appendix was originally published in *Philosophy and Public Affairs,* Winter 1972, 182–203.

12. Karl Marx and Friedrich Engels, "The German Ideology," in Tucker, *Marx-Engels Reader,* 160. Cohen, *Marx's Theory of History,* 133.

13. Jon Elster, *Making Sense of Marx* (Cambridge: Cambridge University Press, 1985), 18.

14. Marx, *Capital,* vol. 1, 72.

15. Marx and Engels, "German Ideology," 172.

16. Ibid., 195. Marx, *Capital,* vol. 1, 609; also see vol. 1, 610.

17. Elster, *Making Sense of Marx,* 464.

18. Cohen, *Marx's Theory of History,* 291.

19. Marx and Engels, "German Ideology," 172.

20. Elster, *Making Sense of Marx,* 20–21, 505.

21. Jon Elster, "Marxism, Functionalism, and Game Theory: The Case for Methodological Individualism," *Theory and Society,* July 1982, 453–82, quote on 458.

22. Ibid.

23. Elster, *Making Sense of Marx,* 413.

24. Maurice Bloch, *Marxism and Anthropology* (Oxford: Clarendon Press, 1983), 10.

25. See Friedrich Engels, *The Origin of the Family, Private Property, and the State,* ed. E. B. Leacock (London: E. Lawrence and Wishard, 1972).

26. Bloch, *Marxism and Anthropology,* 16. Bloch shows that Marx and Engels were "almost totally wrong" in their portrayal of primitive society. His main complaint is that by characterizing primitive society as classless, Marx left himself and his followers little to say.

27. Nor is it hermitic. Private property is the cornerstone of this way of life. See Michael Thompson, "The Problem of the Centre," in Mary Douglas, ed., *Essays in the Sociology of Perception* (London: Routledge and Kegan Paul, 1982).

28. Allen Woods, "Marx and Equality," in John Roemer, ed., *Analytical Marxism* (Cambridge: Cambridge University Press, 1986), 283–303; quote on 284.

29. Marx and Engels, "German Ideology," 160.

30. See Aaron Wildavsky, "On the Social Construction of Distinctions: Risk, Rape, Public Goods, and Altruism," in Michael Hecter, Lynn A. Cooper, and Lynn Nadel, eds., *Toward a Scientific Understanding of Values* (Stanford: Stanford University Press), forthcoming.

31. V. I. Lenin, *What Is to Be Done?* (New York: International Publishers, 1929).

CHAPTER 9

Weber

Of all major social science theorists, Max Weber (1864–1920) is arguably the most famous. Certainly, in universities, he is the most assigned; there is no field, indeed hardly any course in social science, that does not reserve a place for him. This is as it should be. Weber has done more than any other scholar to study and to systematize bureaucracy. His typology of domination—traditional, legal, and charismatic—is used more often than any other today. Ideal types, which he offered as a means of abstracting from the flux of reality, remain a major methodological tool. When we add to that his sensitive discussion of the role of social scientists, together with his valiant efforts to prevent social science from becoming just another form of ideology, his greatness as well as his staying power becomes apparent.

Those accustomed to seeing Weber enlisted as an opponent of "structural-functionalism"[1] may wonder why we bring Weber, however great his contributions to social science, into a review of theorists who make use of functional explanation? Our contention is that Weber's empirical work, as opposed to his methodological strictures, in fact often follows a cultural-functional logic. That is, he explains beliefs and behavior in terms of their consequences for "styles of life."

WEBER AND GRID-GROUP ANALYSIS

There are, we contend, important similarities between Weber's work and Mary Douglas's grid-group analysis. Like Douglas, Weber operates from the premise that total societies are not a useful unit of analysis. According to Reinhard Bendix, Weber posits that "every society is divided into several social strata that are characterized by . . . a specific style of life, and by a distinctive, more or less articulated world view." It is these "status groups" that are "the fountainhead of moral ideas that shape the conduct and world view of the individuals belonging to them."[2] Thus status groups, like our competing ways of life, instruct individuals on what to prefer.

Weber and Douglas also resemble each other in refusing to separate values from social relations. Values, Weber insists, must be related to the mode of social organization they help to legitimate and out of which they emerge. Weber rejects both the Hegelian view of ideas as free-floating, unattached to social relations, and the Marxist view that ideas are mere reflections of social organization. In their stead he substitutes the concept of "elective affinity," a term intended to convey the notion that ideas are both created or chosen by the individual ("elective") and fit in with the individual's social situation ("affinity").[3]

Weber's attention to the "ethos," or "style of life," of status groups, together with the importance he attributed to grounding ideas in social organization, led him to reject arguments based on national character. Such explanations were illegitimate, Weber maintained, because they assumed that individuals mysteriously absorbed a nebulous "folk spirit," thus failing to ground individual beliefs in the social organization that sustains those beliefs. The claim to a common national character also failed, Weber suggested, on empirical grounds. "To ascribe a unified national character to the Englishmen of the seventeenth century," Weber maintained, "would be simply to falsify history." "Cavaliers and Roundheads," Weber continued, "did not appeal to each other simply as two parties, but as radically distinct species of men." By the same token, Weber argued that English merchant venturers and the old Hanseatic merchants, though of different nationalities, exhibited similar "ways of life."[4]

Weber runs into difficulty, however, because every status group seems to have its own style of life. His list of status groups includes Confucian literati, Taoist mystics, Buddhist monks, Hindu Brahmans, Puritan divines, Jewish Levites, and Junkers in imperial Germany. This approach gives us variety but no constraint upon that variety.[´]

To be sure, Weber does say that all forms of authority or domination are "combinations, mixtures, adaptations, or modifications" of three "pure types"—charismatic, traditional, and legal.[5] Traditional domination is based on the belief in the legitimacy of that which "has always existed."[6] Legal domination is founded on a belief in the legitimacy of impersonal laws. Individuals obey the office, not the man. Charismatic domination rests upon a belief in the extraordinary qualities of a leader.

Yet these types seem to be picked out of the air. What are the dimensions, we ask, from which these types are derived? "Tradition" is a historical dimension; "legal" is based on a type of rationality; and "charisma" refers to certain qualities of a leader.

The asymmetry of Weber's three types of authority structures is also evident in the quite different directions his arguments take in each case. In discussing traditional authority, Weber focuses upon differences between subtypes, particularly between patrimonialism and feudalism.[7] The discussion of charisma, in contrast, is concerned with subsequent developments, i.e., with the tendency for charisma to become routinized and transformed into traditional or bureaucratic structures. His examination of legal authority is focused on neither subtypes nor transformation, but instead the examination shifts to the quite different question of how legal-rational authority increasingly penetrates all institutions.[8]

Perhaps the most problematic of Weber's three types is traditional authority, because it assumes that members of certain types of societies rarely question what is handed down to them. Maintenance of social relations thus becomes a matter of course rather than a puzzling phenomenon needing to be explained. The notion of the naturalness of existing social relations, we think, is what all ways of life, whether modern or not, try to instill in their members; because of competition among ways of life, however, it is an achievement that is seldom accomplished.

Legal-rational authority is an unsatisfactory concept, we find, because it does not permit one to distinguish the hierarchical structure of a bureaucracy from the individualist structure of the market. Both bureaucracy and capitalism, in Weber's view, are instances of the historical process of "rationalization," by which he means the displacement of magical elements of thought by "the idea of calculability."[9] Sometimes, as in the *Protestant Ethic,* the march of rationalization is linked with the rise of capitalist exchange relations. Elsewhere in Weber's writings, rationalization assumes the form of the hierarchical authority structure of a bureaucracy. If both hierarchy and individualism are "modern" phenomena, then we need a typology that allows us to distinguish, not only between traditional and modern social orders, but also between different types of modern social relations. As with other theorists working within the tradition-modernity dichotomy, Weber faces the limitation of not being able to compare modern systems (except with respect to their degree of modernity). Weber's only advance is that he throws in the "charisma" wild card.

An additional inadequacy of Weber's typology is its failure to take egalitarianism into account. Weber does refer, albeit only episodically, to "sects." The sect, Weber tells us, is "a group whose very nature and purpose precludes universality and requires the free consensus of its members." Unlike a church, "which includes the righteous and the unrighteous, . . . the sect adheres to the ideal of the *ecclesia pura,*

. . . the *visible* community of saints, from whose midst the black sheep are removed so they will not offend God's eyes." "Pure sects," Weber continues, "insist upon 'direct democratic administration' by the congregation."[10] Weber's description of a sect perfectly matches the type we have identified as egalitarian. How sects relate to other ways of life, however, he does not say.

Weber does attempt to relate sects in an indirect way to his general theme of the rationalization of the modern world, in particular the rise of capitalism. Weber credits sects with having "bred the capitalist spirit."[11] Cast in terms of cultural bias, this argument is striking, for Weber appears to be arguing that egalitarianism contributed to the emergence of individualism.

This paradox is partly explicable in terms of Weber's tendency to talk of "the Protestant Ethic" as if Protestantism were culturally homogeneous. Protestantism, we contend, is predominantly a composite of individualism and egalitarianism. Weber's reference to the Protestant Ethic is unproblematic when he is drawing contrasts between Protestantism and Catholicism. For we would expect that if Protestantism consisted mostly of egalitarians and individualists, these two ways of life would unite, on the basis of their shared low grid (anti-authority) position, against the hierarchical Catholic church.

The seeming paradox of egalitarianism contributing to individualism can be further unraveled by looking more closely at variations within Protestantism. Despite Weber's use of the term "the Protestant Ethic," his own analysis in the *Protestant Ethic* shows that all Protestants were not alike. Most important, Weber distinguishes between Calvinism and the sects growing out of the Baptist movement. The latter sects differed from Calvinism in that they "wished to make the invisible Church of the elect visible on this earth."[12] That is, those sects erected high group boundaries around the elect as a collective, while Calvinism drew boundaries only around the individual. This indicates to us a categorical difference between these two strains of Protestantism, for it is egalitarians, not individualists, who bind their members within strong groups. Weber is unable to relate this critically important distinction to his central thesis about the affinity between Protestant asceticism and the capitalist spirit, except to observe that the connection between the capitalist spirit and the Protestant ethic is much more pronounced among Calvinists than among Baptist and Quaker sects. From Weber's point of view, there are only differences of *degree* between sects and Calvinism; from a viewpoint of ways of life these are differences in *kind*.

The reader attuned to cultural biases can see that the Calvinist doctrine, as described by Weber, is highly individualistic. To reach salvation, each individual "was forced to follow his path alone." There were repeated "warnings against any trust in the aid of friendship of men." "The Calvinist's intercourse with his God," Weber tells us, "was carried on in deep spiritual isolation." Calvinist doctrine, continues Weber, suggested that "God helps those who help themselves."[13] In view of these doctrines, it is not in the least surprising that virtually all of the *Protestant Ethic* draws on Calvinist sources, rather than sects, to support his central thesis about the impact of Protestantism on the spirit of capitalism.

Whenever Weber does introduce non-Calvinist sources, his case noticeably weakens. In discussing the German Pietists, for instance, Weber is compelled to concede that "the desire to separate the elect from the world could, with a strong emotional intensity, lead to a sort of monastic community life of half-communistic character." Or, to take another instance, Weber notes that one Baptist sect, the Dunkers, "has to this day maintained its condemnation of education and of every form of possession beyond that indispensable to life." Not very capitalistic, that. In his discussion of the Quakers, Weber will say only that they fostered "the capitalist principle" of "honesty is the best policy." He concedes that this falls far short of the "influence of Calvinism [which] was exerted . . . in the direction of the liberation of energy for private acquisition."[14] Try as he might, Weber cannot avoid the fact that the sects' strong communitarian ethic impeded this unleashing of the individual. Moreover, the sects' stress upon exclusion is antithetical to the universalistic bidding and bargaining among "consenting adults" that sustains capitalism (and individualism). It seems more plausible, in our view, to argue that "the spirit of capitalism" progressed in spite of and not because of the sects' animating "principle of avoidance of the world."[15] For to build ever-larger personal networks, as entrepreneurs try to do, the whole world must be their "oyster."

In sum, the paradox of religious piety combined with capitalist acquisition that motivates the *Protestant Ethic* turns out to be less puzzling than it originally appears. That Calvinism's "gloomy doctrine," in which each individual should engage in a "deliberate regulation of one's own life,"[16] fosters capitalism is understandable because both were manifestations of the culture of individualist self-regulation. In addition, the sects' low grid position explains why they joined Calvinists in rejecting the many prescriptions of the Catholic church, while their high group position explains why they balked at the unleashing of individual acquisition.

If Weber's thesis about the connection between sectarianism and capitalism does not fare well, he is on firmer cultural ground when he argues that there exists an "elective affinity between the sect and political democracy." This affinity is based on two factors. The first is the sect's insistence upon an internally democratic structure, including "treating the clerical officials as servants of the congregation." Holding governmental authority to account is an essential aspect of democracy. Second, the sect's vulnerable position on the fringes of society makes it a strong advocate of toleration of dissent.[17]

The above examples show that Weber was too keen a student of human history not to notice the importance of the social phenomenon that we have termed "egalitarianism." At the same time, the typology he was working with (which, at bottom, was based on the familiar distinction between tradition and modernity) was too impoverished to permit him to comprehend this phenomenon adequately. A major contribution of Douglas's grid-group typology is to derive the egalitarian mode of organization from social dimensions that can also produce the more familiar categories of market individualism and hierarchy.

WEBER AND FUNCTIONAL EXPLANATION

Just as Weber was a nascent theorist of cultural biases, so too did he employ an incipient (if covert) form of functional explanation. His reliance on functional explanation is particularly evident in his sociology of religion. Weber was fascinated by the question of how and why certain religious conceptions thrive in certain social groups and not others. In attempting to explain the correspondence between social experience and religious doctrine, Weber was often led, despite his dismissal of "functional analysis of the relation of 'parts' to a 'whole,'"[18] to a functional (or consequence) mode of explanation.

Why is it, Weber asks, for instance, that "in the great majority of cases, a prophetically announced religion of redemption has had its permanent locus among the less-favored social strata"? His answer is unmistakably functional: "The oppressed, or at least those threatened by distress, were in *need* of a redeemer and prophet; the fortunate, the propertied, the ruling strata were not in such *need*."[19] The beneficial consequence—feeling one will be compensated in the hereafter for suffering in the here and now—is being used to explain the affinity between a religion of salvation and a particular social stratum.

If those at the bottom of the social heap require a salvation religion that can provide a "release from suffering," privileged groups, in contrast, need a religion that serves the function of "legitimizing their own life pattern and situation in the world."[20] "The fortunate," Weber reasons, "is seldom satisfied with the fact of being fortunate. Beyond this, he needs to know that he has a right to his good fortune. He wants to be convinced that he 'deserves' it, and above all, that he deserves it in comparison with others. . . . Good fortune thus wants to be 'legitimate' fortune."[21] Not redemption but legitimation is thus the function of religion for the privileged strata. Here again it is the beneficial consequence—feeling that one's rule, property, or privileges is just—that is invoked to explain religious conceptions.

Where Weber refers to "needs," the functional character of his argument is clear enough. But what about where Weber talks (as he primarily does) in terms of "affinities" rather than needs? The term "affinity" is used by Weber to denote a correspondence or covariation between social experiences and worldviews. Thus, Weber writes, for example, that "the life pattern of a warrior has very little affinity with the notion of a beneficent providence, or with the systematic ethical demands of a transcendental god."[22] Is this a functional explanation of the religious conceptions of warriors? Indeed is it an explanation at all?

Weber does not rest content with just describing what religious doctrines go with which social strata. As he attempts to explain why certain social strata have an affinity for certain religious conceptions, he gravitates ineluctably toward an explanation in terms of consequences. Warriors, to pursue the example given above, reject certain types of religious ideas, Weber argues, because they would be dysfunctional for the status group. "To accept a religion that works with such conceptions [as sin, salvation, and religious humility] and to genuflect before the prophet or protest," Weber suggests, "would appear plebeian and dishonorable to any martial hero or noble person." Religious beliefs and/or practices are thus rejected or accepted by the warrior class on the basis of their consequences for the ideal and material interests of their group.

Similarly, lurking behind Weber's observation that "a bureaucracy is usually characterized by a profound disesteem of all irrational religion"[23] is an explanation couched in terms of consequences. A charismatic religion is rejected by a bureaucracy because it would disrupt the discipline and routine upon which the bureaucracy depends. In other words, the bureaucracy's antipathy to charisma is explained in terms of the dysfunctional consequences charisma would have for bureaucratic social structures.

As was his wont, Weber was careful to qualify his views. He explicitly denied that he was arguing that religious conceptions were only "a 'reflection' of a stratum's material or ideal interest-situation."[24] One way in which Weber tried to preserve the relative autonomy of ideas was to distinguish between explaining the innovation of religious ideas and explaining the viability of those ideas. Genius, in effect, serves as a generator of possible conceptions, while the social relations select out those ideas that in some way "fit." As Mary Fulbrook puts it, explaining why and where "the seeds of genius" grow and flourish requires an explanation in terms of the "social soil" into which they were planted.[25]

This distinction between innovation and acceptance can be seen in Weber's explanation for why a tradition of ecstatic prophecy was largely unknown outside ancient Palestine. The Israelites' existence as a "pariah people," Weber argues, made them peculiarly susceptible to prophesying ecstatics. Had such prophets emerged in the caste system of India, he maintains, their appeals would have fallen on deaf ears, for they would "have been considered not saintly men but barbarians. They would have no influence." By branding such activity as barbarous or, as with the bureaucratic kingdoms, by having the religious police intervene, hierarchical systems selected against charismatic prophets.[26] Social systems, in short, select for certain types of religious innovations (and leaders).

Weber's understanding of religion thus turns out to be no less functional in character than the analyses offered by avowed functionalists. The difference is that Weber has a much more variegated conception of the way in which religion works. For Radcliffe-Brown, religion (no matter what outward form it took) served only one function, and that was to integrate society. For Weber, the functions religion serves (and hence the forms of religious belief and practice) vary by a group's style of life. We consider this a significant, if unacknowledged, advance.

The functional character of Weber's explanations has been overlooked, we believe, because Weber did not take society as the unit of analysis. Despite the eloquent dissent offered by Robert Merton,[27] social scientists have tended to equate functionalism with those analyses that treat society as an undifferentiated whole. Indeed Weber himself identified functionalism with the interpretations offered by the "organic" school of sociology, so called because it viewed society as akin to a biological organism. Weber's understanding of society as an arena for competing status groups made him understandably skeptical of the utility of an approach based upon an analogy between society and a biological organism.[28] Weber's avoidance of the terminology that has historically been attached to functionalism (with the important exception of "needs"), such as "function," "integration," "cohesion," and "parts and wholes," contributed to the impression that he was not a practitioner of functional explanation.

Weber threw commentators further off the track by his advocacy of "interpretive sociology" as an alternative to functional analysis. Unlike the spleen or liver, Weber points out, people attach meaning to their actions.[29] Social scientists must therefore understand human behavior "from the viewpoint of the subjective experiences, ideas, and purposes of the individuals concerned."[30] Weber's claim is misleading, as a number of commentators have suggested, because his empirical analyses do not, in fact, rest content with explaining behavior in terms of individual motivation.[31] Rather, he explains the subjective dispositions of individuals in terms of the material and ideal interests of the status groups of which they are members.

Weber's methodological formulation is also misleading because it sets up an unwarranted antithesis between intentional and functional explanation. Weber's empirical analyses slide imperceptibly between intended and unintended functions. Consider, for instance, his suggestion that the German Junkers' refusal to associate on equal terms with members of the middle class sustained their "style of life."[32] From Weber's formulation it is difficult to tell whether avoidance of the middle class is consciously motivated by a desire to sustain the Junker ethos, or whether the Junkers were unaware of the consequences of their behavior. The same ambiguity runs throughout Weber's discussion of domination and legitimation. Weber tells us, for instance, that Confucianism functioned to legitimate the material and ideal interests of the literati stratum and to bolster the patrimonial regime, but he equivocates on whether those advocating the Confucian ethic were motivated by, and/or aware of, these beneficial consequences.

A further reason why the functional character of much of Weber's work has been overlooked may be that, alone among his studies of world religions, the central thesis of his most well known work on religion, *The Protestant Ethic and the Spirit of Capitalism,* does not focus on accounting for religion in terms of its consequences. Weber's fundamental argument is that the Protestant Ethic had the unintended effect of ushering in the "spirit of capitalism," not that adherence to Protestantism can be explained by its consequences for capitalists.[33] Unlike Weber's other works that focus on the affinity between social relations and ideas, moreover, the *Protestant Ethic* concentrates much more heavily on ideas (i.e., doctrines). How people said they should live, not how they did live, is the main subject of this work. In both of these respects, the *Protestant Ethic* is atypical of the corpus of Weber's sociology of religion.

Our contention is, not that all social science follows the logic of functional explanation, but rather that in attempting to explain the maintenance of social relations, social scientists are drawn inevitably to functional explanations. We have tried to demonstrate to the reader that when Weber moves from *describing* relationships between ideas and social strata to *explaining* why this "affinity" persists, the logic of his explanation becomes unavoidably functional.

WEBER AND DURKHEIM COMPARED

Weber and Durkheim are often seen as being "at opposite poles as social theorists." A compelling formulation of this view is Reinhard Bendix's essay "Two Sociological Traditions," in which he argues that these two giants represent "diametrically opposed" approaches to sociological analysis.[34] Bendix asserts that Durkheim, who "modeled his sociology after the natural sciences," is representative of the Baconian or Saint-Simonian tradition, in which the major goal is "the discovery of general laws." In contrast, Weber was heir to a tradition dating back to Burckhardt and Tocqueville, in which the major goal is "to discover the genesis of historical configurations."[35]

Bendix is correct in pointing out the divergence between Durkheim's methodological strictures, as laid out in *The Rules of Sociological Method,* and the "Conceptual Exposition" at the opening of Weber's *Economy and Society.* The latter begins with a discussion of the need for "interpretation of meaning" and "the subjective interpretation of action," while the former refers to "the explanation of social facts," and "establishing sociological proofs." Rather than look at what they said about how sociology should be conducted, however, we prefer to compare how they actually conducted their sociological inquiry. A comparison of their practice, we find, reveals striking similarities in their approaches.

Both Durkheim and Weber aimed to ground values and beliefs in social relations. Durkheim's contribution to the social foundations of thought is widely recognized, but Weber is hardly less attentive to the impact that a way of life has on belief. Christianity, Weber argues, for instance, is a product of the social existence of "itinerant artisan journeymen," whereas Judaism is explained as a religion of a "pariah people." Weber was perhaps more prone to emphasize the "elective" nature of the affinity between beliefs and social organization, but it was Durkheim who stated that "because beliefs and social practices come to us from without, it does not follow that we receive them passively or without modification."[36]

Bendix points to Durkheim's and Weber's analyses of religion as illustrative of their fundamental difference in approach. To be sure, Durkheim bases his study on small, technologically primitive, nonliterate tribes, while Weber examines great world religions such as Confucianism, Judaism, and Hinduism. But beneath these surface differences lies a fundamental similarity: Both Weber and Durkheim offer functional explanations of religious belief and practice. Just as Durkheim sees the essence of religion in the latent function it serves to integrate the community, so Weber explains religious behavior functionally in terms of its consequences for a style of life. Where they do differ in an important respect is that while Durkheim focused most of his attention on the cohesive function that religion served in primitive societies, Weber was more attentive to the ways in which a religious belief that is functional for one social group within a society may be dysfunctional for other groups living within that same society.

Weber and Durkheim also differ in the *degree* to which they assume individuals are aware of how their own actions and beliefs contribute to the maintenance of their social relations. For Durkheim, "the reasons with which the faithful justify [social practices] may be, and generally are, erroneous,"[37] whereas Weber tends to place more emphasis on individuals as self-consciously attempting to sustain a *preferred* way of life. Both emphases are justified; people generally intend to justify their way of life, not always successfully, and sometimes justification comes about inadvertently.

CONCLUSION

What we take to be Weber's central strategy of explanation—that variations in belief and practice among status groups can be explained by the functions (both intended and unintended) that these beliefs and practices serve for the material and ideal interests of status groups— clearly prefigures what we have labeled cultural-functional explanation. Though the spirit of much of his work is highly consonant with ours, Weber does not travel far enough down that road. Like a theorist of cultural biases, he examines the "styles of life" within a society, but he classifies groups in terms familiar to contemporary participants— the English merchant, the German Junker, the Puritan divine, and so on—with the result that he ends up with as many ways of life as there are groups in society. Our contribution is to simplify the potentially infinite diversity of Weber's "styles of life" into only a few ways of life.

Reducing the luxuriant diversity of human existence to a manageable number of types, however, is only one-half of our contribution. The other half is to allow for sufficient variation so that there is something to explain. In Chapter 10, we maintain that a typology of ways of life would have made social theory more productive by granting a middle ground between what all social systems share in common (which isn't very interesting) and what is unique to all social systems (which can be fascinating but seems unrelated to anything else). Not Malinowski, not Radcliffe-Brown, and not Parsons, we show in the next chapter, discovered such a middle ground.

NOTES

1. See, for example, Randall Collins, "A Comparative Approach to Political Sociology," in Reinhard Bendix, ed., *State and Society* (Berkeley: University of California Press, 1968), 42–67.

2. Reinhard Bendix, *Max Weber: An Intellectual Portrait* (Berkeley: University of California Press, 1977), 259–60; also see 85–86.

3. Ibid., 64. Also see H. H. Gerth and C. Wright Mills, eds., *From Max Weber: Essays in Sociology* (New York: Oxford University Press, 1946), 62–65.

4. Max Weber, *The Protestant Ethic and the Spirit of Capitalism* (New York: Scribner's, 1958), 88–89. Also see Gerth and Mills, "Introduction," in *From Max Weber,* 65.

5. Weber, quoted in Bendix, *Max Weber,* 329.

6. Ibid., 294–95.

7. By "patrimonialism," Weber meant a system in which the relations between ruler and officials are conducted on the basis of paternal authority and filial dependence. Feudalism, in contrast, is characterized by a contractual relationship between lord and vassal.

8. This paragraph closely follows the analysis in Peter M. Blau, "Critical Remarks on Weber's Theory of Authority," *American Political Science Review* 57 (June 1963): 306–16, quote on 309.

9. Bendix, *Max Weber,* 427.

10. Max Weber, *Economy and Society* (Berkeley: University of California Press, 1978), 1204, 1208; emphasis in original.

11. Ibid., 1208.

12. Weber, *Protestant Ethic,* 130.

13. Ibid., 104, 106, 107, 115.

14. Ibid., 131, 150, 151.

15. Ibid., 146.

16. Ibid., 126.

17. Weber, *Economy and Society,* 1208.

18. Ibid., 15.

19. Weber, "The Social Psychology of the World Religions," in Gerth and Mills, eds., *From Max Weber,* 274, emphasis added.

20. Weber, *Economy and Society,* 491–92.

21. Weber, "Social Psychology," in Gerth and Mills, eds., *From Max Weber,* 271.

22. Weber, *Economy and Society,* 472.

23. Ibid., 476.

24. Weber, "Social Psychology," 270.

25. Mary Fulbrook, "Max Weber's 'Interpretive Sociology': A Comparison of Conception and Practice," *British Journal of Sociology,* March 1978, 71–82, quote on 76.

26. Max Weber, *Ancient Judaism* (New York: Free Press, 1952), 288, 315.

27. Robert K. Merton, "Manifest and Latent Functions," in *Social Theory and Social Structure* (Glencoe, Ill.: Free Press, 1957).

28. Bendix, *Max Weber,* 261–62.

29. Weber, *Economy and Society,* 15.

30. Ibid., 399.

31. See, for example, Fulbrook, "Weber's 'Interpretive Sociology'"; Bryan Turner, *For Weber, Essays on the Sociology of Fate* (London: Routledge and Kegan Paul, 1981); and Gerth and Mills, "Introduction," 57.

32. Bendix, *Max Weber,* 85.

33. Where Weber does consider the question of why certain social strata were attracted to Protestantism (rather than the question of the impact the Protestant ethic had on "the spirit of capitalism"), his explanation does become functional—adherence to Protestantism is explained by the beneficial consequences it had for "the rising bourgeois middle classes" (Weber, *Protestant Ethic,* 37; also see 36, 43, 177).

34. Reinhard Bendix, "Two Sociological Traditions," in Bendix and Guenther Roth, *Scholarship and Partisanship: Essays on Max Weber* (Berkeley: University of California Press, 1971), 282–98, quotes on 283, 286.

35. Ibid., 286, 298.

36. Emile Durkheim, *The Rules of Sociological Method* (Chicago: University of Chicago Press, 1938), lvi n. 7.

37. Emile Durkheim, *The Elementary Forms of the Religious Life* (New York: Free Press, 1965), 14.

CHAPTER 10

Malinowski, Radcliffe-Brown, and Parsons

Though the three theorists considered in this chapter differ in important respects, they share Comte's belief that the task of social science is to state the conditions that all societies must meet to survive. This quest for universal conditions or requisites yielded little beyond definitional lists of system (or, in the case of Malinowski, individual) needs. Our aim in reviewing these authors is to suggest that these unsatisfactory results are not inherent in functionalism but rather stem from a failure to tie functions to types of social relations. More productive, we contend, than the question, What must all societies do to survive? is the question, What must different types of ways of life do to maintain themselves?

MALINOWSKI AND RADCLIFFE-BROWN

Viewed against the backdrop of nineteenth-century anthropology, the functional approach of A. R. Radcliffe-Brown (1881–1955) and Bronislaw Malinowski (1884–1942) constitutes a radical break with the past. Nineteenth-century anthropology had been heavily concerned with tracing the diffusion or migration of cultural traits across societies. Both Malinowski and Radcliffe-Brown adamantly rejected this "shreds and patches" conception of culture[1] on the grounds that a cultural practice was only understandable in terms of the system of which it was a part. Radcliffe-Brown, in his first book, *The Andaman Islanders* (published in 1922), argued that "the ceremonial customs of the Andaman Islanders form a closely connected system, and . . . we cannot understand their meaning if we only consider each one by itself, but must study the whole system to arrive at an interpretation." What was needed, he concluded, was "a new method by which all the institutions of one society or social type are studied together so as to exhibit their intimate relations as parts of an organic system."[2] Malinowski's *Argonauts of the Western Pacific,* also published in 1922, begins with a similar warning that "an ethnographer who starts out to study only religion, or only technology, or only social organization cuts out an artificial field of inquiry, and . . . will be seriously handicapped in his work."[3] Like Radcliffe-Brown, Malinowski regarded "the atomizing or isolating treatment of cultural traits . . . as sterile, because the significance of culture consists in the relation between its elements."[4]

Neither Malinowski nor Radcliffe-Brown was content to analyze interdependence of parts within particular societies. The goal of social anthropology, they both believed, was to construct generalizations that were valid for *all* societies. An anthropology that sought to show only how cultural practices cohered in a specific society (as in the work of Ruth Benedict, who viewed each society as a unique pattern of interdependency[5]) would impede such cross-cultural generalizations. To provide universal laws, Malinowski turned to psychology, whereas Radcliffe-Brown, following Durkheim, looked to sociology.

Malinowski, who coined, or at least popularized, the term *functionalism,* advocated, particularly in his later work, a biopsychological brand of functionalism that found few defenders in social anthropology.[6] All cultures, Malinowski argued, no matter how varied in form, function to satisfy universal biological and psychological needs of individuals.[7] Culture is thus an instrument by which individuals satisfy such impulses as hunger or sexual satisfaction. This is what Malinowski meant when he stated that culture "must be understood as a means to an end, that is, instrumentally or functionally."[8]

Although his brand of functionalism centered on the individual has not proved fruitful, the question that led Malinowski to this formulation is important. Malinowski was rebelling against the assumption, which he associated with "the French school of Durkheim," that "the individual obeys the commands of his community, its traditions, its public opinion, its decrees, with a slavish, fascinated, passive obedience."[9] Anticipating more recent criticisms of functionalism for presenting an "oversocialized man,"[10] Malinowski stressed "man's manipulation and re-setting of his environment."[11] Individuals, in Malinowski's view, were not automatons programmed by society, but rather were actively engaged in manipulating rules.

Any theory that assigns no role to individual agency, Malinowski is surely correct in arguing, is unsatisfactory. His error, in our view, was conceiving individual goals narrowly in terms of the satisfaction of biopsychological impulses. The theory proved unsatisfactory because, as Durkheim taught, the definition of what counts as "satisfied" is largely socially determined. Our theory of cultural biases attempts to leave room for individual discretion by viewing individuals as actively pursuing their preferred way of life, as well as by testing rival ways to determine which is preferable. If the theory were formulated in this manner, one would not have to look to biology and psychology, as Malinowski assumed was necessary, in order to bring the "flesh and blood" individual back in.[12]

True to his Durkheimian heritage, Radcliffe-Brown rejected Malinowski's view that individual psychology could provide the basis for formulating lawlike generalization about social systems. Indeed so vehement was Radcliffe-Brown's opposition to Malinowski's views that he suggested that "as a consistent opponent of Malinowski's functionalism I may be called an anti-functionalist."[13] Contemporary polemics over the appropriate label that each should bear can obscure the fact that it is Radcliffe-Brown's work that most closely resembles what is usually understood today by functionalism, i.e., analyzing a practice for the contribution it makes in sustaining the social whole.

Radcliffe-Brown suggested that social anthropology, by discovering how social usages maintain the social system, could construct universal laws. In order to survive, he argued, "any social system . . . must conform to certain conditions. If we can define adequately one of these universal conditions, i.e., one to which all human societies must conform, we have a sociological law." In an essay on "Patrilineal and Matrilineal Succession," Radcliffe-Brown formulates one such law: Any human social life requires social relations to be structured so that "certain rights and duties" are "defined in such a way that conflicts of rights can be resolved without destroying the structure."[14] Formulated in this way, this "law" is true by definition. But if put in propositional form, e.g., a necessary condition of existence for all social relations is that certain rights and duties be well defined, it can be shown to be false. For we know that egalitarian ways of life are characterized by ill-defined social relations, yet they maintain themselves through, among other mechanisms, accusations of pollution and schism.[15]

More satisfactory than the functional laws offered in "Patrilineal and Matrilineal Succession" is the functional analysis Radcliffe-Brown presented in his celebrated essay "On Joking Relationships." In the latter piece, he comes closest to breaking out of the straitjacket that his search for universal laws imposes upon him. His aim is to identify "the kind of structural situation in which we may expect to find well-marked joking relationships."[16] Joking tends to occur, Radcliffe-Brown finds, in those social relationships where rights and duties are less well defined, and he concludes that joking functions to ease conflict in these areas of "social disjunction."

Radcliffe-Brown was not unaware of the importance of creating typologies of social relations. Social anthropology, he insisted, must begin by addressing "the problems of social morphology—what kinds of social structures are there, what are their similarities and differences, how are they to be classified."[17] Although he made a number of efforts in this direction, such as differentiating types of kinship systems— "father-right" and "mother-right"—and distinguishing modes of alliance: intermarriage, exchange of goods or services, blood brotherhood, and joking, his efforts in this direction were not particularly fruitful.[18] The typology of alliances is haphazard. One is not told from what dimensions the categories are derived, nor why these, and only these, types are important.

Why were Radcliffe-Brown's typologies so sterile? Part of the answer, we suspect, is that Radcliffe-Brown did not appreciate Durkheim's point about how different social structures channel cognition. Lacking Durkheim's interest in different kinds of cognition, Radcliffe-Brown had little motivation to develop typologies of social relations. For Radcliffe-Brown, discovering types of social relations was only a preliminary step to the ultimate goal of stating the functional requisites that were common to all social structures.

Radcliffe-Brown never seemed aware of the tension between a research agenda based on universal laws that held for all societies, and one geared to generalizations based on types of social relations. This becomes particularly evident in his introductory essay to *Structure and Function in Primitive Society,* in which he traces his theoretical approach to both Montesquieu and Comte. Montesquieu's theory, Radcliffe-Brown tells us, "constituted what Comte later called 'the first law of social statics': . . . for any form of social life to persist or continue the various features must exhibit some kind and measure of coherence or consistence."[19] He thus glosses over the fundamental difference between Comte's effort to formulate functional propositions that are universally valid and Montesquieu's attempt to show how different types of society sustain themselves.

In a perceptive review of Malinowski's and Radcliffe-Brown's functionalism, Maurice Mandelbaum has argued that the error they shared was in their "later functionalism," which attempted to construct "global laws" that held for all societies. Mandelbaum suggests that functional analysis should limit itself to the more modest agenda of their "early functionalism," which looked for specific relations of elements within individual societies.[20] Although we agree with Mandelbaum's judgment concerning the failure of the two theorists' attempt to establish functional laws that held for all societies, we are less satisfied with his recommendation that social scientists treat each society as a unique configuration of usages and beliefs. For this leaves us where we began: with an unbridgeable chasm between infinite diversity and total unity. The purpose of a typology of ways of life, as we understand it, is to avoid having to choose between Malinowski's and Radcliffe-Brown's early and late functionalism by producing generalizations tailored to different types of social relations.

TALCOTT PARSONS

In the quarter century following the outbreak of World War II, Talcott Parsons (1902-1979) was the preeminent figure in sociological theory. Since the 1960s, however, his influence has been on the wane, a decline that (not coincidentally) exactly parallels the decline in the reputation of functional analysis. Parsons's central place in the development of functional analysis (and social theory more generally) demands that those who desire, as we do, to revive functional analysis must wrestle with the contributions and deficiencies of his corpus.[21]

At least two paths are open. One can try to resuscitate functional analysis, as Jeffrey Alexander has recently done, by showing that many criticisms of Parsons are misguided.[22] Alternatively, one may concede the validity of these criticisms but show that Parsons's errors were not inherent in a functional mode of analysis. Although we do not concur in all (or even most) of the criticisms leveled at Parsons, we will, by and large, pursue the latter route. More specifically, we shall argue that although Parsons's analysis is in many ways deficient, that deficiency does not signify inherent flaws in functional explanation but rather the failure of a particular brand of universalistic and holistic functionalism dating back to Comte.[23] By tying functions to types of ways of life, we contend, our cultural theory avoids many of the pitfalls of Parsonian structural functionalism.

LINKING THE MICRO AND MACRO

The starting point of Parsons's first (and possibly best) book, *The Structure of Social Action* (1937), is "the problem of order."[24] Nineteenth-century liberal theory, particularly as elaborated in classical economics, Parsons maintains, has no adequate explanation for social order because it assumes that individual ends are random and that the means-ends relationship is governed purely by instrumental calculations. Life in such a society, Parsons agrees with Hobbes, would be "solitary, poor, nasty, brutish and short." Indeed a social system in which preferences varied at random would be "not an order at all, but chaos."[25]

Parsons credits Hobbes with having seen "the problem [of order] with a clarity which has never been surpassed."[26] But he also finds Hobbes' solution—that social order is maintained through coercion exercised by a political authority—"palpably unacceptable."[27] The question is not (or, better, ought not to be), as Hobbes would have it, how to stop people from doing what they want, but rather how it is that what people want is compatible with social order.[28] The solution to the problem of order, Parsons is suggesting, must commence with a theory of preference formation.

Following Durkheim, Parsons contends that social order "concerns not only the conditions under which men act in pursuit of their ends but *enters into the formulation of the ends themselves.*"[29] Individual actors do not exist as isolated social atoms. It is from their involvement with others, Parsons argues, that individuals arrive at their normative conceptions of not only what is preferable but also what are appropriate means to realize desired ends.

The collective, in Parsons's view, is more than the sum of its individual parts. "It is true," he acknowledges, "that in the last analysis all . . . systems [of action] are 'composed' of unit [individual] acts, . . . [but this] does not mean that the relation of the unit act to the total system is closely analogous to that of a grain of sand to the heap of which it is a part." For the macro system has "emergent properties" that "cannot be identified in any single unit act considered apart from its relations to others in the same system."[30] Parsons, in insisting that the macro cannot be reduced to the micro, the social from the individual, is not trying to substitute a one-sided collectivist theory for an equally one-sided atomistic theory. Instead his objective is a synthesis of the dualisms that have "plagued social theory to little purpose for so long."[31] Just as he criticizes theories that ignore the "emergent," supraindividual aspects of social order, so too he has little patience for theories that leave no room for human agency.

Parsons's commitment to preserving individual volition is evident from his criticism of Hobbes, whom he regards as "the first great example of deterministic thinking in the social field." Hobbes, Parsons laments, "set up no ideal of what conduct should be, but merely investigated the ultimate conditions of social life."[32] The reduction of action to objective conditions, principally self-preservation, removes the randomness of ends, but only at the expense of eliminating individual will altogether. Parsons terms this the "utilitarian dilemma": Ends either are random (in which case order is impossible) or are determined by material conditions (in which case individual choice is eliminated).[33]

How can individual discretion be preserved without the sacrifice of the supraindividual character of social order? Parsons's answer, following what he sees as a convergence in the theories of Durkheim and Weber, lies in the internalization of norms. Norms, according to Parsons, are "phenomena of a very peculiar sort." Whether or not a norm is actualized "depends upon the *effort* of the individuals acting as well as upon the conditions in which they act." It is "this active element of the relation of men to norms, the creative or voluntaristic side of it," that distinguishes norms from the unalterable, material conditions of an actor's situation.[34] In contrast to physical or natural constraints, Parsons continues, "one cannot even think of normative rules without implying the possibility of the individual violating them."[35]

The internalization of norms, Parsons claims, provides a way out of the utilitarian dilemma, for no longer does one have to choose between the determinism of external conditions and the randomness of individual ends. By becoming internalized in the individual, Parsons argues, norms "enter directly into the constitution of the actors' ends themselves. . . . The element of ends as it appears in the means-end schema is no longer by definition 'individual' but contains a 'social' element."[36] Internalization is thus the mechanism by which the macro enters into the micro.[37] This formulation, according to Parsons, transcends "the usual distinction between voluntary adherence and constraint," for "while, on the one hand, adherence is voluntary, on the other hand, that adherence is binding on the individual." "The actor is not free to do as he likes, he is 'bound,' but it is a totally different mode of being bound" than is implied in the notion of "subjection to naturalistic causation and that of avoidance of sanctions. . . . It is binding not from physical necessity but from moral obligation."[38]

Parsons misleadingly labels this synthesis of constraint and voluntarism a "voluntaristic theory of action." By this he does not mean, as Jeffrey Alexander correctly points out, that action is exclusively voluntaristic, but rather he intends to signal that voluntarism has been preserved.[39] Perhaps, as Alexander suggests, the term "voluntaristic structuralism" better captures the spirit of Parsons's objective.[40] Whatever the label, we embrace Parsons's aim: to focus on the process of individual negotiation and choice that shape collective arrangements and, at the same time, to analyze the collective ways of life that mold those individual choices.[41]

THE ASSUMPTION OF SOCIETAL CONSENSUS

Although a synthesis of individual action and collective constraints was Parsons's original objective, his subsequent work tends to lose sight of the individual as active negotiator and increasingly substitutes the individual as passive conformist. Norms seem to descend from on high, seeping inexorably into the consciousness of individuals. The socialization process appears to leave the individual little choice but to reproduce the existing social system.[42] Parsons too often theorizes, as Arthur Stinchcombe points out, "as if the values and institutional commitments of a culture stayed that way."[43]

The social system, according to Parsons, is maintained because "the *normal* individual feels satisfaction in effectively carrying out approved patterns and shame and disappointment in failure."[44] It is only the deviant, the pathological or inadequately socialized individual, who disturbs social equilibrium. Parsons can define deviance ("a motivated tendency for an actor to behave in contravention of one or more institutionalized normative patterns"), but he can tell us little about its sources.[45] Deviance, as Ralf Dahrendorf comments, "occurs for sociologically unknown and unknowable reasons. It is the bacillus that attacks the system from the dark depths of the individual psyche."[46] Dissent from "normative patterns" is thus reduced to psychological aberration.

Why is it that Parsons equates normative action with conformity?[47] The answer, we would suggest, is his assumption of consensus at the societal level. By positing a single "common value system"[48] for each society, Parsons leaves open only two possibilities: normative conformity or nonnormative deviance. Were there competing norms for the individual to select from, individual action could be simultaneously normative and nonconforming. Cultural theory, because it provides for competing ways of life within a society, restores the active, negotiating individual by giving him competing norms over which to negotiate.

Where we differ from Parsons, then, is not on the importance of norms but on the extent to which they must be held in common. We agree with Jeffrey Alexander that "one could grant Parsons that normative order is terribly significant, indeed an undeniable factor in the relationship between individuals, without claiming [as Parsons does] . . . that all the individuals in any given collectivity or society share the *same* normative commitments."[49] John Finley Scott makes the same point: "It is one thing to say that there are systems of norms—*Structure* did say this—but another to say that there is consensus on any one system—that is the implication of Parsons's later writings."[50]

In introducing normative themes into the theoretical picture, Parsons seizes the empirical high ground. For, as Ronald Burt has stressed, "empirical evidence, . . . ranging from experiments to surveys within a system of actors to ethnographic studies across systems, . . . supports a normative perspective over an atomistic one. Perceptions and evaluations are significantly affected by the social context in which they are made."[51] But in insisting that "without a system of common values,

. . . there can be no such thing as a society,"[52] Parsons adopts an empirically untenable position. For many (our theory suggests all) societies exist in the face of dissensus on what society should look like and how people should behave.[53]

The deficiencies of the assumption of societal consensus have recently been pointed out by Neil Smelser, whose first book, *Social Change in the Industrial Revolution* (1959), had applied Parsonian theory to the British cotton industry. In *Social Change,* Smelser, following Parsons, assumed that evaluations as to the adequacy of an institution's performance were based upon the "value-system" of a society.[54] In a more recent contribution, however, Smelser indicates that he now believes this assumption is untenable, for "it is possible to envision a number of value-positions, one of which might indeed be dominant, but which stand in competition or conflict with one another as bases for legitimizing expression or dissatisfaction."[55] For instance, British society at the turn of the nineteenth century, according to Smelser, was characterized by at least three competing value systems. The dominant value system legitimated "a hierarchical society in which men took their places in an accepted order of precedence, a pyramid stretching down from a tiny minority of the rich and powerful through ever larger and wider layers of lesser wealth and power to the great mass of the poor and powerless." This value system was challenged by a "Utilitarian value system, which envisioned among other things, a rational society based on principles of free exchange, not status and obligation," and "by political radicalism, which envisioned democratic participation rather than benevolent paternalism."[56]

Given these competing ways of life (which correspond closely to hierarchy, individualism, and egalitarianism), Smelser argues, one "should expect to find conflict and competition over the definition of the situation itself, that is, whether an unsatisfactory state of affairs actually exists."[57] Smelser's comments point the way toward a reorientation of functional analysis around ways of life rather than societies so that differences over the adequacy of an institutional arrangement are seen as derived from conflict between different ways of life. Satisfaction or dissatisfaction with existing institutions, we contend, is expressed not by the value system of society but by adherents of competing ways of life.

THE PATTERN VARIABLES

How is it that Parsons, an incurable typologist, could arrive at such a homogenized view of society? The answer to this question, we believe, is to be found in the limitations of his famous "pattern variables."[58]

The pattern variables stem, in large part, from Parsons's dissatisfaction with Tönnies's gemeinschaft/gesellschaft dichotomy. Believing that this dichotomy obscured as much as it revealed, Parsons introduced the pattern variables as a way of unpacking distinct dimensions that had been lumped together in the tradition/modernity dichotomy.[59]

By far the most prominent of the pattern variables are universalism-particularism (should people be judged according to standards that apply equally to everybody, or should standards be tailor-made for particular groups?) and achievement-ascription (should positions be given according to demonstrated accomplishment or according to qualities that seem unique to a particular person, like family, background, religion, or race?).[60] While analytically distinguishable, these two dimensions correlate so highly that, in practice, they tend to be only slightly different ways of saying the same thing. A social system that values what you do rather than who you are almost invariably has universalistic rather than particularistic rules. By the same token, a social system that rejects treatment based upon generalized rules virtually always treats people according to who they are rather than what they do. If, as we believe, the universalism-particularism and achievement-ascription variables measure the same basic underlying phenomenon, then Parsons's typology does little more than restate the familiar tradition/modernity dichotomy.

Parsons often speaks of an "American value system," which can be "very closely described in terms of the universalism-achievement (or performance) pattern."[61] This formulation is problematic, we believe, for at least two reasons. One is that the universalism-achievement category (like Weber's legal-rational or Tönnies's gesellschaft category) fails to distinguish adequately between hierarchy and individualism. Both hierarchical bureaucracies and competitive markets base decisions on performance. The difference is that performance in hierarchies includes a large measure of following prescribed procedures whereas among competitive individualists performance is judged more on the basis of results (the bottom line). The second deficiency is that this "American value system" omits egalitarianism entirely. The rise of affirmative action in modern America shows that selection based upon group attributes of race or gender is not, as Parsons would have it, a relic from a bygone age. By adopting a cultural bias framework, we can see that egalitarians, in their attempt to diminish differences among people, use affirmative action as a means to prevent the "cumulative inequalities"[62] they believe to be inherent in individualist social relations.

The universalism-particularism and achievement-ascription dichotomies are, of course, only two of Parsons's five pattern variables. The others are affectivity versus neutrality (the gratification-discipline dilemma),[63] specificity versus diffuseness,[64] and self-orientation versus collectivity orientation. Why is it, then, that when characterizing the American value system, Parsons uses only two of the five pattern variables? The answer, we believe, is that five dimensions built in more variation than Parsons (or, for that matter, anyone) could manage. Five pattern variables, after all, yield thirty-two different possible social types.[65] This unwieldy diversity goes a long way toward explaining why the pattern variables have not proven more fruitful.

An additional deficiency of the pattern variables is that despite Parsons's insistence that these five dilemmas of choice are "exhaustive of the relevant logical possibilities,"[66] the choice of dilemmas, as Max Black has pointed out, seems arbitrary.[67] The impression of arbitrariness is bolstered by the fact that Parsons occasionally adds or subtracts a pattern variable from the supposedly exhaustive list. He entertains, for instance, the idea of a sixth dichotomy—long-run versus short-run evaluation[68]—and then later drops the self-orientation versus collective-orientation variable.

From our cultural perspective, it is this jettisoned pattern variable (the private- versus collective-interests dilemma) that holds the most promise. Parsons first explored this distinction in an essay comparing the difference between the medical profession and the business firm. What differentiated action in the two spheres, Parsons argues, is not motivation: "The typical motivation of professional men is not in the usual sense 'altruistic,' nor is that of business men typically 'egoistic.' "[69] Behavior in both realms, Parsons continues, is motivated by a desire to comply with social norms. What differentiates the two is that norms sanctioned the pursuit of self-interest in the business field but not in the medical profession. The pursuit of individual interests is thus no less social action than is the pursuit of collective goals.

This early essay represents Parsons at his best, pursuing the Durkheimian program and relatively unencumbered by his later fascination with conceptual elaboration. The insight that all individual ends are social products enables Parsons to see that even individualism as an ideological phenomenon is a supraindividual product. Individualism, Parsons explains, "is not a mere matter of the removal of social discipline, but of a particular kind of discipline."[70] Individualist social orders, in which "choices are open," no less than collectivist social orders, in which choices are prescribed, are the result of social processes that no single individual can control.[71]

Instead of subsequently elaborating the collective-orientation versus self-orientation category (which completely crosscuts the tradition/modernity distinction), however, Parsons instead relies increasingly on the universalism-particularism and achievement-ascription variables (which only restate the tradition/modernity dichotomy in new language). Having stretched the tradition/modernity dichotomy to its furthest limits, Parsons's work inadvertently reveals the distinction's limitations. If tradition and modernity are the only types of social systems, and if the journey between the two ways is a one-way route, then having reached our destination, as Parsons believed the United States had, the variety of social types immediately shrivels up. The country becomes endowed with a single, integrated "value system." Deviants may temporarily disturb this achievement-universalism pattern, but since there is nothing to change into (having already passed through the gesellschaft stage), the mechanisms of social control quickly reestablish equilibrium.

Cultural theory, in contrast, by opening up the paths of change, suggests that individuals are continually being dislodged from one way of life into another. Cultural theory envisages, rather than a single, static equilibrium, a permanent dynamic imbalance in which adherents are constantly changing positions and, in so doing, transforming the relative strength of the rival ways. To speak of an "American value system" neglects both the constant change that the regime is undergoing and the competing cultural biases within the regime. We argue that the American regime, far from being an integrated whole, is made up of fundamentally incompatible biases. Because the biases that constitute a regime are in conflict, an action that is functional for one way of life may well be dysfunctional for another. Recognition of the rival ways of life that exist within a society, we believe, is the key to resurrecting functional analysis.

FUNCTIONAL REQUISITES

The inadequacy of assuming that functions go with entire societies rather than with ways of life can be seen in Parsons's analysis of organizations. Beginning from the promising premise that it is unsatisfactory "to think of 'bureaucracy' as a kind of monolithic entity which can vary in degree of development but not significantly in type,"[72] Parsons goes on to classify organizations by the function the organization fulfills for society.[73]

It might be suggested that Parsons's approach to analyzing organizations is inherent in functional analysis. Does not functionalism proceed by asking what the part (the organization) does for the whole (society)? Only, we respond, if functions are assumed to belong to societies. Our cultural-functional analysis would study how a way of organizing sustains itself, not society at large. For instance, we explore how the consequences of an egalitarian way of organizing (pollution

Figure 9. Parsons's four-function model

	Instrumental	Consummatory
External	Adaptive Function	Goal-Attainment Function
Internal	Pattern Maintenance Function	Integrative Function

beliefs, for instance) serve to strengthen that pattern and to weaken the patterns of relationships of the other ways of organizing and creating. In asking this question we are able to reveal the fallacy of misplaced concreteness built into all those functionalist theories that take their cue from Comte.

Since our requisite variety condition insists that no single way of life ever has things all its own way, there can be no such thing as *an* organization. Instead, there are just four[74] ways of organizing, each of which is also a way of disorganizing the other three. Ways of life, to be sure, have functions, but they never crystallize out into concrete entities—organizations—that then perform one or other of those functions for some more encompassing but similarly concrete entity: society.

In Parsons's scheme, organizations that regulate relations between members of a society, such as parties, courts, and hospitals, are deemed integrative organizations. Those organizations that he believes serve to maintain the values of society, such as schools and churches, are termed pattern-maintenance organizations. Organizations that function to obtain resources from the environment (i.e., produce wealth), such as the business firm, are adaptive organizations, and those that mobilize societal members to pursue collective goals, such as the government, are goal-attainment organizations.

The value of any classificatory scheme must be measured by at least two criteria: internal, logical coherence and the number and explanatory power of propositions generated. How does Parsons's classification fare on both these counts? The answer, unfortunately, is not very well (Figure 9).

Four boxes do not a typology make. The types must be derivable from dimensions. Parsons's four categories cannot, we believe, be derived from his two dimensions: instrumental versus consummatory and external versus internal.[75] Although the instrumental-consummatory (means-end) dichotomy does distinguish adaptation (mobilizing resources) from goal attainment, it has no bearing on the functional imperatives of pattern maintenance (to "maintain the integrity of that value system and its institutionalization") or integration ("to 'maintain solidarity' in the relations between the units").[76] Why should internal combined with instrumental lead to pattern maintenance, or external and consummatory produce goal attainment? What Parsons offers is not a typology but a list of types. There is thus little reason to think the categories exhaustive. Moreover, the types lack symmetry. Pattern maintenance, for instance, as one commentator observes, "is different from the other three functional requisites" because it serves "to define action, whereas the other three are aspects of ongoing action."[77]

What about the typology's payoff in propositions? Does knowing that an organization fulfills an integrative rather than an adaptive function for society allow us to predict anything about that organization? If this enterprise is to make sense, one must demonstrate the constraint that a particular type of societal function exercises over the organization. But Parsons generates no propositions of this sort. He informs us, for instance, that political parties and hospitals are both integrative organizations, but we are not given a proposition of the sort "because parties and hospitals serve integrative functions, both modes of organization have in common x structure or y dilemma."[78]

Parsons's list of functional requisites proved unproductive, we would suggest, because it aimed to find that which is true of all social systems. What interests Parsons is what *all* societies must do to maintain themselves. In doing so, Parsons followed the path laid by Comte,[79] and taken up by Radcliffe-Brown. The functional requisites Parsons comes up with (integration, pattern maintenance, goal attainment, adaptation) are, by and large, implied in the definition of society and thus only restate what we want to know, i.e., how social life coheres. The result, in Alvin Gouldner's neat phrase, is that Parsons's categories tend to "cover rather than reveal the world."[80]

Parsons deserves credit for having led the way against dualisms. He showed that the micro and the macro were different facets of the same phenomena. From postulating the essential unity of social and individual life, however, he too often swung over to the essential unity of society, which is quite another matter. Believing that society was a relatively integrated entity, Parsons (like Malinowski and Radcliffe-Brown) was led to attach functions to societies as a whole. It was at this juncture that Robert Merton, a former student of Parsons's, entered the picture and took the important step of detaching functions from society considered as a single, integrated organism.

NOTES

1. A. R. Radcliffe-Brown, "On the Concept of Function in Social Science," in *Structure and Function in Primitive Society* (Glencoe, Ill.: Free Press, 1952), 178–87, quote on 186.

2. A. R. Radcliffe-Brown, *The Andaman Islanders* (Glencoe, Ill.: Free Press, 1948), 324; first published in 1922.

3. Bronislaw Malinowski, *Argonauts of the Western Pacific* (London: George Routledge, 1922), 11.

4. Bronislaw Malinowski, "Culture," *Encyclopedia of the Social Sciences* (New York: Macmillan, 1931), 621–46, quote on 625.

5. See Ruth Benedict, *The Chrysanthemum and the Sword* (Boston: Houghton Mifflin, 1946).

6. See, for instance, the vitriolic attack on Malinowski in Max Gluckman, *Malinowski's Social Theories* (New York: Oxford University Press, 1949).

7. Malinowski counted seven "basic needs" that must be satisfied for a human organism to continue: metabolism, reproduction, bodily comforts, safety, movement, growth, and health. See Bronislaw Malinowski, *A Scientific Theory of Culture* (Chapel Hill: University of North Carolina Press, 1944), 91, and passim; and "The Group and the Individual in Functional Analysis," *American Journal of Sociology,* May 1939, 938–64.

8. Malinowski, *Scientific Theory of Culture,* 34.

9. Bronislaw Malinowski, *Crime and Custom in Savage Society* (London: Routledge and Kegan Paul, 1926), 3–4, and passim.

10. See Dennis H. Wrong, "The Oversocialized Conception of Man in Modern Sociology," *American Sociological Review,* April 1961, 183–93; and George C. Homans, "Bringing Men Back In," *American Sociological Review* 29 (December 1964): 809–18.

11. Malinowski, *Scientific Theory of Culture,* 68.

12. Malinowski, quoted in George W. Stocking, Jr., "Radcliffe-Brown and British Social Anthropology," in Stocking, ed., *Functionalism Historicized* (Madison: University of Wisconsin Press, 1984), 174. Malinowski's assumption that a Durkheimian approach must neglect the individual is evident from his assertion that because Radcliffe-Brown was "still developing and deepening the views of the French sociological school . . . [he] thus has to neglect the individual and disregard biology" (Malinowski, "Group and the Individual," 939n).

13. A. R. Radcliffe-Brown, "Functionalism: A Protest," *American Anthropologist,* 1949, 321.

14. A. R. Radcliffe-Brown, "Patrilineal and Matrilineal Succession," in *Structure and Function,* 32–48, quotes on 43–44.

15. Mary Douglas, "Thirty Years After *Witchcraft, Oracles and Magic,*" in Douglas, ed., *Witchcraft Confessions and Accusations* (London: Tavistock, 1970), xiii–xxxviii; Mary Douglas and Aaron Wildavsky, *Risk and Culture* (Berkeley: University of California Press, 1982).

16. A. R. Radcliffe-Brown, "On Joking Relationships," in *Structure and Function,* 90–104, quote on 101.

17. A. R. Radcliffe-Brown, "On the Concept of Function in Social Science," in *Structure and Function,* 180.

18. Radcliffe-Brown, *Structure and Function,* 13, 102.

19. Ibid., 5, 7.

20. Maurice Mandelbaum, "Functionalism in Social Anthropology," in Sidney Morgenbesser et al., eds., *Science, and Method* (New York: St. Martin's Press, 1969), 306–32, esp. 322–25.

21. Jurgen Habermas has recently gone as far as to suggest that "no social theory can be taken seriously today which does not—at the very least—clarify its relationship to Parsons'" (quoted in Jeffrey C. Alexander, "The Parsons Revival in German Sociology," *Sociological Theory* [San Francisco: Jossey-Bass, 1984], 394–412, quote on 395).

22. See Jeffrey C. Alexander, *Theoretical Logic in Sociology,* vol. 4 of *The Modern Reconstruction of Classical Thought: Talcott Parsons* (Berkeley: University of California Press, 1983); and Jeffrey C. Alexander, ed., *Neo-Functionalism* (Beverly Hills, Calif.: Sage, 1985).

23. We would therefore disagree with the assertion, put forth in a recent review of functionalism, that Parsons took functional analysis "to its logical conclusion as a theoretical strategy." If this premise is wrong, then there is no need to accept the authors' conclusion that because Parsons's analysis is deficient, "functionalism as a theory building strategy is also deficient" (Jonathan H. Turner and Alexandra Maryanski, *Functionalism* [Menlo Park, Calif.: Benjamin Cummings, 1979], 83).

24. Talcott Parsons, *The Structure of Social Action* (New York: Free Press, 1937), 91.

25. Ibid., 93.

26. Ibid.

27. Talcott Parsons, "Durkheim's Contribution to the Theory of Integration of Social Systems," in Kurt H. Wolff, ed., *Emile Durkheim, 1858–1917: A Collection of Essays with Translations and a Bibliography* (Columbus: Ohio State University Press, 1960), 118–53, quote on 119. Reprinted as Chapter 1 in Talcott Parsons, *Sociological Theory and Modern Society* (New York: Free Press, 1967).

28. This formulation of Parsons's position is adapted from Brian Barry, *Sociologists, Economists and Democracy* (Chicago: University of Chicago Press, 1978), 77.

29. Parsons, *Structure of Social Action,* 337; emphasis added.

30. Ibid., 739.

31. Ibid., 74.

32. Ibid., 89.

33. Ibid., 64, 90.

34. Ibid., 396; emphasis in original.

35. Ibid., 379.

36. Ibid., 382.

37. See Jeffrey C. Alexander and Bernhard Giesen, "From Reduction to Linkage: The Long View of the Micro-Macro Link," in Jeffrey C. Alexander et al., *The Micro-Macro Link* (Berkeley: University of California Press, 1987), esp. 22.

38. Ibid., 384–85.

39. Alexander, *Theoretical Logic,* 26.

40. Jeffrey C. Alexander, *Twenty Lectures: Sociological Theory Since World War II* (New York: Columbia University Press, 1987), 28.

41. This "multidimensional" aspect of Parsons's theory is emphasized throughout Jeffrey C. Alexander's reconstruction of Parsons's work.

42. See Alexander and Giesen, "From Reduction to Linkage," 14, 25.

43. Arthur L. Stinchcombe, "Why We Have No Theory of Cultural Change," Paper presented at 1984 American Sociological Association Convention, San Antonio, Texas, August 1984, 6.

44. Talcott Parsons, "Professions and Social Structure," in *Essays in Sociological Theory,* rev. ed. (Glencoe, Ill.: Free Press, 1954), 34–49, quote on 45; emphasis added.

45. Talcott Parsons, *The Social System* (New York: Free Press, 1951), 250.

46. Ralf Dahrendorf, "Out of Utopia: Toward a Reorientation of Sociological Analysis," in *Essays in the Theory of Society* (Stanford: Stanford University Press, 1968), 116.

47. See Alexander, *Theoretical Logic,* 442.

48. Parsons, *Structure of Social Action,* 768.

49. Alexander, *Twenty Lectures,* 31; emphasis in original.

50. John Finley Scott, "The Changing Foundations of the Parsonian Action Scheme," *American Sociological Review* 28 (October 1963): 716–35, quote on 734.

51. Ronald S. Burt, *Toward a Structural Theory of Action: Network Models of Social Structure, Perception, and Action* (New York: Academic Press, 1982), 6–7.

52. Parsons, *Structure of Social Action,* 434.

53. The same point is made in Dahrendorf, "Out of Utopia," 115.

54. Neil J. Smelser, *Social Change in the Industrial Revolution* (Chicago: University of Chicago Press, 1959), 16.

55. Neil J. Smelser, "Evaluating the Model of Structural Differentiation in Relation to Educational Change in the Nineteenth Century," in Alexander, ed., *NeoFunctionalism,* 113–29, quote on 119–20. A recent book sympathetic to Parsons and also recognizing functionalism might be better served by dropping the assumption of societal consensus: Robert J. Holton and Bryan S. Turner, *Talcott Parsons on Economy and Society* (London: Routledge and Kegan Paul, 1986), 202–03.

56. Smelser, "Evaluating the Model of Structural Differentiation," 119–20.

57. Ibid.

58. A pattern variable is defined as "a dichotomy, one side of which must be chosen by an actor before the meaning of a situation is determinate for him" (Talcott Parsons and Edward Shils, eds., *Toward a General Theory of Action* [Cambridge, Mass.: Harvard University Press, 1951], 77).

59. See Guy Rocher, *Talcott Parsons and American Sociology* (New York: Barnes and Noble, 1975), 36–37.

60. These definitions are taken from Alexander, *Twenty Lectures,* 54.

61. Talcott Parsons, "A Revised Analytical Approach to the Theory of Social Stratification," in *Essays in Sociological Theory,* 386–439, quote on 399. Also

see Parsons, *Social System,* 107–08; and Parsons, *Social Structure and Person-ality* (New York: Free Press, 1964), 238, 278–79.

62. The phrase is from Robert Dahl's *Who Governs?* (New Haven: Yale University Press, 1961).

63. This pattern variable ("the dilemma of gratification of impulse versus discipline") constitutes a fusion of the gemeinschaft/gesellschaft dichotomy and Freudian psychology. Parsons associates the renunciation of immediate grati-fication with modern society, and indulgence of impulse with preindustrial society. The empirical support for such a correlation is, in our view, nonexistent.

64. This dilemma, Parsons and Shils explain, "consists in whether [the actor] should respond to many aspects of the object or to a restricted range of them" *(Toward a General Theory,* 83).

65. Parsons, *Social System,* 107.

66. Ibid., 66. Also see Parsons and Shils, eds., *Toward a General Theory,* 91.

67. Max Black, "Some Questions about Parsons's Theories," in Max Black, ed., *The Social Theories of Talcott Parsons* (Englewood Cliffs, N.J.: Prentice-Hall, 1961), 268–88, esp. 287–88.

68. Talcott Parsons, "Some Comments on the State of the General Theory of Action," *American Sociological Review,* December 1953, 618–31, quote on 626.

69. Talcott Parsons, "The Professions and Social Structure," in *Essays in Sociological Theory,* 34–49, quote on 45. Also see Parsons, "Some Theoretical Considerations Bearing on the Field of Medical Sociology," in *Social Structure and Personality,* 326–30.

70. Parsons, *Structure of Social Action,* 337. Also see Alexander, *Theoretical Logic,* 41; and Jeffrey C. Alexander, "Formal and Substantive Voluntarism in the Works of Talcott Parsons: A Theoretical and Ideological Reinterpretation," *American Sociological Review* 43 (1978): 177–98.

71. Alexander, *Twenty Lectures,* 80.

72. Talcott Parsons, "Some Ingredients of a General Theory of Formal Organization," in *Structure and Process in Modern Societies* (New York: Free Press, 1960), 59–98, quote on 93.

73. Talcott Parsons, "Suggestions for a Sociological Approach to the Theory of Organizations," in *Structure and Process,* 16–58, quote on 45, 56.

74. Five if we include the hermit, which, for reasons given earlier, we are not doing here.

75. Talcott Parsons, "General Theory in Sociology," in Robert K. Merton et al., *Sociology Today* (New York: Basic Books, 1959), 3–38, quote on 5–6.

76. Talcott Parsons and Neil Smelser, *Economy and Society* (London: Rout-ledge and Kegan Paul, 1956), 15, 17.

77. Leon H. Mayhew, "Introduction," in *Talcott Parsons on Institutions and Social Evolution: Selected Writings* (Chicago: University of Chicago Press, 1982), 27.

78. The low empirical yield of Parsons's approach to organizations is evident from his essay on mental hospitals, which, he tells us, was conceived of as a

"'case study' within the more general framework" proposed in his theoretical essay on organizations (*Structure and Process,* 4). The reader will find no propositions about constraints that integrative organizations share in common. Rather than put forth propositions from the four-function typology, Parsons generates a brand new typology: custody, protection, socialization, and therapy ("Mental Hospital as a Type of Organization," in Milton Greenblatt et al., *The Patient and the Mental Hospital* [Glencoe, Ill.: Free Press, 1957], 108–29). This is vintage Parsons; every time the reader catches up with the deficiencies of an old typology, Parsons is on to a new one.

79. Alvin Gouldner has aptly characterized Parsons as "a latter-day Comte" (*The Coming Crisis of Western Sociology* [New York: Basic Books, 1970], 205).

80. Ibid., 205–09, quote on 209.

CHAPTER 11

Merton, Stinchcombe, and Elster

The predominant reaction among contemporary social scientists to the functionalism championed by Parsons, Radcliffe-Brown, and Malinowski is to dismiss functional analysis as inherently flawed. The very word "functionalism" often sends sociologists and anthropologists running for cover, fearing its utterance almost as one would an ancient curse. A few brave souls have, however, attempted to pick through the wreckage and salvage those bits worth saving while jettisoning those assumptions that are groundless. It is upon some of these efforts to refine and rebuild functional analysis that we focus in this chapter.[1]

ROBERT MERTON

For a reader who could consult only one work on functional analysis, it is likely that most social scientists would recommend Robert Merton's seminal "Manifest and Latent Functions." In this justly famous essay, Merton was primarily concerned with purging functional analysis of what he perceived to be the unnecessary baggage with which previous practitioners, particularly Malinowski and Radcliffe-Brown, had laden it.

Merton's greatest contribution to functionalism, in our opinion, lies in challenging what he calls the "postulate of the functional unity of society," i.e., the view that functions go with "society" in the abstract. Although conceding that the assumption that "standardized social activities or cultural items are functional for the entire social system" may hold true for some nonliterate societies studied by anthropologists, Merton argues that for complex, industrial societies the postulate is blatantly "contrary to fact."[2] Because acts "may be functional for some individuals and subgroups and dysfunctional for others," Merton concludes that it is hopelessly muddled to talk of functions fulfilled for "the society."[3]

Merton demonstrates the implausibility of assuming that functions go with entire societies by showing how functional analyses of religion ignore "commonplace facts regarding the role of religion in contemporary literate societies." Merton asks, "In what sense does religion make for integration of 'the' society in the numerous multi-religion societies?" How, he continues, can religion make for integration of the larger society when its doctrines are at odds with nonreligious beliefs held by other groups in the same society? The assumption that religion serves integrative functions, Merton argues, blots "out the entire history of religious wars, of the Inquisition (which drove a wedge into society after society), of internecine conflicts among religious groups."[4]

Merton demands that a functional explanation specify "the units for which a given social or cultural item is functional."[5] Had functionalists more closely followed Merton's guidance, functionalism might have been spared the criticism that it ignores power. For Merton's brand of functional analysis explicitly addresses the question of who benefits. What is functional for some segments of society, Merton argues, may be dysfunctional for other parts. His analysis makes clear that it is not functionalism per se that ignores power relationships within society but a particular brand of functionalism, typified by Parsons, that posits that practices perform functions for an undifferentiated society.

But if functions don't go with societies, what do they go with? Merton's answer is groups. In his functional analysis of the political machine, for instance, Merton does not ask what the machine does for society but rather identifies the concrete groups—e.g., businessmen and the poor—that benefit from the machine's activities. The question addressed by Merton is how the machine maintains itself in the face of widespread condemnation. In Merton's words, "How [do political machines] . . . manage to continue in operation . . . in view of the manifold respects in which [they] . . . run counter to the mores and at times to the law?"[6] His functional explanation has become a classic in social science: The machine meets the needs of various groups, needs that are not adequately satisfied by the fragmented, formal political structure.

Merton's study of the machine shows the advantages of rejecting society as the unit of analysis. We worry, however, that taking the concrete group as the unit of analysis will produce (indeed has produced), to use Merton's own words, "a buckshot array of dispersed investigations."[7] There is a middle ground, we believe, between the societal monism of Parsons and the frustrating diversity that must result from making specific groups or institutions the unit of analysis.

Types of ways of life, we suggest, provide such a middle ground and perhaps thereby the basis for what, in another sociological classic, Merton terms "theories of the middle range."[8] The political machine, for instance, might be seen as an instance of a wider phenomenon— i.e., individualist networks in the absence of strong hierarchy. Seen in this way, Merton's analysis of the machine could be related to other studies of individualist networks; we could thus make studies cumulative.

One of the noteworthy features of Merton's 1949 essay is that it anticipates and answers many of the criticisms that gained common currency in the 1950s and 1960s. Merton refutes, for instance, the charge that adopting a functional mode of analysis commits one to an ideologically conservative perspective. The basis for this oft-repeated attack upon functionalism is the belief that a focus on the functions of activities for society predisposes the analyst against social change— an argument that an activity has positive consequences easily slips into the view that it is therefore good and should be left alone. Thus functionalism, the argument runs, creates a "disposition to support whatever powers are established."[9]

It is clearly true that past functionalists have been closely linked with a conservative (in the sense of conserving existing institutions) agenda. The tie between functionalism and conservatism can be seen, for instance, in Montesquieu's comment:

> Every nation will here find the reasons on which its maxims are founded; and this will be the natural inference, that to propose alterations, belongs only to those who are so happy as to be born with a genius capable of penetrating into the entire constitution of a state. . . . Could I but succeed so as to afford new reasons to every man to love his prince, his country, his laws; new reasons to render him more sensible in every nation and government of the blessings he enjoys, I should think myself the most happy of mortals.[10]

A preference for social stability (although not necessarily existing institutions) was also prominent in the thought of Comte.[11] The functionalism of Malinowski and Radcliffe-Brown, to take two other instances, was harnessed to a political argument for preserving the customs and institutions of technologically primitive societies.

Merton shows that while many previous functional analyses stand guilty as charged, the errors are not inherent in a functional mode of inquiry. The conservative bias, Merton argues, results only when one accepts "the postulate of universal functionalism" and "the postulate of indispensability." The former postulate, as formulated by Malinowski, holds that "*every* custom, material object, idea and belief fulfills some vital function," while the latter maintains that the item (custom, object, idea, belief) plays an "indispensable part" in sustaining the whole.[12] By jettisoning these two premises—and thus accepting that patterns of behavior may serve no function at all, or even be "dysfunctional"—we can avoid the tendency to "a glorification of the existing state of things"[13] that marred early functionalism.

Despite the compelling nature of Merton's argument, accusations of ideological bias persisted, indeed intensified, in the ensuing decades. Introducing competing cultural biases allows us to illustrate the correctness of Merton's contention that it is not functionalism per se but only bad functionalism that is inclined to ideological conservatism. Our arguing that a belief in a corrupting outside world helps to sustain an egalitarian mode of social relations does not bias us in the direction of wishing to conserve egalitarian social relations.

Indeed we suspect that our example may have raised the opposite suspicion—that cultural-functional analysis is just an ideological smoke screen for undermining egalitarianism. But this too is wrongheaded, for the same mode of analysis can be applied to hierarchy, individualism, or fatalism. Blaming deviants, for instance, functions to sustain a hierarchical structure, whereas self-blame furthers an individualist pattern of social relations. Cultural-functional analysis thus does not bias us, let alone commit us, to a defense of a particular way of life or the practices that sustain it.

Another important contribution Merton made to clarifying functional analysis was to distinguish conscious motivations for social behavior (manifest function) from the objective consequences of such behavior (latent function). Although clarifying much, the distinction is not without its own ambiguity. In the examples Merton presents to demonstrate the distinction, it is the *level of the consequence* that distinguishes manifest from latent functions. In presenting Durkheim's analysis of the social functions of punishment, for instance, Merton refers to the *consequences for the criminal* as the manifest function and the *consequences for the community* as the latent function.[14] If we follow this usage of manifest function, it is difficult to see why manifest functions should be called functions at all, since they are irrelevant to system maintenance. At times, Merton himself seems to agree that manifest functions are not functions at all, as when he contrasts motives or the "end-in-view" with "the functional consequences of action," or when he contrasts the "naive meaning" (i.e., manifest function) with a sociological understanding (i.e., latent function).[15]

Merton's formal definition of the distinction between manifest and latent function, however, suggests that only awareness and intention differentiate the two concepts; the order of the consequence is the same for both types of functions. Manifest functions, according to Merton, "are those objective consequences *contributing to the adjustment or adaptation of the system* which are intended and recognized by participants in the system; latent functions, correlatively, being those which are neither intended nor recognized."[16] If we follow this definition, the category of manifest function includes something more than "naive" common sense.

We have, then, two conceptions of manifest function—manifest functions as intended and recognized consequences unrelated to system maintenance, and as intended and recognized consequences contributing to the maintenance of the system. The proposition that people engage in environmental movements to protect the environment fits the "naive meaning" of manifest function as action unrelated to system maintenance. The proposition that people engage in environmental movements for the purpose of furthering egalitarian social relations uses manifest function in the nonobvious sense of action intended to maintain a way of life. We suggest that the term *intended function* be applied to those acts that sustain, and are intended to sustain, a form of social relations, and manifest function be reserved for the "naive meaning" of behavior unrelated to system maintenance.

We are agnostic on the question of whether people are aware that their actions sustain a particular way of life and undermine rival ways. No doubt, some who propound the view that global warming will have catastrophic consequences are aware that their stand bolsters the egalitarian life of simplicity while undermining the individualist way of life (by drawing into question the entrepreneur's optimistic assumption that no matter how much he knocks nature about, it will bounce back). In such cases it is proper to speak of an individual pursuing a preferred way of life. At other times, however, individuals may be unaware that their behavior is strengthening their way of life. A belief in the evil of the outside world, for instance, helps maintain the boundaries of egalitarian groups and thus keeps together an organizational form in which formal authority is lacking. Most members of an egalitarian community are likely unaware of this function of their shared belief pattern.

The main difficulty posed by the concept of latent functions lies in demonstrating a feedback loop between the consequences of an act and the act's causes. When the consequences are intended, the feedback loop is unproblematic: Action X furthers system Y, and actor Z takes action X in order to further system Y. But how can unanticipated consequences sustain a social system? If an action's consequences for the system are unintended and unrecognized, what impels people to continue to act in this way? The analyst who wishes to demonstrate a latent function seems to have to posit a "group mind," i.e., to endow institutions with human qualities of intention and purpose. It was at this thorny impasse that Arthur Stinchcombe entered the fray.

ARTHUR STINCHCOMBE AND JON ELSTER

The question of how social phenomena can be explained by their consequences without introducing an illegitimate teleology has, as Stinchcombe observes, long been "a sore point in functional theory."[17] Some have attempted to meet this objection to functionalism by shying away from the term *explanation*. Piotr Sztompka, for instance, states that "in order to be valuable and valid, the functional analysis *need not purport to provide explanations* of social phenomena." Instead Sztompka suggests that our aim should be "functional interpretation."[18] Stinchcombe will have none of this terminological retreat. He sets out to show, by identifying "mechanisms which generally select patterns of social behavior according to their consequences," that "there is nothing any more philosophically confusing, nor anything less empirical or scientific, about functional explanations than about other causal explanations."[19] We agree.

Stinchcombe sketches six possible "chains of reverse causation" that can select patterns of behavior by their consequences: biological evolution, social evolution, individual and collective planning to achieve the consequences, satisfaction to the actor from the consequences with consequent operative conditioning, satisfaction to others who reward the actor, and satisfaction to others combined with social selection in a market system.[20] These mechanisms are reducible to three basic types: conscious planning, behavioral reinforcement, and environmental selection.

Planning provides a feedback loop between consequence and cause by introducing conscious intention. "Behavior may be selected by its consequences," Stinchcombe explains, because people "plan their behavior to get the consequences."[21] Although this is undeniably true, it does not help resolve the "sore point" in functional explanation, which is how to demonstrate feedback loops in the *absence* of conscious intentions.

A second mode of social selection identified by Stinchcombe is one in which an act has consequences that are pleasing to others who then reward (and thus reinforce) that behavior. A wife, for instance, "often learns what her family likes to eat by the way they react to what she serves."[22] But this learning process presupposes not only that the link between act and consequence be recognized by the wife, but also that the consequence be intended by the wife. Functional analysis is thus saved from illegitimate teleology by again introducing individual intention.

Only Stinchcombe's third type, environmental selection, provides a "reverse causal link" that does not introduce individual intention or recognition. In a restatement of Herbert Spencer's conception of "survival of the fittest," Stinchcombe argues that "behavior may be selected by the differential survival of social groups with that behavior, because of its favorable consequences." Again like Spencer, Stinchcombe's examples of this type of social selection process are drawn from the economic marketplace (and biology). Stinchcombe argues, for instance, that "firms which level input and output variations in order to run a production line at a steady rate may survive market competition better than those which do not. Hence there could be social selection for those structures within firms which level variations in production."[23]

Stinchcombe's valiant efforts to salvage functionalism have been lauded but nevertheless judged wanting by Jon Elster, who maintains that none of Stinchcombe's mechanisms meet the necessary conditions for a valid functional explanation. Elster offers five criteria—drawn from Merton and Stinchcombe—that a functional explanation of an institutional or behavioral pattern must meet.[24]

1. Y (the function of X) is an effect of X (behavioral pattern).
2. Y is beneficial for Z (the group).
3. Y is unintended by the actors producing X.
4. Y (or at least the causal relation between X and Y) is unrecognized by the actors in Z.
5. Y maintains X by a causal feedback loop passing through Z.

Elster faults Stinchcombe's first feedback mechanism, planning, for violating criteria 3 and 4.[25] Whether one sides with Elster and excludes all explanations that involve intention from the category of functional explanation is a matter of definition. We have tried to show in our prior discussions of Weber and Merton that there is an important place for intended functions in social theory. Elster is correct, however, in arguing that "planning" cannot provide a feedback mechanism for "latent" or unintended functions.

Skinnerian reinforcement, Elster contends, violates criterion 4—that the members of a group must not recognize the consequences of their action. Although conceding that this class of explanations is "empirically important," Elster prefers to call these "filter-explanations." In the case of filter explanations, Elster explains, the feedback loop operates because "the beneficiary is able to perceive and reinforce (or adopt) the pattern benefitting him, although in the first place these benefits played no role in emergence."[26] But, as Russell Hardin has recently noted, "the difference between filter explanations and full-fledged functionalist explanations is often not significant," since the latter often evolve into the former as actors become aware of the consequences of their action. "That it comes later to be recognized," Hardin maintains, "is not a setback for functionalist explanation but rather a demonstration of how compelling it is in the context."[27]

Elster is particularly critical of Stinchcombe's efforts to show that the environment exerts a selective force on behavior. Although Elster agrees with Stinchcombe that the critical link in a successful functional explanation is the feedback loop by which the consequence of an act becomes its cause (criterion 5), in contrast to Stinchcombe he comes to a starkly pessimistic conclusion about the possibility of fulfilling this criterion in the social sciences. Functional explanation, Elster concludes, "has no place in the social sciences, because there is no sociological analogy to the theory of natural selection."[28]

Elster takes functional explanation to task for presuming that when one shows that a behavioral pattern has beneficial consequences for some group, one has thereby explained the maintenance of that pattern of behavior. Consider, for instance, Merton's presentation of Veblen's analysis of the functions of conspicuous consumption. Conspicuous consumption, Veblen argued, has the latent function of a "heightening or reaffirmation of social status." Without specifying the feedback loop by which this beneficial consequence (heightening social status) maintains the pattern of behavior (conspicuous consumption), it is illegitimate, Elster argues, to conclude, as Merton does, that the latent function of reaffirming social status helps "explain the persistence . . . of the pattern of conspicuous consumption."[29]

That a feedback loop that could explain conspicuous consumption has not yet been specified does not necessarily mean that such a functional explanation is impossible. Converting Veblen's thesis into a cultural-functional hypothesis allows us to specify the missing feedback loop. Among individualists, conspicuous consumption on the part of entrepreneurs has the consequence of directing the attention of others in the society toward these Big Men. Giving the promise of limitless resources enables individuals to attract others to their networks.[30] Those unable to afford, or unwilling to indulge in, such extravagance are unable to attract others to their networks and are consequently pushed to the periphery. The result is the selected survival of those members who engage in conspicuous consumption. In terms of Elster's succinct formula:

1. Y (gaining adherents for one's network) is an effect of X (conspicuous consumption).
2. Y benefits Z (Big Men).
3. Y is unintended by actors producing X.
4. Y (or causal connection between X and Y) is unrecognized.
5. Y (gaining adherents) maintains X (conspicuous consumption) through Z, for those able to expand their networks will thrive, while those who don't, won't.

In the following pages, we attempt to show that our theory of sociocultural viability can generate functional explanations of blame and leadership that meet Elster's five criteria for a successful functional explanation (and that, in doing this, it has provided the "sociological analogue to the theory of natural selection"). As we have done elsewhere in this book, we begin where Mary Douglas leaves off.

In *How Institutions Think,* Douglas has gone a considerable distance toward showing that a cultural functionalism is capable of meeting Elster's requirements. Douglas offers the example of the unintended consequences within the egalitarian group of the "threat to withdraw."[31] Having a credible threat to withdraw from the group (X), argues Douglas, creates weak leadership (Y). Weak leadership is beneficial for egalitarians (Z), who wish to live a life free of authority. Moreover, weak leadership, in a feedback loop, maintains the threat to withdraw because it prevents the development of coercive regulations.

Douglas has also shown that "mutual accusations of betrayal of the founding principles" function in egalitarian groups to foster "a shared belief in an evil conspiracy," a belief that is beneficial for the group because it unites the normally fractious members of the group against an evil outside. Believing that those in the outside world are trying to undermine their way of life heightens a sense of their precarious position as a "city on the hill," thus reinforcing their sensitivity of betrayal from within.[32] Put into Elster's five-point formula, Douglas's functional explanation of betrayal accusations takes the following form:

1. Y (shared belief in an evil conspiracy) is an effect of X (mutual accusations of betrayal of the founding principles of the society).
2. Y is beneficial for Z (egalitarian group).
3. Y is unintended by actors producing X.
4. Y is unrecognized as an effect of X.
5. Y maintains X through Z.

Blame as a mechanism for sustaining a way of life is not, of course, unique to egalitarians. When things go badly, as they must, the question of who is to blame is invariably raised in all ways of life. An institution or way of life that cannot deflect blame, particularly when times are hard, cannot be sustained. The analysis of blame is thus a natural candidate for functional analysis.

The individualist norm of self-reliance, for instance, diverts blame away from the system of exchange.[33] When the economy turns sour, the belief that an individual's performance is within the control of that individual allows the system to resist those who might wish to increase regulation of transactions or put safety nets under individuals—if you don't break the fall, individualists believe, the bounce back will be that much faster and higher. In the absence of the ethic of self-reliance, an individualist system would be rapidly transformed into one of the competing social systems. Self-blame, moreover, is sustained (and explained) by the belief that transactions should be unburdened by regulation.

1. Y (belief that regulations of transactions should be kept to a minimum) is an effect of X (attributing personal failure to bad performance).
2. Y is beneficial for Z (individualists).
3. Y is unintended.
4. The causal connection between Y and X is not perceived.
5. Y maintains X.

Hierarchies are renowned for their blame-shedding techniques. Responsibility is hidden or (the same thing) diffused among numerous offices. Subordinates avoid blame by explaining, "I was only following orders." Superiors point the finger at subordinates. In passing the buck, each individual intends to absolve only himself from blame, but the unintended effect is to so diffuse blame that the hierarchy itself escapes blame. Because those willing to accept blame are more likely to be fired, buck passing becomes a mode of behavior that is selected for.

1. Y (diffusion of blame) is an effect of X (passing the buck).
2. Y benefits Z.
3. Y is unintended by actors producing X.
4. Y is unrecognized by those in Z.
5. Y maintains X.

Another mechanism used in the hierarchy that deflects blame away from the system is labeling dissenters as deviants, misfits, malcontents, troublemakers. Hierarchies punish their dissenters by throwing them into asylums, quarantining them, reeducating them, or otherwise stigmatizing them as having passed the bounds of reason. Identifying deviants sustains the hierarchical organization by reinforcing in its members a sense of the bounds of acceptable activity.[34] This public reminder of the bounds of intolerable behavior, in turn, reinforces the member's desire to punish deviance. Transcribed into Elster's formula, a functional explanation of the punishment of deviance would look like this:

1. Y (maintaining well-defined rules of behavior) is an effect of X (punishment of deviants).
2. Y is beneficial for adherents of hierarchy (Z), who want it well defined who can do what to whom.
3. Y is unintended by actors producing X.
4. The causal connection between X and Y is not perceived by members of Z.
5. Y maintains X, for a heightened sense of what is unacceptable behavior reinforces the will to punish transgressors.

Fatalists blame fate when things go badly. The effect is to instill in these people a sense of resignation that nothing they can do will change their existence. Although they hope things will improve, they make no effort to better their condition; things thus rapidly go from bad to worse as the other cultures manipulate them for their own purposes. As misfortune is heaped upon the heads of fatalists by the other cultures, fatalists are led more and more to account for their situation by blaming fate. And so the circle continues. In Elster's terms:

1. Y (resignation to whatever occurs) is an effect of X (blame fate).
2. Y benefits Z (fatalism).
3. Y is unintended by actors producing X.
4. The causal connection between X and Y is unrecognized.
5. Y sustains X through Z.

Leadership too can be accounted for in terms of a functional explanation. Charismatic leadership, we argue, can be explained by the function it serves in egalitarian collectives. Because an egalitarian group requires that every individual participate in, and consent to, every decision, consensus is a prerequisite to collective action. But the egalitarian antipathy toward authority makes it illegitimate for one member of the collective to make decisions for another member. Consequently, when an issue arises on which there is disagreement within the collective, the group is often unable to reach a consensus, and hence unable to act.

This imbalance between the egalitarian group's limited capacity to produce agreement and the members' critical need for agreement continually threatens the viability of the group. Endowing a person with charismatic qualities solves the organizational dilemma by allowing the members to abandon their personal decision premises in favor of those of the leader. Following a charismatic leader is not perceived as coercion, because the charismatic is following the right path. The charismatic's disregard for all written law or standard practices—the charismatic's dictum, Weber tells us, is, "It is written, but I say unto you"—moreover, prevents the buildup of any formal, routinized mechanisms—such as majority vote—that would make it easier for the group to reach agreement. Written in Elster's formula, a functionalist explanation of charismatic leadership takes the following form:

1. Y (group cohesion without building up a body of rules) is an effect of X (followers endowing leaders with charisma).
2. Y is beneficial for Z (egalitarian group), because in the absence of agreement the group will fall apart or, at a minimum, be unable to act and achieve objectives.
3. Y is unintended by actors producing X.
4. Y or the causal relation between X and Y is unrecognized by actors in Z.
5. Y maintains X, for charisma, by preventing the buildup of institutionalized means for resolving disputes, sustains the very conditions it requires to flourish.

We are not suggesting that charisma is a functional requisite for survival of egalitarian groups. Egalitarian groups do survive in the absence of charisma. Schism is one alternative mechanism (functional alternative, if you prefer) for restoring agreement within egalitarian collectives without resorting to charisma or transforming the egalitarian nature of the group's social relations. By dividing into two (or more) relatively homogeneous units, the original group may survive in a smaller form. The real-world experience of egalitarian organizations suggest that schism is in fact a common way of coping with unmanageable disagreement.

If blame and leadership, neither of which is likely to be regarded as an activity of only peripheral significance in the human experience, can be explained by their unintended beneficial consequences, then functionalism is more relevant to social science than Elster suggests. If Elster errs in concluding that functional explanations are of little value in social science, he is undoubtedly correct that most purportedly functional explanations do not satisfy the conditions he spells out.

Our sociocultural theory supplies what was missing in structural-functionalism, namely a typology of viable ways of life. Rather than merely exhort others to study the functions of structures (i.e., patterns of behavior), our theory provides a theory about how different ways of life cohere. Absent some theoretical guidance about what cultural biases go with what social relations, even the conceptual shoring-up that functional analysis received from Merton and Stinchcombe could not prevent it from being discredited.

Structural-functionalism also failed, as we have argued throughout, because it too often remained at the level of "the society." Abandoning society as the unit of analysis does not commit us, however, to following Elster down the path of methodological individualism. In between society and the individual are ways of life that channel thought and behavior in often unintended and unanticipated directions.

Elster's recommended program of methodological individualism is fine as far as it goes. We have no objection to explaining human behavior in terms of individual efforts to realize objectives. Our difficulty, instead, is with the assumption that the objectives themselves require no explanation. Rather than a theory that takes preferences for granted, we have proposed a cultural theory that explains why it is that people want what they want in the first place. This need to explain objectives opens up a space for functional explanation.[35]

The examples Elster gives (building on Merton) of bad functionalism are his most powerful arguments against functional explanation. He despairs of ghostlike apparitions called "society," predicates without subjects, groups for which any bit of behavior may be deemed functional if only the context is vague enough and the time elongated sufficiently. He intends methodological individualism to be an antidote to lack of explanatory specificity—say who, say whom, say why, say when, say how, specify the causal mechanism by which whatever you wish to explain comes about. To all of this we say, Bravo!

We see no need, however, to follow Elster in rejecting methodological collectivism, the view that "there are supra-individual entities that are prior to individuals in the explanatory order."[36] If one can explain more of a person's behavior by examining his personality rather than his social context, it is likely that the individual is seriously sick. For most individuals, our cultural theory holds, much is given by the existing pattern of social relations. Notions of what is expected, what is valued, what is natural, what is just, and so on are given to us by our social relations. That these collective phenomena are themselves the products of individual actions, aims, and aspirations in no way contradicts (let alone invalidates) the collectivist thesis that individual preferences are shaped by social relations.

Our attempt to show that functional explanations can be valid in the absence of individuals being aware of, or intending, the cultural consequences of their action should not be taken as an endorsement of the proposition that all (or even most) people are unaware of the functions they are performing. Some are quite explicit about their long-range goals: Their aim in pursuing a particular policy, they will tell you, is to create an "enterprise culture"[37] or a "new age society,"[38] or to redistribute power, or to bolster authority. Many of the policy preferences of these people who self-consciously seek to further their way of life may be derived in a straightforward intentional manner: The policy preference is selected by the individual as the best available means of realizing his cultural preference. For these "culturally conscious" individuals, there may be less need to resort to latent functions in explaining much of their behavior (although the question of why they prefer one cultural bias over another still remains to be answered).

Other individuals, however, will be unable to articulate many of the cultural consequences of their actions.[39] For them an action just seems right or necessary. How is it that those people who do not ponder the long-range implications of their actions (which is most of us most of the time) nevertheless come to have so many preferences? Our answer, following Durkheim, is that having chosen to live a particular way of life (or having had that choice foisted upon them), individuals unintentionally commit themselves to a much larger set of beliefs and behavior, including ideas of physical and human nature, perceptions of risk, notions of responsibility, conceptions of desirable leadership, and on and on. Having ordered the way of life, the way of life then orders for the individual.

We refer to "functions" rather than simply "unintended consequences" because we wish to draw attention to the ways in which the behavioral patterns generated by a way of life in turn sustain that way. Functional explanations suggest that the unintended consequences generated by social life are not random but instead serve to bolster the way of life that spawned them. To reject the concept of function leaves one ill equipped to account for system maintenance except as a chance occurrence or a concerted conspiracy. Chance and conspiracies do, of course, occur, but not with sufficient regularity to account for social stability. Little wonder that the masters of sociological theory we surveyed have all resorted to functional analysis in explaining how social life coheres.

By comparing our theory with that of the great social theorists of the past, we have tried throughout Part 2 to show what is added by our framework, namely, a more variegated and logically coherent typology that distinguishes among ways of life within a society. In the third and final section, we extend our comparisons with other theoretical approaches by reanalyzing a number of classic works in political culture. If in Part 2 we have shown that the great theorists have largely limited themselves to hierarchy and individualism, our aim in Part 3 is to demonstrate that this oversight was due to theoretical blinders and not to the absence of these ways of life in the real world. And just as we have argued that functional explanation went awry in its effort to attach functions to whole societies rather than to their constituent ways of life, so we suggest that the concept of political culture floundered because it was assumed that a nation (or race or ethnic group or tribe) had a single political culture. The difference is that while functionalism was marred by banal universality (functional requisites that held for all societies), political culture often suffered from a bewildering diversity (each nation with its own unique culture). All the more credit, then, to those intrepid souls who have sought, against the odds of those who claim each society is different, to find patterns amidst the eternal flux.

NOTES

1. Other important contributions not covered here include Ernest Nagel, "A Formalization of Functionalism," in *Logic Without Metaphysics* (Glencoe, Ill.: Free Press, 1956); Carl G. Hempel, "The Logic of Functional Analysis," in Llewellyn Gross, ed., *Symposium on Sociological Theory* (Evanston, Ill.: Row, Peterson, 1959), 271–307; and Dorothy Emmet, *Function, Purpose and Powers* (London: Macmillan, 1957).

2. Here, we think, Merton concedes too much to Malinowski and Radcliffe-Brown. Except in rare instances, even technologically primitive societies, we maintain, will likely be characterized by competing ways of life.

3. Robert K. Merton, "Manifest and Latent Functions," in *Social Theory and Social Structure* (Glencoe, Ill.: Free Press, 1957), 25, 27, 52. All subsequent page references to this book, unless otherwise indicated, are to this edition.

4. Ibid., 29.

5. Ibid., 30.

6. Ibid., 71.

7. Merton, "The Bearing of Sociological Theory on Empirical Research," in ibid., quote on 100.

8. Merton's purpose in propounding "theories of the middle range" was to create theories "that lie between the minor but necessary working hypotheses that evolve in abundance during day-to-day research and the all-inclusive systematic efforts to develop a unified theory that will explain all the observed uniformities of social behavior, social organization and social change" ("On

Sociological Theories of the Middle Range," in *Social Theory and Social Structure,* enlarged ed. [New York: Free Press, 1968], 39–72; quote on 39).

9. Alvin W. Gouldner, *The Coming Crisis of Western Sociology* (New York: Basic Books, 1970), 333. For an extreme version of the "functionalism is conservative" thesis, see Don Martindale's observation that "the rise of sociological functionalism thus coincides with the return of the Republican Party to power, the return to religion, the rise of McCarthyism, and other typical manifestations of a postwar conservative reaction" (*The Nature and Types of Sociological Theory* [Boston: Houghton Mifflin, 1960], 520).

10. Baron de Montesquieu, *The Spirit of the Laws,* trans. Thomas Nugent (New York: Hafner, 1949), 92–93.

11. This aspect of Comte's thought is emphasized in Gertrud Lenzer's introduction to *Auguste Comte and Positivism: The Essential Writings* (New York: Harper & Row, 1975). According to Lewis Coser, Comte "was, above all, a man attached to order" (Coser, *Masters of Sociological Thought: Ideas in Historical and Social Context* [New York: Harcourt Brace Jovanovich, 1977], 14).

12. Merton, *Social Theory,* 30, 32.

13. Ibid., 39.

14. Ibid., 61.

15. Ibid., 51, 61, 69. Similarly, Merton writes, "it is precisely at the point where the research attention of sociologists has shifted from the plane of manifest to the plane of latent functions that they have made their *distinctive* and major contributions" (66, emphasis in original).

16. Ibid., 51, emphasis added; also see 63.

17. Arthur L. Stinchcombe, *Constructing Social Theories* (New York: Harcourt, Brace & World, 1968), 85.

18. Piotr Sztompka, *Robert K. Merton: An Intellectual Profile* (New York: Macmillan, 1986), 140; emphasis in original.

19. Stinchcombe, *Constructing Social Theories,* 85, 90.

20. Ibid., 99.

21. Ibid., 86.

22. Ibid.

23. Ibid., 86.

24. Jon Elster, *Ulysses and the Sirens: Studies in Rationality and Irrationality* (Cambridge: Cambridge University Press, 1979), 28.

25. Ibid., 32.

26. Jon Elster, *Explaining Technical Change* (Cambridge: Cambridge University Press, 1983), 58, and *Ulysses and the Sirens,* 30.

27. Russell Hardin, "Rationality, Irrationality and Functionalist Explanation," *Social Science Information,* 1980, 755–72, quote on 759.

28. Jon Elster, "Marxism, Functionalism, and Game Theory: The Case for Methodological Individualism," *Theory and Society,* July 1982, 453–82, quote on 463. Maybe there is now. The scholarly discussion of methodological individualism has taken place with the understanding that there is no such appropriate analogy. New ideas, however, suggest a reconsideration is in order.

Cultural theory and the theory of natural selection come together, we have argued, around the notion of evolutionarily stable strategies: ways of life (largely genetic, no doubt, in the biological case, culturally shaped in the sociological case). Cultural theory does not reduce the sociological to the biological; rather, it points to the same kinds of dynamics that underlie both systems. Game theory is the framework that has opened up our understanding of evolutionarily stable strategies, and as Maynard Smith has observed, game theory was originally developed with the aim of explaining human social behavior. There were, however, two obstacles in its way; obstacles that were absent in the biological case. "First, the theory requires that the value of different outcomes (for example, financial rewards, the risks of death or the pleasures of a clear conscience) be measured on a single scale. In human application, this measure is provided by 'utility'—a somewhat artificial and uncomfortable concept. In biology Darwinian fitness provides a natural and genuinely one-dimensional scale. Secondly, and more importantly, in seeking the solution of a game, the concept of human rationality is replaced by that of evolutionary stability" (John Maynard Smith, *Evolution and the Theory of Games,* [Cambridge: Cambridge University Press, 1982], vi).

Cultural theory's central axiom—that an act is rational if it strengthens the way of life of the actor—provides us with both a single scale (support for a way of life) and a definition of rationality as plural, in the sense that there are five, and just five, social contexts in which the definitions of what is rational and irrational can interact with those contexts in an evolutionarily stable way. With these two obstacles removed, sociology would have its analogy to the theory of natural selection. Because these ideas are new and have yet to be tested, our discussion in the text proceeds as if we accepted the "no analogy" position.

29. Merton, *Social Theory,* 69.

30. For examples drawn from anthropology, see Ruth Benedict, *Patterns of Culture* (Boston: Houghton Mifflin, 1934) on the potlatch ceremonies of the Kwakiutl, and Leopold Pospisil's description of New Guinea tribes giving away their cassowaries, in *Kapauku Political Economy* (New Haven: Yale University Press, 1963). Also see Andrew Strathern, *The Rope of Moka: Big-Men and Ceremonial Exchange in Mount Hagen, New Guinea* (Cambridge: Cambridge University Press, 1971), 187–227.

31. Mary Douglas, *How Institutions Think* (Syracuse: Syracuse University Press, 1986), 38. Douglas mistakenly identifies this as "a functional explanation of weak leadership." Weak leadership in her example is the function or consequence (Y), not the behavioral pattern (X) to be explained. It is not difficult, however, to reverse the variables and make "weak leadership" the explanandum (X) and "the threat to withdraw" the function (Y). (1) Weak leadership (X) has the consequence of enabling members to threaten to withdraw from the group (Y). (2) Y is useful to members of the group (Z) because the threat to withdraw keeps other members from extracting unwanted contributions. (3) Having a credible threat to withdraw (Y) maintains weak leadership (X) because leaders who try to make demands on their followers will lose their followers via exit from the group.

32. Ibid., 40.

33. Paul M. Sniderman and Richard Brody, "Coping: The Ethic of Self-Reliance," *American Journal of Political Science* 21 (August 1977): 501–22.

34. Functional analyses of deviance can be found in Robert Dentler and Kai T. Erikson, "The Functions of Deviance in Groups," *Social Problems,* Summer 1959, 98–107; and Kai T. Erikson, *Wayward Puritans: A Study in the Sociology of Deviance* (New York: John Wiley, 1966).

35. The same point is made in Paul Wetherly, "Marxist Functionalism: Some 'Problems' Considered," Paper delivered at the PSA Conference, Plymouth Polytechnic, April 12–14, 1988.

36. Jon Elster, *Making Sense of Marx* (Cambridge: Cambridge University Press, 1985), 6.

37. A Thatcherite phrase.

38. Mark Satin, *New Age Politics: Healing Self and Society* (New York: Delta, 1978).

39. We ignore for the moment the practical difficulty of getting people to articulate their underlying objectives publicly for fear of losing support from those who might not share their "hidden agenda."

PART THREE

POLITICAL CULTURES

Introduction to Part Three:
Cultures Are Plural, Not Singular

The concept of political culture swept the field of political science in the late 1950s and early 1960s. Intimately linked with the so-called behavioral revolution, it signaled a turn away from the study of formal institutions to the study of the informal behavior that breathed life into them. Political culture was heralded as a concept capable of unifying the discipline. By relating the behavior of individuals to the system of which the individual was a part, it promised to "bridge the 'micro-macro' gap in political theory."[1] In the 1970s, however, the concept of political culture, like that of functionalism, fell out of academic fashion amidst criticism that it was conservative, static, tautological, that it ignored power relations and could not explain change.[2]

Our aim in Part 3 is to show that these criticisms miss the mark. This is not to say that the political culture literature has never been guilty of some of these sins, but that these difficulties are not inherent in the concept of political culture. Rather it is to say that analyzing phenomena in terms of ways of life (each made up of a distinctive cultural bias justifying a distinctive pattern of social relations) can explain both change and stability in a way that neither ignores power relations nor commits one to ideological conservativism.

In reanalyzing some of the classic works on political culture, we have several goals in mind. The first is to demonstrate that these works have a great deal of merit, much of it unacknowledged. Building upon them, our second objective is to show that they can tell us even more if their ethnographic material is ordered according to the categories of cultural theory. Our third aim is to show that each of these studies, whether it be focused on China, Germany, Mexico, Great Britain, Italy, or the United States, supports our view that competing ways of life exist within a single nation. No matter what their level of technology, literacy rate, or type of political system, countries are constituted of competing political cultures, not a single political culture.

ON THE POLITICAL IN POLITICAL CULTURE

What, we begin by asking, does the "political" in political culture refer to? Defining political culture as patterns of orientation to political action or objects sidesteps the question of what is to count as political. Some insist that all action is political. So, for instance, Leslie Gottlieb of the Council on Economic Priorities declares: "Shopping is political. Buying a product means casting an economic vote for that company."[3] If "political" denotes power relations, then there is nothing that is not political, from child-rearing to marriage to attending school. If culture is by definition political, then the term *political* is superfluous. To avoid this redundancy, students of political culture have attempted to define political culture as orientations toward government (as opposed to, say, the economy, religion, or the family).[4] This conception includes attitudes about what government does (or should do) together with what people outside of government try to get it to do.

As these competing definitions of the "political" attest, the boundary between political and nonpolitical is not graven in stone, inherent in the nature of things. Definitions of what is political are themselves culturally biased. When one person accuses another of "politicizing" a subject, the disagreement is about how far the governmental writ should run. Constructing the boundary between political and nonpolitical is thus part of the struggle between competing ways of life. Rather than join in a debate about what is "really" political, we prefer to show how different culturally biased definitions of the political support different ways of life.[5]

Egalitarians desire to reduce the distinction between the political and nonpolitical. Defining the family or firm as nonpolitical or private, egalitarians believe, is a way of concealing and hence perpetuating unequal power relations. Egalitarians view the public sphere, in which all can actively participate and give their consent to collective decisions, as the realm in which the good life can best be realized.

Because individualists seek to replace authority with self-regulation, they are continually accusing others of politicizing issues. Their interest is in defining politics as narrowly as possible so as to maximize behavior that is considered private, and thus beyond the reach of governmental regulation. Hence their reluctance to admit the egalitarian charge that private resources influence public decisionmaking, for this admission would imply capitulation.

If egalitarians see the political sphere as the realm in which human beings most fully realize their potential, fatalists regard the political with nothing but fear and dread. Fatalists respond to their plight by trying to get as far out of harm's way as possible. Unlike individualists, however, fatalists do not discriminate sharply between the private and public spheres. Whether called public or private, the blows come without apparent pattern or meaning. The task of fatalists becomes personal or at most familial survival, and they cope as best they can without trying to distinguish between the sources of their difficulties.

For the same reasons that they approve of putting people and products in their properly ordered place, hierarchists approve of differentiating the public and private spheres. They frequently harbor an expansive view of state functions, hence their conflict with individualists, but they insist, contra the egalitarians, that politics is not for everyone and everyday for the rest of us, but rather reserved for a qualified and privileged few full-timers and for one day every four or five years. Where hierarchists draw the line between the public and private will vary, but that boundary is likely to be well defined.

Running through these four ways of life shows that the type of behavior or institution that is deemed political, or whether a boundary is even drawn at all, is itself a product of political culture. This suggests that the study of *political* culture (as distinct from culture generally) should pay special attention to the ways in which the boundary between political and nonpolitical is socially negotiated. More important, it also means that political scientists must give up the notion that the distinction between politics and other spheres (whether economic, social, or something else) is "out there" in the world, ready-made to be picked up and used. If, moreover, the boundaries between the political and nonpolitical are socially constructed, then the study of political culture must assume a central place in the discipline.

CULTURE AND ITS CRITICS

Before political culture can regain its position of prestige within political science, it must be shown that conventional criticisms of the concept have been misguided or, at a minimum, that the errors inhere in the past practice, not in the concept itself. We sympathize with those who complain that political culture is often treated as a residual variable, an explanation of last resort dragged in to fill the void when more conventional explanations fail. A recent study appearing in the preeminent political science journal typifies this usage of culture. The authors show that standard demographic variables (income, education, religion, race, age, gender) cannot explain intrastate variation in party identification and ideological identification, and then attribute the unexplained variance to political culture.[6] Invoking political culture in this way is little better than saying, "I don't know."

The most common criticism levied against the political culture literature is that it takes values as a given. Culture, critics insist, is a consequence, not (or at least not only) a cause, of institutional structures. Typical is Brian Barry's argument that a democratic political culture is a learned response to living under democratic institutions rather than, as he claims Gabriel Almond and Sidney Verba argue in their seminal work, *The Civic Culture,* a prerational commitment exerting a causal force upon those institutions.[7] Similarly, Alessandro Pizzorno criticizes Edward Banfield's classic study, *The Moral Basis of a Backward Society,* for explaining the absence of collective action in southern Italy as a product of an irrational "ethos" rather than in terms of a rational response to their "marginalized" position in the economic and political structure.[8]

To deny that political culture is shaped by structure, critics continue, makes the concept of culture deeply mysterious and unfathomable. As Peter Hall argues, "unless cultural theories can account for the origins of . . . attitudes by reference to the institutions that generate and reproduce them, they do little more than summon up a *deus ex machina* that is itself unexplainable."[9] We agree that political culture must not be treated as an uncaused cause purportedly explaining why people behave as they do, yet incapable of itself being explained. To do so is to posit a world in which values are disembodied, unattached to human subjects. People's continued adherence to certain doctrines and habits must themselves be explained.[10] This adherence is precisely what our sociocultural theory of preference formation, presented in Chapter 3, is designed to explain.

Political culture is transmitted from generation to generation, but it is not transmitted unchanged, nor is it transmitted without question or by chance. Cultural transmission is absolutely not a game of pass-the-parcel or musical chairs. It is a lively and responsive thing that is continually being negotiated by individuals. A plausible theory of political culture must not turn the individual into an automaton, passively receiving and internalizing political norms.

A first step in this direction is to allow for the importance of adult, rather than only childhood, experience in shaping individual orientations. Experience with institutions counts.[11] That is why immigrants who migrated from Banfield's southern Italy to the United States no longer behaved as fatalists. A second step is to allow for competing norms and values within a society. Ways of life are continually making promises that may not be fulfilled, predicting consequences that may prove false, creating blind spots that may lead to disaster. That is why during the Cultural Revolution, as Pye shows, Chinese elites could change from hierarchy to egalitarianism and back again. If one way of life falters, others are available to fill in the vacuum. Justifications or beliefs that once seemed powerful gradually (or perhaps even suddenly) seem to lose their hold. Witness, for instance, the significant rise of cynicism about government in the United States in the decades since *The Civic Culture.* To stay as we were requires vast energy. There is no reason why political culture, conceived as ways of life that are continually being negotiated, tested, and probed by individuals, cannot make sense of political change, long considered the Achilles heel of cultural theories.[12]

POLITICAL CULTURE AND NATIONAL CHARACTER

Research in political culture had its intellectual roots in the studies of "national character" pioneered by Ruth Benedict, Margaret Mead, and Geoffrey Gorer.[13] This literature focused upon the unique configuration of values, beliefs, and practices that constituted a nation's culture. The Russians were different from the Japanese were different from Chinese were different from the English were different from the Americans and so on. Comparison seemed beyond hope. By assigning cultures to nations or races, moreover, advocates of the culture concept forfeited all claim to being able to account for conflict within societies or racial groups. Explaining conflict was left largely to those armed with political economic categories of class and self-interest.

If the concept of culture was to be of utility to political scientists, some classification of cultures was necessary. The significance of Almond and Verba's typology of parochial, subject, and participatory orientations to politics was that it offered a classificatory scheme that enabled scholars to make cross-national comparisons among what had hitherto been seen as totally unique political cultures.[14] Although political scientists contributed to making political cultures comparable, the analytic focus largely remained, as in past works on national character, at the level of the nation-state. Differences between nations, rather than differences within nations, remained the central focus of inquiry.[15] Conflict within nations remained largely unexplained, if not inexplicable.

The tendency to attach culture to nations persists despite strong evidence suggesting that variation in political attitudes and values within countries are often greater than those between countries. Introducing a recent book of essays on European democracies, Mattei Dogan, for instance, finds that there is not a British civic culture nor a German, French, or Italian one. The differences among countries are differences in degree, not of kind, differences of a few percentage points. The differences within nations appear greater than the differences among nations. There are more similarities in the beliefs of a French and German social democrat than between a French socialist and a French conservative or between a German social democrat and a German Christian democrat.[16]

This conclusion accords with our contention that every nation contains a diversity of ways of life. We attempt to bolster this claim by showing that classic works in political culture, often in spite of their predisposition toward finding a national culture, uncover a variety of political cultures within each country and that these variations correspond to our five ways of life. We begin with the two "missing" ways of life, egalitarianism and fatalism.

NOTES

1. Gabriel A. Almond and G. Bingham Powell, *Comparative Politics: A Developmental Approach* (Boston: Little, Brown, 1966), 51–52. Also see Gabriel A. Almond and Sidney Verba, *The Civic Culture: Political Attitudes and Democracy in Five Nations* (Princeton: Princeton University Press, 1963), 32ff; and Lucian W. Pye, "Introduction: Political Culture and Political Development," in Lucian W. Pye and Sidney Verba, eds., *Political Culture and Political Development* (Princeton: Princeton University Press, 1965), 9.

2. Political culture is currently undergoing something of a revival, a trend noted in Lucian Pye, *The Mandarin and the Cadre: China's Political Cultures* (Ann Arbor: University of Michigan, 1988), 175 n. 3; and Robert Putnam with Robert Leonardi and Raffaella Y. Nanetti, "Institutional Performance and Political Culture: Some Puzzles About the Power of the Past," *Governance* 1, 3 (July 1988): 221–42, quote on 225. The renewed interest is also evident in Ronald Inglehart, "The Renaissance of Political Culture," *American Political Science Review* 82, 4 (December 1988): 1203–30; and Harry Eckstein, "A Culturalist Theory of Political Change," *American Political Science Review* 82, 3 (September 1988): 789–804.

3. Tony Bizjak, "New Dictums of the 'Politically Correct,'" *San Francisco Chronicle,* March 17, 1989, B5.

4. See, e.g., Almond and Verba *The Civic Culture,* 13. Almond and Verba readily concede that the boundary between political and nonpolitical cultures "is not as sharp as our terminology would suggest." They find, for instance, that "the political orientations that make up the civic culture are closely related to general social and interpersonal orientations," so close that at one point they refer to "social trust and cooperativeness" as "a component of the civic culture" (13, 493, 490).

5. This argument is further elaborated in Aaron Wildavsky, "On the Social Construction of Distinctions: Risk, Rape, Public Goods, and Altruism," in Michael Hecter, Lynn A. Cooper, and Lynn Nadel, eds., *Toward a Scientific Understanding of Values* (Stanford: Stanford University Press), forthcoming.

6. Robert S. Erikson, John P. McIver, and Gerald C. Wright, Jr., "State Political Culture and Public Opinion," *American Political Science Review* 81, 3 (September 1987): 797–814.

7. Brian Barry, *Sociologists, Economists and Democracy* (London: Collier-Macmillan, 1970), 48ff. Rereading *The Civic Culture* shows that although for analytic purposes, Almond and Verba primarily treat culture as the independent variable and democracy as the dependent variable, they allow the causality to go both ways. This point is brought out strongly in Arend Lijphart's excellent essay, "The Structure of Inference," in Gabriel A. Almond and Sidney Verba, eds., *The Civic Culture Revisited* (Boston: Little, Brown, 1980), esp. 47–49.

8. Alessandro Pizzorno, "Amoral Familism and Historical Marginality," *International Review of Community Development*, 1966, 55–66.

9. Peter Hall, *Governing the Economy: The Politics of State Intervention in Britain and France* (New York: Oxford University Press, 1986), 34.

10. See Mary Douglas, "Cultural Bias," in *In the Active Voice* (London: Routledge and Kegan Paul, 1982), esp. 184–85; and Mary Douglas and Baron Isherwood, *The World of Goods: Towards an Anthropology of Consumption* (London: Allen Lane, 1979), 31.

11. Although one might not be able to tell from reading critics of *The Civic Culture,* it was Almond and Verba who were among the first to draw attention to the fact that previous research had "seriously underemphasized . . . the importance of . . . experience with the political systems" (34).

12. Eckstein reaches the same conclusion (although by a different route), that political culture can account for change, in "A Culturalist Theory of Political Change."

13. Ruth Benedict, *Patterns of Culture* (Boston: Houghton Mifflin, 1934), and *The Chrysanthemum and the Sword: Patterns of Japanese Culture* (Boston: Houghton Mifflin, 1946); Geoffrey Gorer, *The American People: A Study in National Character* (New York: Norton, 1948), and *Exploring English Character* (New York: Criterion, 1955); Margaret Mead, *And Keep Your Powder Dry: An Anthropologist Looks at America* (New York: Morrow, 1942), and "National Character," in Alfred L. Kroeber, ed., *Anthropology Today: An Encyclopedic Inventory* (Chicago: University of Chicago Press, 1953).

14. Almond and Verba, *Civic Culture.* Also see Gabriel A. Almond's seminal piece, "Comparative Political Systems," *Journal of Politics* 18 (1956): 391–409.

15. Political cultural variation within nations is explicitly recognized in *The Civic Culture.* Almond and Verba caution the reader that "our classification does not imply homogeneity or uniformity of political cultures. Thus political systems with predominantly participant cultures will, even in the limiting case, include both subjects and parochials"(20). Still their primary focus undeniably remains at the level of nations as a whole.

16. Mattei Dogan, ed., *Comparing Pluralist Democracies: Strains on Legitimacy* (Boulder, Colo.: Westview Press, 1988), 2–3.

CHAPTER 12

The Missing Ways of Life:
Egalitarianism and Fatalism

Hierarchy and individualism are familiar to most social scientists. Egalitarianism and fatalism, not to mention autonomy, are considerably less so. They are recognized, perhaps, as attitudes, but not as fundamental ways of life on a par with individualism and hierarchy. We demonstrated in Part 2 that the great social theorists focused almost exclusively on individualism and hierarchy. In this chapter, we show that two of the more acclaimed empirical works on political culture, Edward Banfield's *The Moral Basis of a Backward Society,*[1] and Lucian Pye's lifework on Chinese political cultures, now memorialized in his recent *The Mandarin and the Cadre,*[2] uncover the neglected ways of life, fatalism and egalitarianism.

THE MORAL BASIS OF A BACKWARD SOCIETY

Banfield's *The Moral Basis of a Backward Society* is the finest study of fatalism known to us. Through an intensive examination of a single village (to which he gives the fictitious name Montegrano) in southern Italy, Banfield attempts to show how a fatalistic cultural bias impedes the collective action necessary to sustain economic development and a democratic political order.[3]

At first Banfield throws us off the track by suggesting that the people of Montegrano are not fatalistic because they do want to get ahead in the world. Our concept of fatalism, however, does not require individuals to relinquish their aspirations for a better life; only the hermit, who neither manipulates nor is manipulated, truly is satisfied with sufficiency and does not want more. What distinguishes fatalists from adherents of other ways of life is that although they desire a better life, they feel that fate conspires to prevent them from improving their condition. As Banfield himself puts it, although "getting ahead" is a central theme of a Montegrano peasant's existence, "he sees that no matter how hard he works he can never get ahead. . . . He knows . . . that in the end he will be no better off than before."[4]

Banfield's criticism of explanations of Montegrano behavior that resort to "melancholy fatalism" as an explanation is, in large part, an attack on employing culture as an uncaused cause. In trying to explain why the Montegranesi do not organize to get their roads improved, for instance, Banfield rejects the popular explanation that "the southern Italian is a despairing fatalist."[5] Used in this way, Banfield shows, the concept of fatalism blocks inquiry. Banfield explains that

> the merchants of Montegrano are well aware of the importance to them of good roads. They would not, however, expect to be listened to by the authorities who decide which roads are to be improved. A Montegrano man might write a letter to the provincial authorities in Potenza or to the newspaper there, but it is unlikely that his doing so would make any difference. In fact, these officials would be likely to resent what they consider interference in their affairs.[6]

Their passivity is rooted in their social (or political) relations, in this case, their relations with governmental officials. A fatalistic orientation (the attitude that nothing one can do will influence the government to fix the roads) is thus a learned (and rational) response to a distant, capricious, and unresponsive power imposed from without.

The peasants' melancholy (the local expression is *la miseria*), Banfield concedes, is partly a consequence of a poor resource position. Yet, Banfield points out, there are other people whose biological level of well-being is worse but who are cheerful or, at least, not perpetually unhappy. "What makes the difference between a low level of living and *la miseria*," Banfield concludes, "comes from culture." A Montegrano peasant "feels himself part of a larger society which he is 'in' but not altogether 'of.'"[7] Controlled by outside forces, the fatalist is unable, or so he believes, to help himself.

Through thematic apperception tests (TAT), which ask people to tell stories about a picture, Banfield was able to obtain a more systematic gauge of Montegranesi attitudes. Even more valuable were the results of similar tests given to peasants in northern Italy and farmers from Kansas. These tests show, for instance, that the themes of calamity and misfortune figure much more prominently in the psyche of the Montegranesi than among the respondents in rural Kansas or northern Italy (see Table 1). Banfield elaborates on the content of the Montegranesi stories:

No matter how hard the parents struggle, the family may suddenly be destroyed or reduced to beggary. The peasant expects some dreadful calamity to befall it at any moment. In this view a mountain of woe hangs over the family by a slender thread. Ninety percent of the TAT stories told by Montegrano people had themes of calamity or misfortune; in some stories the calamities and misfortunes were averted; in many more they were not.[8]

Disaster can wreck even the best laid plans. One Montegrano resident, shown a *blank* card, told a story of

a lovely house with a garden and small fountain in front. There was a man who with much effort and many sacrifices succeeded in making a small pile. He bought a bit of land and at the same time continued to work hard and to profit. Then with many sacrifices he succeeded in building the house, very beauteous and commodious. But he was not able to enjoy it because just as it was being finished he unexpectedly died.[9]

Table 1
TAT stories having themes of calamity or misfortune (in percentages)

	Southern Italy[1]	Northern Italy[2]	Rural Kansas[3]
Calamity: Story ends in death, insanity, or blighting of all hope.	44	13	9
Misfortune: Story ends with injury of "hero," loss of money, death of live-stock, etc.	20	11	7
Calamity or misfortune averted or miti-gated: Story deals with an escape, fears that prove unfounded, tribulation fol-lowed by eventual success or alleviation.	26	38	26
Safety: Story is not necessarily happy, but there is no theme of peril.	7	29	50
Unclassifiable: Story is fragmentary or purely descriptive.	3	9	8
ALL	100	100	100

[1] 320 stories by 16 persons (seven married couples and two youths) in Montegrano; all laborers.

[2] 200 stories by 10 persons (five married couples) in the province of Rovigo (bounded by Verona, Padova, and Venice); all laborers.

[3] 386 stories by 30 persons (15 married couples) in Vinland, Kansas; farm owners.

In the face of such a capricious world, Banfield reasons, an individual "cannot count on achieving anything by his own effort and enterprise."[10] In only 2 of the 320 stories told by the Montegranesi peasants, Banfield tells us, "did a family prosper by thrift or enterprise."[11] Dramatic success invariably requires the fortuitous intervention of a benevolent patron.

Faced with a TAT picture of a boy contemplating a violin lying on a table before him, the Kansan farmers (and northern Italian peasants) commonly tell a story in which success comes from individual initiative and hard work ("he worked and slaved day after day . . . studied at night . . . [and] today he is one of the nation's leading conductors."[12]) In the stories told by Montegranesi peasants, however, success is usually attributed to the chance intervention of a patron. One man, for instance, constructs a story in which "a gentleman . . . who was much moved with compassion by him . . . took the boy home and let him study. The boy knew very well how to profit by his good fortune and indeed became a very fine maestro." Another envisioned a sad child, who is "thinking that he was born to this earth only to bear sorrows . . . but one day his fortune changed because a gentleman interested himself in the boy, took him off the street, and put him in college to study." And yet another related the tale of "a young boy in a poor family, who wanted very much to study, but there was no possibility . . . [but] then finally it was his fortune that an uncle from America sent him money so that he could study and he became a fine professional."[13]

The Montegranesi wait for nature to disgorge in their direction. They wait, for instance, for the "call" that will enable them to take their family to the more prosperous regions of the north or, even better, for the "call" from a relative in America that will enable them to migrate to the United States.[14] There is nothing they can do, or so they believe, to bring about the desired outcome. Banfield's understated conclusion is indisputable: "The idea that one's welfare depends crucially upon conditions beyond one's control—upon luck or the caprice of a saint—and that one can at best only improve upon good fortune, not create it—this idea must certainly be a check on initiative."[15] As we argued in Chapter 2, the conception of the world as a lottery-controlled, rather than a skill-controlled, cornucopia is one of the primary mechanisms by which fatalism reproduces itself as a way of life.

The Montegranesi social construction of the physical world explains much about why they put so little stock in collective action. As Banfield states: "Where everything depends upon luck or Divine intervention, there is no point in community action. The community, like the individual, may hope or pray, but it is not likely to take its destiny into its own hands."[16]

Nor are fatalists likely to build up the leaders that might help them better their collective condition. Banfield reports that "apparently there has never been in Montegrano a peasant leader to other peasants." Indeed, Banfield flatly predicts that "there will be no leaders and followers" in such a society. For even in the unlikely event that an individual takes the initiative to offer leadership, according to Banfield, "the group would refuse it out of distrust."[17] The absence of leadership, in turn, impedes the very collective organization the peasants need to break out of their cycle of despair and distrust.

Fearful of being exploited by others—employers, thieves, landlords, politicians, neighbors—the fatalist, Banfield contends, will prefer authoritarian political systems, in which people are "looked after" and laws are rigorously enforced.[18] No value is placed on participation or competition. In the view of the people of Montegrano, "a regime which uses its power solely to enforce the law and not to exploit the citizen comes into being only when the rich and powerful take it into their heads to indulge themselves in the virtues of charity and justice."[19] People, like nature, are seen as capricious, occasionally benevolent but much more often bad. Unable to predict when power will be abused and when it will not, the fatalist is predisposed to support authoritarian systems, which give them predictability without responsibility.

The genius of Banfield's book lies in specifying the reciprocal relationships between social relations and cultural biases that make the fatalistic way of life viable. The way of life, we see from Banfield, is self-reinforcing and self-replicating. No efficacy, no collective action, no pooling of resources, no economic growth, no defenses against adversity, no efficacy. No trust, no cooperation, no democracy, no defenses against arbitrary authority, no trust. The consequence of a fatalistic orientation is to sustain a mode of social organization that inhibits economic growth and democracy, thereby leaving the adherents vulnerable to the caprice of nature and people, and thus refueling the existing fatalistic bias.

THE MANDARIN AND THE CADRE

"Both the speed and the ease of China's dramatic changes suggest that there must somehow be 'two Chinas,' or maybe it is 'one China, and two political cultures.'"[20] So suggests Lucian Pye in his distillation of a lifetime of observation and study, *The Mandarin and the Cadre: China's Political Cultures* (note the plural). Pye's book comports with our argument that there are competing ways of life within a single nation. We summarize his findings to make two points: One is that whenever a knowledgeable and insightful ethnographer describes ways of life, the same cultural biases appear; the other is that placing well-realized descriptions within the ambit of a theory of cultural viability adds to explanatory power, in this instance the ability to understand the Cultural Revolution. First the cultural biases.[21]

Four Ways of Life

Pye's account makes clear that the two strongest ways of life in China have been hierarchy and egalitarianism. Pye argues that

> the fundamental polarity of China's traditional cultures was between . . . an elitist high Confucian culture that glorified the established authority of the better educated and rationalized their claims of superiority on the basis of possessing specialized wisdom, and a passionate, populist heterodox culture that glorified the rebel and trusted magical formulas to transform economic and social reality.[22]

In the hierarchical China, "the Chinese instinctively think that all authority should be arranged in a single pecking order, and that the only way that authority can be properly divided is between acknowledged superiors and inferiors." Hierarchy in China, Pye points out, is a structure not just of command but of status, a structure whose rationale is not only to get individuals to perform their assigned duties but also to allow their members to gain prestige through titles. Following on "the intense Chinese fear of *luan* [chaos], disorder and confusion," they turn to "the classical Confucian assumption that all will be right with the world if everyone conscientiously performs his or her assigned role."[23] So far, so hierarchical.

Alongside hierarchy, however, Pye finds a rival tradition that glorified the rebel and celebrated "the idea of egalitarian brotherhood." This traditional rebel culture, Pye maintains, was "at the core of Maoism." It "idealized more egalitarian values, despised formal education and the pretensions of those who thought themselves to be the moral and intellectual betters."[24] In contrast to the hierarchical culture, which values the "masterly performance," the egalitarian tradition values "the purity in beliefs . . . [and] the passions of commitment."[25] Whereas the hierarchical Chinese tradition emphasizes the value of institutions for molding behavior and channeling emotions, the egalitarian culture stresses the need to unleash the unlimited potential and natural goodness of human beings.

Although the differences between these two ways of life are profound, the cultures do share one important feature. "Both cultures," Pye explains, "stress the importance of the group over the individual,"[26] or as we would say, both hierarchy and egalitarianism have strong group boundaries. Both cultures, Pye finds, place a high premium on sacrificing for the collectivity. Just as the hierarchical culture teaches the virtue of "sacrificing the smaller self to fulfill the greater self," so the egalitarian, rebel culture extols those who commit "supreme sacrifices" for the cause.[27]

Although these two collectivist modes of social organization take up much of China's cultural landscape, they do not exhaust the possibilities. Pye also comments on the Chinese belief in "the propriety and wisdom of controlling feelings and accepting one's situation fatalistically." In China, "fatalism is associated with the impossibility of questioning ways of authority; at best it is pointless to challenge the whims of the powerful, at worst it is dangerous to attract the attention of amoral authorities." Life, for these people, is like a lottery. They have "been taught that discrimination is a natural condition of life, and therefore it is foolish not to accept one's lot and hope that in good time fortune will, in its random way, come around and bless one's life."[28] It is the resentments of this group that the egalitarians, whether Maoist or traditional rebel, have tried to harness in order to discredit established authority.

Fatalism, egalitarianism, and hierarchy are all, in their different ways, organized so as to restrict individual autonomy. Is there no cultural bias in China celebrating the individual? According to Pye, there is. "Opposed against this idealizing of self-sacrifice," Pye informs us, "is the equally respected vision of the prospering notable who has combined good luck, quick wits, and hard work to advance himself."[29] Another long-time China scholar, Robert Scalapino, refers in passing to his belief that "in China, the entrepreneurial spirit is deeply implanted in the culture."[30] To assert individualism's presence is not to deny its weakness. Rather, our message is that those who seek will find at least four ways of life. Indeed, as our strong reliance on the poet Po Chu-i has already made clear, those who seek diligently will find all five.

Understanding the Cultural Revolution

"Two decades after Mao Zedong ignited the Great Proletarian Revolution [called the Cultural Revolution, beginning circa 1968]," Pye declares, "there is still no satisfactory accounting for the upheaval that Beijing now says caused millions of deaths and left some 100 million people scarred victims." Why, Pye wonders, did Mao's call to purify the Party and root out conspiracies meet with such extraordinary enthusiasm; how was it "that long-time friends and associates, from classmates to office workers, were so quickly brought to the state of attacking each other in life and death struggles"?[31]

Here our understanding is aided by Lowell Dittmer's recent account of "the inner logic" of the Cultural Revolution. Dittmer finds that the Cultural Revolution was characterized by a "structure of polemical symbolism" in which "the world of appearance, full of light, purity, public spirit and virtuous action . . . concealed a world of darkness, selfishness, defilement, passive dependency." Because the enemy was hidden behind "masks" or in "holes," the response was to ruthlessly strip away disguises. Moreover, because evil was hidden and therefore threatened to corrupt the inner purity of the group, the proponents of the Revolution felt impelled "to reinforce the barrier between the two worlds, decry any attempt to obscure or extenuate this barrier as hypocrisy or subversion, and to drive invaders from the subterranean world back out of sight."[32]

We can see from Dittmer's account that the inner logic of the Cultural Revolution is only an instance of a broader phenomenon: the inner logic of an egalitarian group. Belief in a pure inside and an impure outside impels egalitarians to build up the "wall of virtue" that separates them from the outside world. As the wall becomes ever higher, the antagonism between "us" and "them" is heightened. Because evil is masked, moreover, there is a continuous search for hidden enemies and concealed conspirators within the group. Fearing betrayal from within, friends are unmasked as counterrevolutionary enemies.

Pye observes that after Mao left the scene, the obsession with enemies subsided. This prompts Pye to suggest that Mao Zedong's "borderline personality" explains much of the Manichaean cosmology exhibited during the Cultural Revolution. A fundamental characteristic of the borderline personality, Pye tells us, is "the need always to have an 'enemy' to battle against." Moreover, "the possessor of a borderline personality may suddenly 'split' with others; an apparently normal, friendly relationship can with little apparent cause become an adversarial one. Friends suddenly are seen as enemies."[33]

It may be that Mao fits this personality type. But a psychological explanation by itself, we argue (and Pye no doubt would agree), is inadequate. For, as Mary Douglas has commented, although "leaders may well have psychological traits which enable them to express very sharply these fears and resentments, . . . only a sociological analysis can explain why they find their followings in predictable niches."[34] Only by shifting from a psychological analysis of individual neuroses to a cultural analysis of collective biases can we hope to explain why so many people responded with such enthusiasm to Mao's call to attack a hidden enemy and ferret out counterrevolutionaries. We believe the syndrome exhibited in Maoism—conflict viewed as a struggle between the wholly good and the utterly evil, the conversion of erstwhile friends into enemies, endemic schism—is a product of, rather than a "border-line personality," the egalitarian (or, as Douglas and Wildavsky label it in *Risk and Culture,* the "border"[35]) way of life.

Sociocultural theory suggests another reason why egalitarian followers were willing to follow Mao blindly and to endow him with superhuman qualities. One cannot mix and match just any kind of leader with just any way of life. Charismatic leadership, which seeks to replace the body of the law with the person of the leader as the source of authority, we argue, can be sustained only in an egalitarian culture. The charismatic's disregard for routinized practices makes such leadership anathema to hierarchists; charisma's demand for unquestioning devotion is rejected by individualists, who wish to negotiate transactions for themselves; fatalists cannot muster the devotion that the charismatic calls for. Only egalitarians, who find their desire for enacting social justice stymied by their antipathy to leadership, have an incentive to invest leaders with extraordinary qualities. Pye's analysis indicates the predicted affinity between charismatic leadership and the Chinese egalitarian tradition. "The ideal leader of the traditional rebel culture," Pye informs us, "was one with superhuman powers and a tactical cleverness that set him apart from ordinary mortals."[36]

Viewed through a cultural lens, there is nothing particularly novel about the Cultural Revolution, except its extremity, a fact that is due to egalitarians' ability to seize near total power. In that respect, however, it is matched (and perhaps exceeded) by another egalitarian movement, the Cambodian Khmer Rouge.[37] Neither Pye nor we claim that egalitarianism is more violent than other ways of life (thinking about the German Nazi and Soviet Communist hierarchies would immediately disabuse anyone of that notion). The paths to repression are as various as the paths to democracy. What we are saying is that the Cultural Revolution was initiated and carried out by egalitarians (in a context where rival political cultures were weak), and that its trajectory and content are characteristic of radical egalitarian movements.

NOTES

1. Edward C. Banfield, *The Moral Basis of a Backward Society* (New York: Free Press, 1958).

2. Lucian W. Pye, *The Mandarin and the Cadre: China's Political Cultures* (Ann Arbor: University of Michigan Press, 1988). His other major works on Chinese political culture include *The Spirit of Chinese Politics* (Cambridge: MIT Press, 1968) and *Asian Power and Politics* (Cambridge: Harvard University Press, 1985).

3. Banfield, *Moral Basis of a Backward Society,* 8–10.

4. Ibid., 64.
5. Ibid., 36.
6. Ibid., 18–19.
7. Ibid., 63–64.
8. Ibid., 105.
9. Ibid., 107.
10. Ibid., 107.
11. Ibid., 64.
12. Ibid., 185.
13. Ibid., 177, 179.
14. Ibid., 58–59, 88.
15. Ibid., 109.
16. Ibid.
17. Ibid., 97.
18. Ibid., 92–93.
19. Ibid., 135.
20. Pye, *Mandarin and the Cadre,* 37.
21. Aside from some confusion of individualism and autonomy, the cultural biases within Chinese society have been mapped, altogether independently from Pye's analysis, by Katrina C.D. McLeod, "The Political Culture of Warring States in China," in Mary Douglas, ed., *Essays in the Sociology of Perception* (London: Routledge and Kegan Paul, 1982), 132–61.
22. Pye, *Mandarin and the Cadre,* 39.
23. Ibid., 32–34.
24. Ibid., 39–40, 44.
25. Ibid. 50.
26. Ibid., 41.
27. Ibid., 58–59.
28. Ibid., 54–57.
29. Ibid., 58.
30. Robert Scalapino, "Reflections on Current Soviet and Chinese Revolutions," typescript, February 7, 1987, 8.
31. Pye, *Mandarin and the Cadre,* 109, 119.
32. Lowell Dittmer, *China's Continuous Revolution: The Post-Liberation Epoch, 1949–1981* (Berkeley: University of California Press, 1987), 86–88.
33. Pye, *Mandarin and the Cadre,* 160–61.
34. Mary Douglas, *Natural Symbols: Explorations in Cosmology* (New York: Pantheon, 1982), 119.
35. Mary Douglas and Aaron Wildavsky, *Risk and Culture* (Berkeley: University of California Press, 1982).
36. Pye, *Mandarin and the Cadre,* 61.
37. Karl D. Jackson, ed., *Rendezvous with Death: Democratic Kampuchea, 1975–1978.* See also the review of Pin Yathay, *L'utopie meurtrière* (Paris: Robert Laffont, 1980), by Ferenc Feher, *Telos,* no. 56 (Summer 1983): 193–205.

CHAPTER 13

American Political Subcultures

The bulk of political culture research, reflecting its origins in studies of "national character," has been concerned with cross-national comparisons. A notable exception to this pattern is Daniel Elazar's pioneering work on American political subcultures.[1] Through intensive studies of state politics, Elazar and his students have attempted to demonstrate the existence and importance of cultural variation within the United States.

In spirit, Elazar's work is close to our own. Like Elazar, we hope to show that there are important cultural variations within a nation, and that knowing these variations will lead to more powerful explanations of behavior. We also follow Elazar in attempting to go beyond the familiar categories of modern individualism and traditional hierarchy, categories handed down by the masters of social thought. In substance, there are striking parallels between his categories (individualism, traditionalism, and moralism) and our own. Our aim in presenting Elazar's typology is to offer the reader a competing categorization of political cultures that can be compared with ours both for coherence and payoff.

Elazar's individualistic subculture corresponds closely to our individualist way of life. The individualistic political culture, according to Elazar, "emphasizes the conception of the democratic order as a marketplace . . . [and] places a premium on limiting community intervention—whether governmental or nongovernmental—into private activities to the minimum necessary to keep the marketplace in proper working order."[2] This description isolates the two features—bidding and bargaining, and self-regulation—that we have identified as the distinguishing characteristics of the individualist way of life.

Elazar's description of the traditionalistic political culture suggests a strong affinity with the way of life we have termed hierarchical. The traditionalistic culture, Elazar tells us, is characterized by "an ambivalent attitude toward the marketplace coupled with a paternalistic and elitist conception of the commonwealth." This political culture, he explains, "reflects an older precommercial attitude that accepts a substantially hierarchical society as part of the ordered nature of things, authorizing and expecting those at the top of the social structure to take a special and dominant role in government."[3]

"Traditionalism," we believe, is an unfortunate label for this way of life, for it suggests that at its core is a commitment to doing things the way they have been done in the past, regardless of the substance of those past behaviors and beliefs. This is unsatisfactory because (1) it is not parallel with "individualism," which suggests a commitment to a particular set of substantive beliefs, and (2) it does not correspond to the description offered by Elazar that focuses on the culture's ambivalence toward the self-regulation and competition of markets as well as its distrust of popular participation. We prefer the designation "hierarchical" because we believe it more accurately denotes the way of life (as defined by Elazar) that its adherents believe in.[4]

Elazar's moralistic political culture is the most ambiguous of his three categories. The confusion begins with the label "moralistic," which suggests that moralism is the peculiar province of one political culture. The question, in our view, is not which culture is moralistic, but what counts as morality (and moralism) in different ways of life. Is the individualist who lectures the poor on how they have no one to blame but themselves for their plight any less moralistic than the egalitarian who lectures the rich that they are responsible for the oppression of the poor? Every way of life, we maintain (along with Durkheim, Marx, Weber, and other classical authors), is held together by moralizing about how not to behave.

The "moralism" label is also misleading because it does not adequately convey the characteristics that Elazar offers as the defining features of this way of life. Elazar argues that the political cultures of moralism and individualism represent "two contrasting conceptions of the American political order." In contrast to the individualistic political culture, where "the political order is conceived as a marketplace in which the primary public relationships are products of bargaining among individuals and groups acting out of self-interest," Elazar tells us, the moralistic culture conceives of the political order as "a commonwealth—a state in which the whole people have an undivided interest—in which the citizens cooperate in an effort to create and maintain the best government in order to implement certain shared moral principles."[5] This description suggests that Elazar conceives of these two cultures as existing at opposite poles of a single continuum based on the degree to which individuals believe political life should be oriented toward a collective public good. This dimension might be seen as roughly coincident with our group dimension. Rather than use the designation "moralism" (which seems to denote a *style* of expressing one's beliefs, in contrast to individualism, which refers to the *content* of those beliefs), it would better capture Elazar's meaning if we referred to this culture as "communitarian" or "communalism."[6]

How then does moralism (or communalism) relate to traditionalism? Both, according to Elazar, indicate belief in the commonwealth. The difference is that whereas the traditionalistic culture harbors a deferential conception of the commonwealth, the communitarian culture adheres to a participatory vision of the collective. Politics, from the communitarian perspective, is "ideally a matter of concern for every citizen, not just for those who are professionally committed to political careers. Indeed, it is the duty of every citizen to participate in the political affairs of his community."[7] This difference, we would suggest, is the difference between hierarchical collectivism and egalitarian communalism.

If we adhere to this definition of a moralistic political culture as both participatory and communitarian, it becomes evident that much of what Elazar classifies as moralism is actually better described by the traditionalistic category (deferential and communitarian). Consider the case of Massachusetts, the state that Elazar identifies as the seedbed of the moralistic culture. The political culture of eighteenth- and early nineteenth-century Massachusetts was, as Elazar posits, strongly communitarian. But that collectivity was predominantly deferential, not participatory. In no other state in the Union (except perhaps Delaware) was the Federalist party, the party of hierarchy, more powerful than in Massachusetts. If distrust of widespread political participation and suspicion of an unregulated free market are the hallmarks of a traditionalistic culture, then the Federalist party of Massachusetts was the embodiment of the traditionalistic (we would say hierarchical) culture.[8]

James Banner's classic study of Massachusetts federalism, *To the Hartford Convention,* richly evokes that party's hierarchical (or, in Elazar's language, traditional) propensities. "The basic motifs of Massachusetts Federalist thought," Banner tells us, "were harmony, unity, order, solidarity." Federalists conceived of society "both as a structure of harmonious and mutually interdependent interests and as a collectivity in which individuals, by occupying fixed places and performing specified tasks, contributed to the health and prosperity of the whole community." A Federalist cleric explained:

> The social body is composed of various members, mutually connected and dependent. Though some may be deemed less honorable, they may

not be less necessary than others. As the eye, the ear, the hand, the foot of the human body, cannot say to the other, I have no need of you, but all in their respective places have indispensable uses; so in the Commonwealth, each citizen has some gift or function, by which he may become a contributor to the support and pleasure of the whole body.[9]

Although each member of the collectivity has a role to play in the whole, each must keep to his proper sphere. Participation in the political sphere was ideally limited to the few who were virtuous, wealthy, and wise. "The Commonwealth's well-being," Federalists believed, "was directly proportionate to the participation of the better sort in public affairs." As the clergyman Jedidiah Morse taught, "distinctions of rank and condition in life are requisite to the perfection of the social state. There must be rulers and subjects, masters and servants, rich and poor. The human body is not perfect without all its members, some of which are more honorable than others; so it is with the body politic." It has pleased God, lectured another, "to place mankind in different stations and to distinguish them from each other by a diversity of rank, power, and talent."[10] Evident here is both group (abiding by the collective decision) and grid (socially imposed prescriptions on behavior).

Deference to one's betters, which was a defining feature of the Massachusetts Federalists' political culture, was instilled at an early age. It was common for children of Federalist families to bow before their parents and address them by a deferential "Honored Papa" and "Honored Mama." The "tightly regulated and patriarchal family," Banner shows, was seen as "the best place . . . to initiate this training in deference." Children were taught, Banner continues, "to honor and obey their elders, control their whims, and restrain their youthful energies in the general interest of the whole household. It was within the home that the growing child must first be exposed to the necessary distinctions among men and taught that only a few possess the privilege to rule." Such "habits of subordination" were also to be inculcated in school. Schools were to teach people "to confide in and reverence their rulers." The purpose of education, according to one Federalist, was "to inculcate on . . . expanding minds the necessity of sub-ordination and obedience to their superiors."[11]

Elazar is correct in calling attention to the deep suspicion of competitive individualism that existed in Massachusetts political culture. Massachusetts Federalists, as Banner points out, "spiritedly rejected the argument that the general welfare of a republican society was enhanced by uninhibited competition and the pursuit of self-interest." The quest for individual gain, Federalists charged, diverted individuals' attention away from sacrificing for the collectivity. But the roots of the Federalists' critique of market capitalism (like the critique that emerged in Virginia and South Carolina) were not egalitarian but hierarchical. Their complaint against individualism was, not that it created inequalities, but rather that it subverted the natural order of social rankings: "Rather than trying to better his condition, a man was to keep his place; rather than striving to transcend his station, he was to transfer to his betters the authority to decide at what moment he was to be permitted to rise."[12]

The limitations of Elazar's moralistic category can be more clearly seen by comparing the radical abolitionism of William Lloyd Garrison and the conservative Whiggery of Daniel Webster. Elazar considers both of these New Englanders as representatives of the moralistic (or, as he sometimes calls it, Yankee) political culture.[13] In our view, however, Garrison and Webster adhered to fundamentally different ways of life. Webster was an advocate of hierarchical collectivism, in which the many should defer to the few and the few should display a "paternal sympathy"[14] for the many, whereas Garrison championed egalitarian communalism, in which all had an obligation to participate and no one had the right to exercise control over another.[15]

In his acclaimed study, *The Political Culture of the American Whigs,* Daniel Walker Howe selects Webster as an archetypal representative of Whig conservatism.[16] Like their Federalist predecessors, conservative Whigs upheld a politics of deference and noblesse oblige. They defended authority, whether in the form of teacher, husband, parent, or political leader. Many, including Webster, relied on an analogy between the human body and the social and political system. Just as there was a need in the body for the higher faculties of conscience and reason to restrain the lower animal passions, so in society it was necessary for the more responsible at the upper end of the social stratum to discipline and regulate the profligate at the lower end.[17]

Garrisonian abolitionists, by contrast, were committed to egalitarian social relations, in which no person would exercise power over another. As Lawrence Friedman shows in *Gregarious Saints,* abolitionists organized their lives differently from the rest of northern society. "Small groups," Friedman finds, were "at the heart of the immediatist crusade." Each group, moreover, contained a tension between "harmonious collectivity" and "unfettered individuality."[18] Abolitionism, echoes another historian, simultaneously "contained an anarchic appeal and a collectivist call, a command to shun evil and consult only conscience, and a mandate to join with the like-minded and look outward for perfect fellowship."[19] "A world in ourselves and in each other" is the way one of the abolitionists aptly characterized their life of weak prescriptions and strong group boundaries.[20] The combination of strong group ("harmonious collectivity," "collectivist call," "a world in each other") and low grid ("unfettered individuality," "anarchic appeal," "a world in ourselves") produces an egalitarian way of life.

Their commitment to egalitarianism led Garrisonians to call into question traditional gender roles. "Our object," Garrison revealed, "is *universal* emancipation—to redeem woman as well as man from a servile to an equal condition." A member of the Garrison-led Boston Clique, Maria Lydia Child, explained that she and her husband "despised the idea of any distinction in the appropriate spheres of human beings." Garrison and his followers were highly critical of familial authority relations, whether between husband and wife or parent and child. A radical Garrisonian went as far as to liken "every family" to "a little embryo plantation." Another explained that she was always "very conscientious not to use the least worldly authority over her child." Perhaps the abolitionist marriage that most closely approximated the egalitarian ideal was that of Garrisonian followers Abigail Kelley and Stephen Foster. Both agreed that either could withdraw from the marriage whenever they chose, and the farm they bought after their marriage was deeded to Foster and Kelley jointly. While Abigail was out lecturing, moreover, Stephen would often stay home and take care of the farm and child. To an admiring abolitionist, the Foster home was a place in which there could be "seen the beauty and the possibility of a permanent partnership of equals."[21]

The Whig attitude toward the family was radically different. Whigs not only defended the husband's control over the wife, and parents' authority over children, but also generalized from these familial relationships to the ideal political relationships. The patriarchal family, Howe points out, was identified by a number of conservative Whigs as the ultimate origin of the state.[22] Leaders, in the Whig view, should assume the same attitude toward the citizenry that "a parent holds to a child, or a guardian to a ward." By the same token, the citizenry was obligated to show the same deference toward political leaders that children owed to their parents and wives to their husbands. The government ought to be "the parent of the people," exerting "a beneficent, paternal, fostering usefulness upon the industry and prosperity of the People" as well as protecting and guiding "the weak and disabled and . . . more dependent members of society." The nation, in the words of Webster, was a "family concern."[23]

Whereas Whigs saw each member of society, from the mightiest to the meekest, as an integral although unequal part of the whole, abolitionists tried to separate themselves from the wider society, which they believed was shot through with corruption. In the view of Garrisonian abolitionists, black slavery was "only the worst example of American reliance on force—on man oppressing his fellow man rather than partaking in mutual love. Oppression of man by man in all its forms, not simply southern racial bondage, made up the American slave system." Using this expanded definition of slavery, Garrison could proclaim "that Pennsylvania is as really a slave-holding state as Georgia."[24] Believing that the "slaveholding spirit" suffused government, Garrisonians refused to vote or hold political office. Participation in the system could only result in co-optation and defilement.

The different ways of life adhered to by New England Whigs and abolitionists also led them, despite a common Puritan heritage, to radically different views of religious institutions. Whereas Garrisonian abolitionists employed religious conscience as a standard by which to question authority, Whigs looked to religion to uphold authority. The predominantly Whig Congregational Association of Massachusetts, for instance, defended "deference and subordination [as] essential to the happiness of society, and particularly so in the relation of a people to their pastor."[25] Garrisonians, by contrast, attacked Protestant churches for being "the bulwarks of American slavery" and indicted the clergy for its "truckling subservience to power . . . clinging with mendicant sycophancy to the skirts of wealth and influence." The churches' corruption stemmed, in their view, from the "desire among clergy to assert their authority." Faced with a conflict between their preferred way of life and church membership, many Garrisonians withdrew from their church, thus escaping what they perceived as their "spiritual bondage."[26]

Whigs and immediatist abolitionists also differed in their views of human nature. Consistent with their hierarchical predisposition, Whigs had a pessimistic view of human nature. "The weakness, the follies, and the vices of human nature" were an unquestioned axiom of Whig thought. Because human nature was "so strongly inclined to go astray," Whigs believed it was safer to rely on institutions to "keep it on a path approximate to the parallel of rectitude, than to give it unlimited freedom to go right or wrong."[27] Garrisonian abolitionists believed in the ultimate perfectibility of man. By renouncing membership in the corrupt (i.e., hierarchical) institutions of this world and joining with other like-minded brethren, they believed they could recreate heaven on earth and man's basic goodness would emerge.[28]

The abolitionists' view of the world as a battleground for a cosmic struggle between good and evil is often adduced by historians as evidence of an alleged psychopathology. But, as Mary Douglas argues in her analysis of "The Problem of Evil," this Manichaean cosmology is a predictable concomitant of an egalitarian mode of social organization.[29] Because internal roles are ill defined, members of an egalitarian group are perpetually engaged in building up the boundary separating themselves from others. Since it is not easy to keep together organizations that reject authority, a rigid dichotimization between an evil outside and a good inside functions to help keep this way of life's centrifugal tendencies under control. Life inside the egalitarian collective may have its faults, members are reminded, but life outside is much worse. The abolitionists' division of the world into good and evil is not, therefore, a product of individual psychology but, rather, is an organizational phenomenon resulting from the attempt to sustain an egalitarian way of life.

Elazar deserves credit for recognizing that abolitionism was not simply a variant of the dominant culture of competitive individualism, merely capitalists with a conscience, but instead represented a distinct cultural type. So, too, we believe, he has made a valuable contribution in pointing out that the collectivist orientation of Whig political culture (as well as Federalist) distinguished it from individualism. But as Elazar is right to point out that individualism cannot encompass the variety of American experience, his moralistic category, in our view, is inadequate because it tends to run together two distinct ways of life, egalitarianism and hierarchy. It will not do, we maintain, to throw the radical abolitionism of William Lloyd Garrison and the hierarchical Whiggery of Daniel Webster, the patriarchal Mormonism of Joseph Smith and the egalitarian communalism of Hopedale, the leveling of the Populists and the paternalism of the Mugwumps, into the same cultural melting pot.[30]

Why, despite Elazar's theoretical statement of the distinction between participatory and deferential cultures, does he tend to merge these two ways of life in practice? The reason, we believe, is that his categorization does not adequately distinguish the particular historical manifestation of a type from the type itself. The traditionalistic culture, for instance, is made virtually synonymous with the political culture of the southern states. The result is to leave the analyst insensitive to the occurrence of hierarchy (i.e., collectivism combined with deference) among northern Yankees. A related consequence is that cultural variation within the South is overlooked. Alabama and Virginia, for instance, are both identified as traditionalistic cultures by Elazar. Yet V. O. Key's seminal study of southern politics suggests that

the political distance from Virginia to Alabama must be measured in light years. Virginian deference to the upper orders and the Byrd machine's restraint of popular aberrations give Virginia politics a tone and a reality radically different from the tumult of Alabama. There a wholesome contempt for authority and a spirit of rebellion akin to that of the Populist days resist the efforts of the big farmers and "big mules"—the local term for Birmingham industrialists and financiers—to control the state. Alabamians retain a sort of frontier independence, with an inclination to defend liberty and to bait the interests.[31]

Elazar's otherwise penetrating discussion of the "three constitutional traditions" indicates the same limitation of his categories. One Elazar labels the "Whig tradition," which emphasized a "communitarian polity and the importance of republican virtue," including "direct, active, continuous, and well-nigh complete popular control over the legislature and government in general." A second tradition, which he identifies with James Madison, "placed greater emphasis on balancing individual and group interests." The final tradition he terms "managerial" and identifies with Alexander Hamilton. The managerial view, according to Elazar, "conceptualized politics as a matter of executive leadership and rational administration within a hierarchical system."[32]

The first two constitutional traditions correspond closely to Elazar's communitarian and individualistic subcultures (and our egalitarian and individualist ways of life), but the Hamiltonian constitutional tradition seems to bear no relation to any of Elazar's three cultures. Having relegated hierarchy to the premodern South (under the rubric of traditionalism), Elazar is ill equipped to account for the hierarchical character of the Hamiltonian tradition. The only choice that Elazar's categorization seems to leave is to merge the "managerial" tradition into the moralistic subculture. Again, we see that when hierarchy is conceptualized too narrowly, the moralistic category becomes a holding tank for all nonsouthern ways of life that do not fit the individualistic mold.

Many of the difficulties that accompany these categories, we believe, are a product of the fact that the categories are not derived from dimensions. Instead the types are derived inductively from regional variations in the United States: Traditionalism is drawn from the plantation-centered system of the South, and moralism from New England Puritanism. As a result the categories are neither mutually exclusive nor exhaustive.

Uncertainty about where these categories come from and how they relate to each other is evident in the confusion over how to represent these three categories spatially. Perhaps the most common way, following Ira Sharansky, is to conceive of Elazar's categories as lying on a single continuum, running from moralism to traditionalism, with individualism as the midpoint.[33] David Haight agrees that Elazar's categories are best represented as constituting a single continuum, but he argues the continuum runs from moralism to individualism, with traditionalism as the midpoint.[34] More recently, Frederick Wirt has suggested a continuum running from traditionalism to individualism, with moralism as the midpoint.[35] Elazar himself has waded in and tried to settle the debate by arguing that a single continuum is inappropriate, and that the relationship is best represented by a triangle.[36] No rationale is offered, however, for why political cultures arrange themselves in this triangular fashion.

Elazar's categories have been subject to extensive testing. Researchers have looked for relationships between his political cultures and the incidence of corruption, levels of voter turnout, the quality of metropolitan life, level of taxing and expenditure, content of political advertising, orientations to civic duty, efficacy, political interest, social change, race relations, and on and on. How well Elazar's scheme has withstood this intense scrutiny is a matter of continuing debate. For every study that claims to have found Elazar's theory vindicated, there is another that claims to find it of little use.[37] (So it is, the reader may recall, with Durkheim's theory of suicide and Weber's efforts to connect Protestantism to capitalism.) To be validated at all is a considerable accomplishment.

Elazar has argued, correctly in our view, that many of these "tests" based on simple correlations or even complex multiple regression miss a critical component of his theory. The same public policy, Elazar points out, may be adhered to for different reasons by adherents of different cultures. In *Cities of the Prairie,* for instance, Elazar suggests that adherents of the individualistic culture embraced the council-manager plan and nonpartisan elections in order to take the politics out of government, while in moralistic settings those arrangements represented an effort to make local politics more effective by separating local elections from the state and national parties.[38] Our own research has turned up any number of instances, from supporting the 1986 tax reform package to endorsing the Monroe Doctrine,[39] in which adherents of different cultures, as Elazar suggests, "do the same things for different reasons."

Whether the ambiguous results that have been produced in testing propositions derived from Elazar's categories are a result of inadequacies in the tests or the categories, or both, we cannot say.[40] Perhaps a better question than whether Elazar's categorization is "true" is how it stacks up against existing alternatives. For those unwilling to accept either that every state is culturally unique or that every state is culturally alike, Elazar's categories until now have been the only game in town. By throwing our hat into the ring, our hope is that researchers will compare Elazar's typology with our own to see which better captures and explains the American political cultural landscape.

NOTES

1. See Daniel J. Elazar, *American Federalism: A View from the States* (New York: Crowell, 1966), and *Cities of the Prairie: The Metropolitan Frontier and American Politics* (New York: Basic Books, 1970); Elazar and Joseph Zikmund II, eds., *The Ecology of American Political Culture* (New York: Crowell, 1975); and Elazar, *Cities of the Prairie Revisited: The Closing of the Metropolitan Frontier* (Lincoln: University of Nebraska Press, 1986).

2. Daniel J. Elazar, *American Federalism: A View from the States,* 2d ed. (New York: Crowell, 1972), 94; all page references are to this edition.

3. Ibid., 99.

4. In addition, "traditionalism" carries with it baggage from the modern/ tradition dichotomy, a dichotomy that cannot accommodate the occurrence of competitive individualism among such "traditional" societies as the tribes of New Guinea and American Indians. See Mary Douglas, *Natural Symbols: Explorations in Cosmology* (New York: Pantheon, 1982), chap. 9. Also see E. Adamson Hoebel, "The Political Organization and Law-Ways of the Comanche Indians," *Memoirs of the American Anthropological Association,* no. 54, 1940, Supplement to *American Anthropologist* 42, 3, Pt. 2, 4–142.

5. Elazar, *American Federalism,* 13–14. A roughly equivalent formulation can be found in William A. Schambra, "The Roots of the American Public Philosophy," *Public Interest,* Spring 1982, 36–48.

6. Elazar himself uses the term *communalism* in giving us an incisive portrayal of the difference between egalitarianism and hierarchy. "The distinction they [moralists] make (implicitly at least)," Elazar explains, "is between what they consider legitimate community responsibility and what they believe to be central government encroachment, or between 'communalism' which they value and 'collectivism' which they abhor" (*American Federalism,* 97). He also posits that the major difficulty faced by adherents of the moralistic culture "in adjusting bureaucracy to the political order is tied to the potential conflict between communitarian principles and the necessity for large-scale organization" (ibid., 98).

7. Ibid., 97.

8. On the hierarchical nature of Massachusetts political culture, see James M. Banner, Jr., *To the Hartford Convention: The Federalists and the Origins of Party Politics in Massachusetts, 1789–1815* (New York: Knopf, 1970); David Hackett Fischer, "The Myth of the Essex Junto," *William and Mary Quarterly,* April 1964, 191–235; and Ronald P. Formisano, *The Transformation of Political Culture: Massachusetts Parties, 1790s–1840s* (New York: Oxford University Press, 1983).

9. Banner, *To the Hartford Convention,* 53. Also see Fischer, "The Myth of the Essex Junto," 191–235.

10. Banner, *To the Hartford Convention,* 57, 65.

11. Ibid., 54–55.

12. Ibid., 60–61.

13. Elazar, *American Federalism,* 109, 115.

14. Ronald P. Formisano, *The Transformation of Political Culture,* 271.

15. The egalitarian character of the abolitionists is elaborated in Richard Ellis and Aaron Wildavsky, "A Cultural Analysis of the Role of Abolitionists in the Coming of the Civil War," *Comparative Studies in Society and History* 31, 1 (1990): 89–116. On the hierarchical nature of Whiggery, see Richard Ellis and Aaron Wildavsky, *Dilemmas of Presidential Leadership: From Washington Through Lincoln* (New Brunswick, N.J.: Transaction, 1989), chap. 6.

16. Daniel Walker Howe, *The Political Culture of the American Whigs* (Chicago: University of Chicago Press, 1979), chap. 9.

17. Ibid., 29–30.

18. Lawrence J. Friedman, *Gregarious Saints: Self and Community in American Abolitionism, 1830–1870* (New York: Cambridge University Press, 1982), 63–67, 197.

19. John L. Thomas, "Antislavery and Utopia," in Martin Duberman, ed., *The Antislavery Vanguard: New Essays on the Abolitionists* (Princeton: Princeton University Press, 1965), 247.

20. Friedman, *Gregarious Saints,* 44.

21. John L. Thomas, ed., *Slavery Attacked: The Abolitionist Crusade* (Englewood Cliffs, N.J.: Prentice-Hall, 1965), 79. Blanche Glassman Hersch, *The Slavery of Sex: Feminist Abolitionists in America* (Urbana: University of Illinois Press, 1978), 234, 225, 236; Lewis Perry, *Radical Abolitionism: Anarchy and the Government of God in Antislavery Thought* (Ithaca: Cornell University Press, 1973), 230; Ronald G. Walters, *The Antislavery Appeal: American Abolitionism After 1830* (Baltimore: Johns Hopkins University Press, 1976), 72.

22. Howe, *Political Culture of American Whigs,* 45, 86.

23. John Ashworth, *'Agrarians' and 'Aristocrats': Party Political Ideology in the United States, 1837–1846* (Atlantic Highlands, N.J.: Humanities Press, 1983), 54–55; Formisano, *Transformation of Political Culture,* 275–76, 458.

24. Friedman, *Gregarious Saints,* 27, 63–64.

25. Walters, *Antislavery Appeal,* 43.

26. Ibid., 41–48; Perry, *Radical Abolitionism,* 57, 105–06.

27. George A. Lipsky, *John Quincy Adams: His Theory and Ideas* (New York: Crowell, 1950), 82; Ashworth, *'Agrarians' and 'Aristocrats,'* 60.

28. Thomas, "Antislavery and Utopia," 247; Ronald G. Walters, *American Reformers, 1815–1860* (New York: Hill and Wang, 1978), esp. 69–70.

29. Douglas, *Natural Symbols,* chap. 8.

30. The egalitarianism of Populists is persuasively argued in Gary Lee Malecha, "Understanding Agrarian Fundamentalism: A Cultural Interpretation of American Populism," Paper prepared for delivery at the 1988 Annual Meeting of the American Political Science Association, Washington, D.C., September 1–4, 1988. The hierarchical character of the Mugwumps is clear from Geoffrey Blodgett, *The Gentle Reformers: Massachusetts Democrats in the Cleveland Era* (Cambridge: Harvard University Press, 1966).

31. V. O. Key, Jr., *Southern Politics* (New York: Knopf, 1950), 36. The absence of deference in antebellum Alabama is highlighted in J. Mills Thornton III's fine study, *Politics and Power in a Slave Society: Alabama, 1800–1860* (Baton Rouge: Louisiana State University Press, 1978).

32. Daniel J. Elazar, "The Principles and Traditions Underlying State Constitutions," *Publius: The Journal of Federalism* 12 (Winter 1982): 11–25, quotes on 13.

33. Ira Sharkansky, "The Utility of Elazar's Political Culture: A Research Note," *Polity*, Fall 1969, 66–83.

34. Elazar's continuum, Haight argues, is based upon the scope of goals held by political participants, running from society as a whole (moralism) to one's own group (traditionalism), to the individual (individualism). David Haight, "Collectivists, Particularists and Individualists: An Emerging Typology of Political Life," Paper presented at the Annual Meeting of the Midwest Political Science Association, 1976.

35. Frederick Wirt, "Does Control Follow the Dollar? Value Analysis, School Policy, and State-Local Linkages," *Publius* 10 (Spring 1980): 69–88.

36. Daniel J. Elazar, "Afterword: Steps in the Study of American Political Culture," *Publius: The Journal of Federalism* 10 (Spring 1980), 127–39, quote on 129, and *Cities of the Prairie Revisited*, 86. In the original formulation, Elazar had suggested that "the continuum is actually circular" *American Federalism* (1966 ed.), 110.

37. For a flavor of the debate, see Timothy D. Schiltz and R. Lee Rainey, "The Geographic Distribution of Elazar's Political Subcultures Among the Mass Population: A Research Note," *Western Political Quarterly* 31 (September 1978): 410–15; Robert L. Savage, "Looking for Political Subcultures: A Critique of the Rummage-Sale Approach," *Western Political Quarterly* 35 (June 1981): 331–36; David Lowery and Lee Sigelman, "Political Culture and State Public Policy: The Missing Link," *Western Political Quarterly*, September 1982, 376–84.

38. Elazar, "Afterword," 135, and *Cities of the Prairie Revisited*, 104–05.

39. Dennis Coyle and Aaron Wildavsky, "Requisites of Radical Reform: Income Maintenance Versus Tax Preferences," *Journal of Policy Analysis and Management* 7, 1 (Fall 1987): 1–16; Ellis and Wildavsky, *Dilemmas of Presidential Leadership*, 97–98.

40. More work, in our view, needs to be done, to ascertain whether the cultural clusters that Elazar designates do indeed exist (either at the mass or elite level). This step, it seems to us, should precede attempts to link public policy outputs with political cultures. Unfortunately most work has started with the second step and assumed the first. This practice is forcefully criticized in Lowery and Sigelman, "Political Culture and State Public Policy."

CHAPTER 14

The Civic Culture Reexamined

The Civic Culture addresses itself to one of the great questions of postwar social science: Why, in the period between the world wars, did democracy survive in Britain and the United States while collapsing on the European continent?[1] Following Aristotle (as so many of us do), Almond and Verba suggest that a stable democratic polity requires a balanced political culture (the civic culture), which combines both a participatory and a deferential orientation to politics. Were everyone to participate in every decision, they argue, the political system would be overloaded and governing would become impossible; were everyone to defer to their superiors, democracy would cease to be responsive to citizen needs and thus give way to authoritarianism.

Even today, more than twenty-five years after it was first published, *The Civic Culture* remains a model of social scientific inquiry. Not only do Almond and Verba make their evidence speak to a profound theoretical issue, but also their empirical work is both rich and systematic, allowing others to test, and refine or reject, their hypotheses.

Almond and Verba's characterization of political cultures in the five nations of Italy, Mexico, Germany, the United States, and Great Britain is based on two key attitudinal variables: commitment and involvement. The first taps the individual's attitude toward the political system and distinguishes between allegiant and alienated orientations. The second, measuring attitudes toward participation in the political system, differentiates between deferential and participant orientations.[2] Combining these two dimensions reproduces the four cultural biases that we have derived from the grid-group typology. An allegiant-deferential orientation is the bias of the hierarchist; an allegiant-participant orientation is the bias of the individualist; an alienated-participant orientation is the bias of the egalitarian; and an alienated-deferential orientation belongs to the fatalist.

The Civic Culture's research design—explaining divergent institutional outcomes in different countries—dictated that Almond and Verba stress differences between rather than within nations. Our reanalysis of some of their interviews suggests, however, that the differences within each country are at least as striking as the variation among countries. Although there is nothing wrong with characterizing a national culture as "alienated," "allegiant," "deferential," or "participatory" as a sort of shorthand for more of one way of life than another, this usage does tend to obscure the fact that each of the viable political cultures can be found within a nation, albeit in varying proportions. In addition, this usage slights the change over time in the strengths of these rival ways of life, without which we cannot count for either the collapse or the rebirth of democracy in continental Europe.

ITALY

Italian political culture, according to Almond and Verba, is characterized by "relatively unrelieved political alienation." In grid-group terms, Italy is characterized by a fatalistic way of life, in which group involvement is low and social prescriptions are high. Our theory of cultural viability tells us, however, that fatalists cannot exist on their own. If our theory is correct, we should find that "Italian political culture" is not a single political culture, but an amalgam of competing ways of life. The four individual case histories that Almond and Verba present support our thesis.

The first is a Communist housewife, whom they characterize as "an alienated participant." Signora M. combines a hostile attitude to the present system, which she believes oppresses the people, with a high degree of political involvement. Religion, Signora M. believes, "is a fraud for those that believe in it," masking the oppression perpetrated by those in power. Our religion, she states, "is in the ideas of the party." Her entire family are Communists, and the solidarity among this group of believers is high. She would approach any part of the central government, Almond and Verba report, only as a member of a group. This thumbnail sketch makes clear that Signora M. is not a fatalist at all—she has no shortage of personal efficacy—but an egalitarian, who believes that the political system is to be avoided because it is inequitable and hence immoral and corrupting.[3]

The second example is a tailor from southern Italy, who is also described by Almond and Verba as an alienated participant. In fact, however, there is little about this man to warrant the label participant. According to Almond and Verba, he has "a sense of futility about his ability to influence the government." If a local law is passed that is unjust, Signor S. explains, "we have to accept. There is not much we can do." Only those who have money or family connections, he believes, can hope to influence government. In contrast to the Communist housewife, who is part of a band of ideological brothers, Signor S. is largely isolated, on the periphery of other people's networks—his tailor business, for instance, does very poorly, and we are told he finds it difficult to make ends meet. Living in the South, itself on the periphery, exacerbates his sense of isolation and alienation—"the government of Rome is not interested in the South," he laments. Though egalitarians might be able to recruit this individual, he is at present not an egalitarian but a fatalist.[4]

The next example is that of a "parochial housewife." Signora O. is a lowerarch in the hierarchy who feels a part of the system even though she has no direct contact with the hierarchs. She does not feel it is her place to participate in politics, but she does feel that a government is necessary because "a country needs a guide, just as a family needs a father or mother." Although she has no idea how tax funds are being spent, she is sure they are being spent "in the right way." A good citizen, this housewife believes, is the person "who minds his own business and does his job without bothering anyone."[5]

The final example presented by Almond and Verba is that of a town messenger, whom they characterize as an "allegiant subject." Signor B. is a government employee who expresses an unflagging loyalty toward the political system. At home, moreover, he is the hierarch: "I make the decisions as the head of the family. . . . The children listen and keep quiet. . . . My wife is sure that whatever I say is correct." He is a devout Catholic who believes religion is of immense importance as a social glue. He approves of the Christian Democratic party because, among other things, it is effective, benevolent—it established a pension system that keeps the truly destitute from dying of hunger. The party upgraded the importance of religion—it has "given a better living to the priests by augmenting their salaries, . . . has built new offices, . . . and has instituted works of charity." In short, Signor B. feels himself part of a hierarchy that takes care of all its members, from the mighty to the poor.[6]

These examples belie talk of "an Italian political culture," as if all Italians were the same, or even similar. To say that Italy is an "alienated political culture" is to ignore the critical distinction between egalitarianism and fatalism. Both egalitarians and fatalists may express alienation from the political system, but their ways of life are radically different: One is active, desiring to transform the political system along voluntaristic lines, the other passive, expecting no more from the revolution than from the powers-that-be. *Che sarà, sarà.* Moreover, labeling Italy an alienated culture misses important hierarchical (as well as individualist) elements within the country.

The importance of cultural variation within Italy is further bolstered by the exhaustive studies undertaken by Robert Putnam and his associates.[7] In 1970, Italy established fifteen regional governments, and ever since that time Putnam and his colleagues have followed the development of six of them through an impressive array of studies, from election results to surveys of mass opinion to elite interviews to criteria of administrative effectiveness (the measures of which included making the budget on time, cabinet stability, proportion of legislation introduced that passed, innovation in law making). They have discovered substantial variation among regions in political attitudes, participation, associationism, governmental effectiveness, economic growth, and much else. For instance, "in the efflorescence of their associational life, some regions of Italy rival Tocqueville's America of congenital 'joiners,' while the inhabitants of other regions are accurately typified by the isolated and suspicious 'amoral familists' of Banfield's Montegrano."[8] Although these findings contradict the idea of a single, uniform national political culture, they bolster Almond and Verba's contention that political cultures have a significant impact upon institutional performance.

Like Almond and Verba, the broader purpose of Putnam and his associates is to assess the prospects for stable and effective democratic government. High levels of socioeconomic development, they find, were necessary for stable and effective government, but not sufficient; something else was needed. That something else is political culture, more specifically, a tradition of civic involvement.[9] Particularly among the more economically developed regions, political culture helps explain otherwise inexplicable differences in institutional performance.[10] Even more striking, they show that past political culture is a powerful predictor of present levels of socioeconomic development (measured by industrialization, wealth, literacy, and public health), while past levels of socioeconomic development have no impact whatsoever on political culture. Moreover, past political culture is at least as good as (and often better than) past socioeconomic development as a predictor of present socioeconomic development.[11] A more decisive vindication of the position that culture matters would be difficult to imagine.

GERMANY

German political culture, Almond and Verba instruct us, is a blend of feelings of subjective competence and political detachment. Germans tend to be informed about politics and satisfied with the performance of their government, but—other than voting, which they regard as a civic responsibility—they do not believe it is proper for them to participate actively in politics. This package of values is readily recognizable as a hierarchical culture in which individuals identify with the system but believe their participation should be limited to its proper sphere.

Almond and Verba first introduce us to a forty-eight-year-old German businessman whom they label a "detached subject." Herr R. is a reserved man who still works for his father in a business that is described as "secure" and who lives in the same "secure" neighborhood that he grew up in as a child. He keeps aloof from partisan politics and hopes for a united Europe. Competition, in the view of Herr R., is messy and conflict ridden. Herr R., Almond and Verba report, "votes out of a sense of duty, but without any feeling of personal involvement." He orients himself to the government as a subject who receives orders from above. "After all," he explains, "every regulation has the force of law and must be obeyed. . . . We must do exactly as ordered. Think of the draft: The younger man must serve. Think of taxes; and so on." There can be little doubt that hierarchy is this man's preferred way of life.[12]

The second example we are offered is of a headwaiter who is characterized as an "allegiant participant." Herr Q. has worked his way up from hotel trainee to headwaiter in charge of table service for the entire hotel, able now to buy a nice house with a number of modern conveniences. He applauds the changes that have taken place in Germany over the past several decades for opening up more opportunities for his children: "Chances are better today, there is more scope socially, class barriers have disappeared." Herr Q. also supports the changes in child-rearing because "children are [now] being brought up to be independent human beings, and they are being permitted far more freedom in their choice of an occupation." Herr Q. backs the CDU (Christian Democratic Union) because it stands for "the creation of a democratic Germany in which freedom and law and the desires of the individual stand in first place." In sum, Herr Q. is a committed individualist who desires to decrease the prescriptions that he sees as having restricted equal opportunity and individual expression in prewar Germany.[13]

A third example presented by Almond and Verba is a farmer's widow who is termed "a subject/parochial." Frau P. regards politics as something that is best left to the men. It is not her station to discuss, let alone, participate in this realm. Her support for the CDU reflects her devout Catholicism: "We are all Catholics here, after all." In family life, she believes that children are not competent to participate in making decisions until they are eighteen; even then they cannot be expected to have the experience necessary to decide wisely. A committed adherent of hierarchy, Frau P. knows her place, and works to make sure that others know their place as well.[14]

The fourth example, a refugee housewife identified by Almond and Verba as "a subject," is more complex. Like Frau P., Frau A. believes politics is not a proper domain for women. Women, Frau A. states, ought to be more feminine, more passive, the "soul" of the family. But in contrast to Frau P., who lives in an isolated rural village where life remains pretty much the same, Frau A. lives in a Bavarian tourist town where the hierarchical life as she knew it seems to be collapsing. Frau A. bemoans the rise of the modern "career woman," the declining standards among children, and the flashiness and luxury of the tourists. Her life as a refugee, moreover, has left her feeling that she is no longer a part of the hierarchy. Indeed she left the Catholic church because she felt it had abandoned her in her hour of need. Here is a case of a lowerarch losing a sense of identification with the group and thus slipping into fatalism.[15]

These sketches tell us a number of things about political cultures in Germany. First, there is no such thing as a unitary German political culture. Second, egalitarianism appears to be notable by its absence during this period (if the research for *Civic Culture* were to be repeated today it would be easy to find instances of egalitarianism, e.g., the Greens). Third, hierarchy was strong in Germany, but as the story of Herr Q. makes evident, there was a growing individualistic challenge to hierarchical dominance.[16]

MEXICO

Political culture in Mexico, Almond and Verba argue, is a combination of alienation and aspiration. Mexicans are alienated, distrusting and avoiding what they view as a corrupt and arbitrary government. In this respect, they resemble a fatalistic population. Almond and Verba introduce the concept of aspiration to account for some "civic aspirational tendencies," such as the pride Mexicans express in the presidency and the revolution. We find this concept unsatisfactory, not only because it has been derived ad hoc to fit anomalous observations, but also because the case histories they offer do not show it to be particularly important.

The first Mexican we are introduced to is a master stonemason who has five men working under him. Almond and Verba categorize Señor M. as "an alienated subject/aspiring citizen," but their description of him fails to support their view that he is alienated from the government.

Though he pays little attention to current politics and public affairs, Sr. M. believes the national government is doing an admirable job of keeping internal order, providing jobs and keeping prices down. He has a low opinion of his fellow human beings and thus believes government is necessary because "even with a government, people kill each other. Without a government, people would kill and kill without fear." The same appreciation for authority is evident in his ideas about the preferred pattern of family relations. He bemoans the fact that "nowadays, young people do not show respect to anyone, even their parents." The man of the house, Sr. M. continues, must have the final word in family decisions and children need not be consulted because "they still cannot reason and cannot give opinions." From this, we conclude that it seems most plausible to place Sr. M. in the hierarchist category.[17]

The next example presented by Almond and Verba is of a farm worker whom they also characterize as "an alienated subject/aspiring citizen." This individual more clearly warrants the alienated label. Sr. P. describes his work as a "dead-end" job, and while he wishes he were an auto mechanic or sculptor, this remains a wish rather than something he is striving toward. On the farm, he has to obey without question the orders of a short-tempered, arbitrary farm owner. Government is alien: "them," not "us." "All those in the government," he complains, "don't worry about the lower classes." He refuses to support any party, but is particularly hostile to the PRI, the Mexican Institutional Revolutionary party, which he believes "imposes its candidates" on us. He expresses a vague longing for a "party of the people" (just as he does for becoming a sculptor), but in his view this is something that will just happen rather than something that he can make happen. Faced with a harmful local or national law, he believes he would be powerless to do anything about it. Sr. P. has the earmarks of a fatalist.[18]

The third example, a radio technician, is also labeled an instance of "an alienated subject/aspiring citizen." Here the "alienated" label seems even more out of place than with the stonemason. Sr. C. has been quite successful in his life and hopes and believes that his children, because of increased educational opportunities, will do even better. He believes in a democratic family life. Children should participate in family discussions "as soon as they can use their reason, at five or six years of age." He worries that his children are too deferential toward him—that they "allow themselves to be guided too much by me." Decisions, he believes, should be based on whichever alternative is "the logical and reasonable one." He believes that people are basically good, honest, and cooperative. This is a very different cultural bias than that which we are offered in the previous two sketches. Absent is the fatalistic resignation of the farm worker or the deference to authority that we saw in the stonemason. Instead this is a voice that combines a mixture of egalitarianism and individualism.[19]

Finally, Almond and Verba introduce us to a housewife, whom they describe as "parochial/alienated." Sra. S. is a classic fatalist. She resents her poverty but doesn't believe there is anything she can do about it. She is poor, she explains, "because God wanted to give me a poor life." God, she concludes in resigned disgust, "gives more to some than others." Life is full of suffering—"Today I suffer more than before. One suffers a great deal in marriage"—that must be borne stoically. Sra. S. has no pride in her country—the Mexican Revolution was "nothing more than going around stealing and violating girls"—but has no vision of a better alternative. Nor does she have any understanding of, or involvement in, politics. The political realm she regards as hostile and alien. She explains, for instance, that she wouldn't want her children to support a political party because "it's better to keep out of trouble." Faced with an unjust law, she says she would do nothing, "because what can you do when you know nothing about such matters?"[20]

Almond and Verba's categorization scheme lumps the first three Mexican citizens under the label "alienated subject/aspiring citizen," yet their descriptions of these three individuals point to what we have shown are culturally distinct beliefs and behaviors. Moreover, the final example of the Mexican housewife, although given a new label "parochial/alienated," is, in our view, culturally indistinguishable from the fatalistic farmhand.

THE UNITED STATES AND GREAT BRITAIN

Both the United States and Great Britain, Almond and Verba argue, "closely approximate the model of the civic culture." By the term *civic culture* they denote an allegiant orientation toward politics in which participant orientations are balanced by deferential ones. Whereas both the United States and Britain "achieve a balance of the active and passive roles," Almond and Verba suggest that in the former, the cultural mix tends to be weighted somewhat more toward the participant pole, while in the latter there is a slight tilt in the direction of the deferential pole.[21]

Mr. H., a working-class Tory, best illustrates the "deferential civic culture" that Almond and Verba maintain is characteristic of the British political culture. When family problems arise, the whole family discusses them but as the father he has the last word. Mr. H. supports the Conservative party because "they are the right people in the right place." His working hours prevent him from participating actively in politics, but he does try to "keep up" with what is happening in the political world. Although ill informed on such issues as taxes, Mr.

H. has faith that the pressing issues facing the nation are in capable hands. The government, he believes, can be trusted to do the right thing. A firm patriot, Mr. H. is "proud of the way his country is run and of the policy to help those who cannot help themselves."[22]

An eighteen-year-old American girl, working as a stenographer in a small southern town, is offered by Almond and Verba as an example of the American "participant civic culture." Although accustomed to having her father have the final word in family decisions, Miss E. feels free to state her views and thinks that perhaps young people should have more voice in family decisions. Miss E. belongs to a number of organizations, including two church organizations and the YWCA. Although still too young to vote, she considers herself a Democrat— "I've always thought it stands for the little people"—but feels that "when I have children they can make up their own minds. If they felt like being Republicans, I'd feel they had good reasons." Miss E. is very satisfied with government at the local, state, and national level, and takes great pride in her country: "We have freedom. It's a democracy. We can worship as we feel we want to. We have a good government, and we are one of the great powers in the world." A good citizen, she feels, should not only vote but also participate in community, church, and school affairs, as well as being "patriotic, proud of his country, and do whatever he can to keep it free." Miss E., as we would predict from the "allegiant-participant" label that Almond and Verba assign to her, most closely resembles an individualist (certainly she is neither fatalist nor egalitarian).[23]

The American "participant civic culture" and the British "deferential civic culture" described by Almond and Verba closely resemble what we have identified as an "establishment" alliance of individualism and hierarchy. These case studies of Mr. H. and Miss E. illustrate some of the ways in which the American regime is skewed in the direction of individualism and the British regime is biased in the direction of hierarchy. Though both ways of life share an allegiant attitude toward the political system, the larger dose of hierarchy in Britain entails a greater emphasis on deference to authority (and a downgrading of individual autonomy) than tends to be found in the more individualistic political culture of the United States. In neither instance is the apparent absence of egalitarianism considered remarkable.

THE CULTURAL REQUISITES
OF DEMOCRATIC STABILITY

Both the American and British cultural blends, Almond and Verba maintain, facilitate democratic stability.[24] In contrast, the political cultures of Mexico, Germany, and Italy, they argue, are inconsistent with democratic institutions. Does viewing *The Civic Culture* through our cultural categories enable us to draw additional lessons about the preconditions of democracy?

The Mexican experience shows that where fatalism (the combination of deferential and alienated orientations) is endemic, democracy cannot survive. Fatalism generates (and is generated by) authoritarian political systems. A population that is withdrawn from the political sphere increases the scope for the exercise of arbitrary governmental power, thus further fueling the citizenry's withdrawal from politics. This self-replicating pattern leaves a grim outlook for democracy in societies with predominantly fatalistic political cultures.

That fatalism is not the only recipe for authoritarianism is evidenced by the German example. Support for the system (allegiance), the German experience suggests, is insufficient for democratic stability. When combined with deferential orientations, allegiant orientations can produce repressive, authoritarian government. The assumption within hierarchical political cultures that authority can be trusted to do the right thing leaves people ill equipped to check the abuse of that trust. Democracy, we learn, requires the participatory norms that come with the low-grid cultures of individualism and egalitarianism in order to check the abuse of power.

Fatalism, hierarchy, and egalitarianism are well represented in Almond and Verba's description of Italian political culture. What stands out is the weakness of the individualist way of life in which allegiance toward the political system is combined with a commitment to civic participation (although Putnam's research shows that this deficiency is both time and region bound). This suggests (as, incidentally, does the experience of Argentina) that one of the conditions for a democracy is a vibrant, individualist way of life. Individualism is essential to democracy because, among other things, individualism inculcates in its adherents the value of competition for its own sake. From this way of life comes the willingness to leave office when voted out, perhaps the most basic requirement of a democracy. Without the presence of a way of life legitimating competition (and conflict) as a good in itself, the calls for unity, cooperation, or solidarity that inevitably accompany adversity may overwhelm democratic procedures.

As described by Almond and Verba, Britain and the United States, the two "relatively stable and successful democracies,"[25] share an establishment blend of individualism and hierarchy (that is, allegiant attitudes are prevalent, and deferential and participant orientations are balanced), from which both egalitarianism and fatalism are excluded. We agree with Almond and Verba that democracy requires a balance of individualism and hierarchy. So too do we agree that fatalism in large quantities is lethal to democracy. Where we diverge is in our evaluation of the relationship between egalitarianism (the combination of alienated and participant orientations) and democracy.

In moderation, egalitarianism is a tonic, or perhaps better, an astringent for the establishment cultures. Just as a balance between passivity and involvement is necessary for democracy, so we would suggest a blend of allegiance ("my country right or wrong") and skepticism ("question authority") is healthy for democracy. A willingness to oppose authority is as essential as a willingness to support authority. Egalitarianism punctures authority's pomposity. It criticizes the establishment's connivances, exposing its hypocrisies and cover-ups. The incessant criticism of authority prevents governmental power from growing arrogant or domineering. Because, moreover, there is always the danger that egalitarianism may grow by recruiting fatalists, the establishment has an added incentive to placate minorities to keep down discontent. That which we today identify as free societies—those with the rule of law, alternation in office, and the right to criticize— are a product of the interpenetration of hierarchy, individualism, *and* egalitarianism.

Too much egalitarianism, to be sure, may reverse these democratic benefits. If egalitarians become dominant, they may enforce draconian measures (viz., the Khmer Rouge and the Chinese Cultural Revolution) to achieve equality of condition. Or, pace Weimar, their criticism may lead to collapse by delegitimating existing, albeit imperfect, democratic authority. We can all argue about just how much of a good thing is too much, but we can all agree that the nature of the relationship of each of the ways of life to democracy is always curvilinear. Paracelsus's dictum, "The poison is the dose," applies to the body politic as well.

The idea that the balance between cultures is as important as the content in explaining democratic success has been most fully developed by Harry Eckstein in his classic *A Theory of Stable Democracy.* Eckstein argues that democracy requires authority that "contains a balance of disparate elements." Like Almond and Verba, he points to Britain as an exemplar case that combines, among other things, popular participation, governing by elites, and the rule of law. Testing this theory, Eckstein concludes, requires "a much better set of categories for classifying authority patterns that we now possess." Such categories, he continues, "ought to be applicable to any kind of authority pattern not just to government."[26] No one will be surprised to learn that we think our ways of life fill the bill. They are built around authority relationships, yet are sufficiently general to be applied in or out of government. In addition, they cover the types that have emerged from scholarly study, while alerting the user to other types that may have gone unnoticed. By showing that all ways of seeing are biased, moreover, our theory provides an explanation for why balanced democracies do better. Excluding cultural biases, we can now see, weakens democracy by enlarging its blind spots.

NOTES

1. Gabriel A. Almond, "The Intellectual History of the Civic Culture Concept," and Sidney Verba, "On Revisiting the Civic Culture: A Personal Postscript," in Almond and Verba, eds., *The Civic Culture Revisited* (Boston: Little, Brown, 1980), 22, 407.

2. We have simplified Almond and Verba's typology by dichotomizing dimensions that they trichotomized. Instead of participant-subject-parochial, we use participant-deferential; and instead of allegiant/apathetic/alienated, we employ allegiant-alienated.

3. Gabriel A. Almond and Sidney Verba, *The Civic Culture: Political Attitudes and Democracy in Five Nations* (Princeton: Princeton University Press, 1963), 404–07.

4. Ibid., 407–09.

5. Ibid., 410–11.

6. Ibid., 411–14.

7. Robert D. Putnam et al., "Explaining Institutional Success: The Case of Italian Regional Government," *American Political Science Review* 77 (1983): 55–74; Robert D. Putnam et al., "Institutional Performance and Political Culture: Some Puzzles About the Power of the Past," *Governance* 1, 3 (July 1988): 221–42.

8. Putnam et al., "Institutional Performance and Political Culture," 231.

9. Unlike Almond and Verba, Putnam et al. operationalize political culture in terms of behavioral (rather than attitudinal) variables such as electoral turnout, newspaper readership, and union membership ("Explaining Institutional Success," 64). Also see Putnam et al., "Institutional Performance and Political Culture," 237.

10. Putnam et al., "Explaining Institutional Success," 66.

11. Putnam et al., "Institutional Performance and Political Culture," 232–34.

12. Almond and Verba, *Civic Culture*, 429–32.

13. Ibid., 432–35.

14. Ibid., 435–37.

15. Ibid., 437–39.

16. On the changing patterns of German political culture, see David Conradt, "Changing German Political Culture," in Almond and Verba, eds., *Civic Culture Revisited*, 212–72.

17. Almond and Verba, *Civic Culture*, 416–18.

18. Ibid., 418–20.

19. Ibid., 420–23.

20. Ibid., 426–28.

21. Ibid., 493.

22. Ibid., 463–67.

23. Ibid., 441–44.

24. Almond and Verba suggest that the British cultural mix "to some extent . . . represents a more effective combination of the subject and participant roles" (ibid., 455). The more deferential political culture of Britain, Almond and Verba reason, tends to prevent the excessive levels of participation that can overload and immobilize a political system.

25. Ibid., 473.

26. *A Theory of Stable Democracy,* a monograph originally published in 1962, is reprinted as an appendix in Harry Eckstein, *Division and Cohesion in Democracy: A Study of Norway* (Princeton: Princeton University Press, 1966), Appendix B: quotes on 262–63, 284–85.

CHAPTER 15

Hard Questions,
Soft Answers

Having made their way through this book, even our most sympathetic readers may feel we have raised as many questions as we have answered. If ways of life are so different, how is it possible for adherents of these different ways to communicate (let alone to cooperate) with each other? Why do ways of life not borrow from each other until they become indistinguishable? Do individuals internalize rival ways of life, or do different individuals internalize different ways of life? What place does our scheme leave for historical contingency? Such questions provide an opportunity for us both to recapitulate and to extend our theory.

Less sympathetic readers may question the wisdom of introducing yet another grand classificatory system. Was not the lesson of Parsons that such sweeping efforts are foreordained to failure? We are in agreement with Robert Brown that "when someone produces a 'bulky system,' he must also answer the implied question 'A system for what?' He cannot merely reply, 'It organizes the data.' *Any* criterion will organize data—will order items in classes—but only some classifications will be scientifically useful."[1] That is why we insist that typologies must be based on dimensions that form categories, not on categories by themselves. The disadvantage of categories as designations rather than as compounds of at least two dimensions is a loss of explanatory power. Even if, as in Elazar's pioneering work, the categories plainly capture a good deal of the variety in the phenomena, the categories, being only designations, stop there. Why an individualist behaves differently from a moralist under similar conditions and circumstances, aside from what is implied in the names of these categories, remains unknown or requires supplementary explanation. There is a typology but it is not embedded in a theory. Hence the paucity of explanation.

The difference between dimensions and designations comes out in our discussion of the Cultural Revolution in China. To show that Mao

Zedong and his followers were radical egalitarians is worthwhile, indeed an essential beginning for analysis. In order to explain why egalitarians (or adherents of any of the five ways of life) behave as they do (erecting rigid boundaries between inner purity and external corruption, demanding 100 percent participation, tearing down established authority, and so on), it is necessary to understand their internal dynamics. And to get at these dynamics it is necessary to know the dimensions of their internal organization. When people construct a way of life combining strong group boundaries with weak prescriptions, they must reconcile collective choice with individual autonomy. This reconciliation can be accomplished only by institutionalizing the principle of equality of condition, for if all have to give their consent, each will demand equal power.

The question of compulsion (Why *must* people who live in a given mode of social relations behave in the way we say they do?) is answered by the interaction of the two dimensions. A single dimension is insufficient to compel anything. It is the organizational imperatives created by the interaction of the grid and group dimensions that compel people to behave in ways that maintain their way of life.

Showing that residents of Banfield's Italian village can be designated as fatalist is our starting point, not the end point. Explaining their behavior entails understanding the sociocultural dynamic that generates fatalistic attitudes. Weak group boundaries combined with a strong prescriptive grid generate a social context in which individuals find themselves without the autonomy to decide, but also without the protection and privileges that come with membership in a group. The result is that plausibility is lent to those attitudes, such as fatalistic resignation and distrust of others, that seem so irrational to those who find themselves in different social contexts.

The package of individualist values and beliefs is made credible (and workable) by a social context in which prescriptions are weak and group boundaries nonexistent. Only in such a context do individuals have the freedom to contract with whomever they please and make their way up (or if they are less fortunate or skillful, down) the ladder of prestige and influence. Were prescriptions increased or were the individual to be bound by group decisions, the opportunities for bargaining would be circumscribed and self-regulation would become less possible.

Those behaviors we classify as hierarchical (sacrifice of the parts for the whole, deference to superiors, belief in the value of order) are generated by the interaction of strong group boundaries and restrictive prescriptions. Only by propagating the belief that some people are more virtuous, experienced, knowledgeable, or otherwise more deserving than others can hierarchists justify separating individuals into ranked levels and stations. Were this belief to be undermined, individuals would begin to demand an equal say in collective decisions, thus transforming the way of life into an egalitarian one.

STOLEN RHETORIC AND CULTURAL TRAITORS

Cultural theory tells us about what social contexts prevent the sharing of which values. Thus arises the question: whether it is possible for adherents of culture A to use the rhetoric of culture B to support the positions of culture A. In answering this question, we have adopted Mary Douglas's distinction between rhetoric that binds and rhetoric that leaves people free to do whatever they please.[2] Peace and brotherhood do not bind; espousing competition, equality of condition, fixed statuses, fatalistic resignation, or renunciation of all desires does bind. For Soviet leaders to proclaim equality of condition as the guiding norm of their society, for instance, would threaten the legitimacy of their rule. Consequently they both preach and practice inequality (reserving equality for some distant future).[3]

To use the core values of one's opponents in order to undermine those opponents and broaden one's own appeal is a path fraught with danger. Witness, for instance, antiabortionists who attempt to discomfort their prochoice opponents and appeal to those on the fence by referring to "the equal rights of the fetus." By insisting on the equal rights of all, antiabortionists abandon (and hence undermine) their hierarchical commitments to the community's right to make distinctions among its members and its duty to regulate the morality of its members. If it is illegitimate to make distinctions between a fetus and a child, then perhaps egalitarians are justified in claiming that it is illegitimate to discriminate between humans and animals, men and women, old and young.

The perils of stealing rhetoric are further evidenced by the experiences of the American Whig party. Repeated failures in national presidential elections led many hierarchical Whigs to adopt the antiauthority rhetoric of the more successful Jacksonian party. Aping Jacksonian rhetoric did help the Whigs become more electorally competitive, but at the same time capitulation to Democratic rhetoric and categories of thought meant that the Whigs subverted their own preferred way of life. Within a decade the Whig party disintegrated, and the hierarchical belief system it institutionalized receded from the American political scene. In winning the electoral battle, the Whigs lost the cultural war.[4]

Look at stolen rhetoric in reverse. Were is possible for adherents of each way of life to steal at will the more successful rhetoric of the rival ways, we would have a great deal less variation than is apparent in the world today. Every individual or group would come to sound much like every other. Such a world would be not only homogeneous but also unpredictable, for there would be little constraint in individual belief systems. Yet all of us know of people, whether we number them among our personal acquaintances or hear about them as public figures, whose actions and speech are so predictable that we can say what is on their mind and in their speech before they have an opportunity to reveal themselves. We can do this because values and beliefs come in packages.

If it is not easy to steal rhetoric and to use it effectively, is it still possible for individuals to adopt a position at variance with their current cultural bias without going over to one of the other ways of life? Our view is that to take a position not in accord with one's way of life on an occasional issue does not a cultural traitor make. Were an individual to move beyond occasional disagreement into a pattern of disagreements, however, his cultural allegiance would be suspect. Were an individualist to feel, for instance, that there ought to be more environmental protection against oil spills and less logging of old stands in the forests, that person could probably still maintain an individualistic identity. But if that person went on to join the antinuclear movement, became upset about the release of genetically engineered organisms into the environment, saw water and air pollution as major threats to human health, and on and on, it would become increasingly difficult for him to maintain his original cultural identity.

The reasons for this are both social and cognitive. Joining several environmental and safety groups, for instance, would put our individualist in contact with many people who not only shared his views on deforestation but also held anti-individualist views on system blame, on poverty, on social programs, on foreign policy, and on a panoply of other issues. Anyone who has sat in a room for some time with people who differ on not only one or two issues but also on a wide spectrum of issues knows that this is difficult to bear. Caught between rival ways of life, the would-be cultural traitor will feel pressured either to move back to the position from which he came or to become something quite different.

The other constraint on individuals stems from the interconnected character of belief systems. For an individualist to accept the proposition that the forest industry must be regulated is to make an exception to his preference for untrammeled self-regulation. If the exceptions multiply, however, the rule itself at some point begins to be thrown into question. To suggest, moreover, that the unfettered cutting of trees is bad is to acquiesce, even if unintentionally, in the egalitarian view that nature is essentially fragile and to call into question the individualist conception of nature as resilient. And if one comes to believe that the least little upset is sufficient to lead Mother Nature to wreak vengeance on the human species, it becomes difficult to justify to oneself and to others the decentralized system of trial and error upon which the individualist life of self-regulation depends. The interdependence of beliefs thus makes it difficult to reject a part without unraveling the whole.

THE MULTIPLE SELF

We often hear, in conversation and from readers of our work, because these people see parts of themselves in all or most of these five ways, that our classification of individuals into five ways of life cannot be correct. This comes as no surprise to us, for we too feel that our existence is not taken up entirely in a single way of life. We do not agree, however, that this invalidates our classification of ways of life or the cultural theory on which it is based.

Our theory asserts that cultural bias depends on social context (and vice versa). If this is so, then we would expect that an individual's bias will be consistent only to the extent that his social context is consistent. An individual may find himself in cutthroat competition with his business rivals, hierarchical relations in the military, egalitarian relations at home, while treating certain areas of life, say inability to carry a tune, with fatalistic resignation. In this sense each individual, although certainly not "an island, entire of itself," is a self-contained regime.

Can we go beyond the unobjectionable, but not overly illuminating, observation that it all depends on the social context? Let us imagine two extreme cases, one in which an individual perceives each object of attention equally through the five cultural biases and another in which an individual perceives all objects through the same cultural bias. In the former instance, it is difficult to see how such an individual could ever act. Just as to the man in Dostoyevsky's famous novel *Notes from the Underground,* evidence for all positions would always appear equally compelling, so that we could never make up our minds. We would find ourselves like Larry Slade in *The Iceman Cometh,* who "was born condemned to be one of those who has to see all sides of a question. When you're damned like that, the questions multiply for you until in the end it's all question and no answer."[5]

In the case of the individual who sees everything through the same cultural bias, it is hard to imagine him ever cooperating with anyone. In a world full of such people, the alliances among ways of life that we have discussed would be impossible. This is not to say that such extreme individuals do not sometimes exist—uncompromising fanaticism and chronic indecision do occur—but only that most of us most of the time are somewhere in between seeing every object through a single bias and seeing each object equally through five biases.

Given that individuals find themselves in different social contexts in different areas of their lives, the interesting question is how they cope with this situation. Is there a strain to consistency on the part of individuals or do individuals compartmentalize the rival ways of life? The challenge for future research lies in specifying the conditions under which one is more likely than the other.

We would expect that individuals will make significant efforts to bring consistency to their social environments. This strain to consistency explains why people are not randomly distributed in social contexts. Individuals often seek out social relationships that are compatible with their preferred bias and shun those relations in which they feel less at home. For instance, a member of the Clamshell Alliance, an organization in which decisions depend on the consent of all, is unlikely to volunteer for service in the armed forces, where decisions are handed down by those at the apex of the hierarchy. Many Garrisonian abolitionists, to take another example, attempted to bring congruence to their social context by withdrawing from churches that were hierarchically organized and by transforming their familial relations in an egalitarian direction.[6] Similarly, in his *Theory of Stable Democracy,* Harry Eckstein suggests that individuals accustomed to authoritarian relations in the home and in the workplace may find themselves out of place and unsure how to behave in a democratic political system.[7]

Congruence is a direction only, however, never a final destination. "Contradictory beliefs," as Jon Elster has pointed out, "may coexist peacefully for a long time, if they belong to different realms of life."[8] So, for instance, the eighteenth-century Scottish entrepreneur felt no inconsistency in adopting competitive individualist principles in his relations with his business associates while supporting a highly deferential, hierarchical set of social relations in the domestic sphere. Similarly, in the early years of the American republic, many citizens had little difficulty reconciling their insistence on egalitarian political relations between whites and their enslavement of blacks.[9] This "compartmentalization of the self" is an important means by which individuals cope with multiple social contexts.[10]

The compartmentalization of biases may come about either through an individual's failure to perceive contradictions between competing biases (what Robert Lane called "morselizing"[11]) or through a positive belief that different biases in different spheres are beneficial. So, for instance, the Scottish entrepreneur may feel that the imposition of prescriptions at home may enhance his competitiveness in the market-place, or it may simply never occur to him that there is any tension between behaving one way with his wife and another with his business associates. Similarly, the early American may see no inconsistency between relating to black men in one way and white men in another (perhaps because he believes that blacks are something less than human), or he may feel that the subjugation of blacks helps make it possible to sustain egalitarian relations among whites.

Yet for all the means by which biases are compartmentalized and morselized, most individuals do find themselves inhabiting one way of life more than the others. As within Goethe's Faust, there may be more than one soul dwelling within an individual's breast, but the competing allegiances are not equally divided among the possible ways. Were this not so, we could not account for the patterning and predictability that we observe in human affairs. The strain to consistency can never completely eliminate, however, the diversity of an individual's social contexts and preferences. It is partly because of this overlap in social contexts that individuals find it possible to cooperate with inhabitants of other ways of life. This leads us directly to our next question: How do adherents of rival ways communicate with each other?

HOW DO ADHERENTS OF RIVAL WAYS OF LIFE COMMUNICATE?

If it is true that the five ways of life are fundamentally distinct ways of perceiving the world, how is it that adherents of these competing ways can communicate with each other? If there are plural rationalities, how can individuals operating under one form of rationality make sense of what is said in another rationality? How can individuals in different ways of life ever come to agreement, or even agree on what they disagree about, if what counts as evidence differs among opposing ways?

We begin by observing that communication between different cultures does take place. Anthropologists do not, as Ernest Gellner points out, come back from exotic and faraway places, saying that their concepts are so alien that it is impossible to describe or explain any of what the natives are doing. Although one often hears of partial failures of comprehension, what is noteworthy, Gellner suggests, is that anthropologists and travelers have, on the whole, been remarkably successfully in explaining culture A in the language of culture B.[12] Given that people do communicate (albeit imperfectly) with those who live very differently, the question then becomes: What makes this communication possible?

Alasdair MacIntyre has confronted this question head on in his recent book *Whose Justice? Which Rationality?* MacIntyre assents to the relativist proposition that "there is no standing ground, no place for enquiry, no way to engage in the practices of advancing, evaluating, accepting, and rejecting reasoned argument apart from that which is provided by some particular tradition or other." But he then goes on to argue that "it does not follow from this that what is said from within one tradition cannot be heard or overheard by those in another."[13] How is it that adherents of different traditions (we would say ways of life) can make sense of what is being said in rival traditions?

For starters, MacIntyre maintains, all traditions "agree in according a certain authority to logic both in their theory and their practice. Were it not so, their adherents would be unable to disagree in the way in which they do."[14] Agreement on the rules of logic (noncontradiction, for instance) is insufficient, of course, to resolve disagreements between traditions, but it does provide a basis for communicating what is being disagreed about.

Against those relativists who would insist that because each tradition "provides its own standards of rational justification, [it] must always be vindicated in the light of those standards,"[15] MacIntyre contends that the viability of a tradition is constrained by the need to be both internally consistent and externally effective. When adherents of different traditions meet threatening challenges, which MacIntyre calls "epistemological crises"[16] and we designate as cumulative failures to meet internally generated expectations, these must be overcome by new concepts and practices that, as Cardinal Newman argued in *An Essay on the Development of Christian Doctrine,*[17] must still remain true to the historical development of the tradition. "It is in respect of their adequacy or inadequacy in their responses to epistemological crises," MacIntyre suggests, "that traditions are vindicated or fail to be vindicated."[18] Persistent anomalies, as we argued in Chapter 4, together with the appearance of promising alternatives, encourage individuals to reconsider their commitment to one way of life and compel them to seek out rival ways that offer a more adequate explanation of events.

Thus that no enquiry is possible outside of a tradition does not mean that traditions cannot be invalidated or are invulnerable to criticism from without. Each tradition, MacIntyre suggests, can be evaluated and criticized from the standpoint of its rivals. He avoids relativism's slippery slopes by positing an active, interrogating individual in the midst of these coexisting traditions. Each individual, according to MacIntyre, must test dialectically the theses proposed to him or her by each competing tradition, while also drawing upon these same theses in order to test dialectically these convictions and responses which he or she has brought to the encounter. Such a person has to become involved in the conversation between traditions, learning to use the idiom of each in order to describe and evaluate the other or others by means of it.[19]

We would add that communication between our ways of life (and MacIntyre's traditions) is further facilitated because the ways are limited in number. Were frames of reference infinite (with every nation, ethnic group, or individual endowed with his own rationality), the impediments to communication between individuals in different ways would be virtually insuperable. If we never heard the same argument twice, it is difficult to see how we could ever understand anyone outside our frame of reference. But because the different biases are limited to a small number, individuals encounter the same arguments over and over. Repeated contact with the rationales and beliefs of rival ways of life helps individuals to make sense of much of what is said from within these rival ways. Ours (and MacIntyre's) is thus a theory of constrained relativism, not only in the sense that every way of life is constrained by the real world (and rudimentary rules of logic), but also in the vital sense that the different ways of organizing social life are strictly limited in number.

Testing each way of life (or tradition) by means of the perspectives offered by the others also establishes the basis for a genuinely critical theory. Too often work that goes under the rubric of "critical theory" is critical of only a single way of life, that of liberal capitalism. Habermas's claim,[20] for instance, that the ideal speech situation requires equal access to and possession of resources gives egalitarianism a privileged position and delegitimates hierarchy, individualism, and fatalism. A critical theory worthy of its name, we insist, must be critical of all biases. MacIntyre shows (and we agree) that it is possible for adherents of each way to criticize the others and for interested people to overhear these arguments. There is no transcendental way of life, superior to all the others in all respects, but there is the possibility of mutual criticism under which no single way is sacrosanct. Bias is inevitable, but failure to learn about biases is not.

WHAT CULTURAL THEORY LEAVES OUT

Is cultural theory an explanatory panacea, a universal nostrum, good for all problems, like some quack medicine? "Not a sparrow falls,"

Clifford Geertz comments (part in exasperation, part in admiration), but that action is said to be caused by or harnessed in the service of some cultural bias.[21] Cultural theory's applications have ranged from the rules for keeping kosher,[22] to why and what institutions forget,[23] to the practices of different types of criminals,[24] to how mathematicians deal with anomalous results.[25] We think of this less as overambition than as fulfillment of an important canon of scientific work by providing ever greater opportunities for falsification.

Surely, however, there must be subjects not amenable to cultural analysis. Suppose, for instance, a wall of water rushes toward us; presumably we would not need a cultural theory to tell us to get out of the way. The human instinct for self-preservation would be sufficient. Or would it? For even in this most extreme instance, where all involved are likely to agree on the danger, culture can have a critical role in explaining behavior. Cultural theory may tell us why some individuals adopt an attitude of "each for himself and the devil take the hindmost," while others advocate "women and children first" or "follow the leader," while still others decide that "it's no use, I'll stay here."[26]

A distinguishing characteristic of cultural theory is that it is a theory of multiequilibria. Instead of positing a single, optimal equilibrium, as is the case with theories that make survival or maximizing utility the criterion for individual choice, cultural theory insists there are five rational and sustainable solutions to every problem. Following Parsons and Shils, we ask "not what does [the individual actor] have to strive for in order to survive as an organism . . . [but] what does this actor strive for . . . [and] to what consequences has this actor been committed by his selection of choices?"[27] How people choose to live (and the consequences that follow from those choices) is what we take to be the domain of cultural theory.

What is culturally rational may conflict with (and even lose out to) individual self-interest. Consider, for instance, the business firm that seeks governmental subsidies, thereby enriching itself at the expense of weakening competitive individualism. The NIMBY ("not in my back-yard") syndrome for the location of potentially dangerous facilities might be another example of self-interest overriding cultural bias. But lest we concede too much, we hasten to add that determining what is in one's interests is often an exceedingly difficult task. Deciding whether a nuclear facility endangers one's safety, for instance, depends on one's perception of risk, which in turn is a function of one's cultural bias.[28] Cultural theory does not try to deny the operation of self-interest as a motivation, but it does insist on asking how individuals come to know where those interests lie.[29]

Where there are disagreements within a nation over the extent of danger or the appropriate public policy, cultural theory (because of its attention to the competing ways of life existing within a country) is obviously a promising explanatory candidate. But what about those situations in which policies are agreed upon or perceptions of danger are shared across ways of life? Can cultural theory account for such agreements, or must the theory inevitably slight cooperation in favor of conflict?

Admittedly, because of the essential pluralism of ways of life, cultural theory might appear to lend itself to explanations of divergent more readily than of convergent outcomes. But convergence on policy issues between competing ways of life is not necessarily incompatible with cultural theory. For adherents of different ways of life need not agree on ultimate ends in order to agree on particular issues. Convergence on policy outcomes may be achieved through overlap, complementarity, and integration.

Overlapping or shared dimensions is one way of producing similar policy preferences among adherents of competing ways of life. Egalitarians and individualists, for instance, score negatively on the grid dimension, and consequently proponents of both these ways of life tend to agree on the need for opposing governmental laws regulating individual morality. Because hierarchists and egalitarians score positively on the group dimension, they may agree on redistributive measures, hierarchists to manifest the concern of the higher for the lower echelons and egalitarians to reduce what they conceive of as unwarranted differences among people in power and income.

Convergence in policy preferences is also possible among ways of life that complement each other. Both hierarchists (positive group, positive grid) and individualists (negative group, negative grid) are attracted, for instance, to a relatively positive view of technological innovation. Individualists see technology as a means to expand opportunities, while hierarchists view it as a way to make good on the promise of a better life if the experts and procedures it validates are followed.

There are also occasions, far more rare, when adherents of all three active ways of life get together for different reasons on the same policy. These integrative solutions (so named by Mary Parker Follett at the turn of the century) require creative leadership. A good example is the convergence on the 1986 tax reform in the United States by egalitarians who wanted millions of low-income people off the tax rolls, individualists who wanted fewer tax preferences to level the economic playing field, and hierarchists who hoped to relegitimate the tax code.[30] Thus cultural theory does not predict that adherents of each way of life must end up with wholly distinct policy preferences, but rather that the ultimate ends guiding the route by which the policy is reached will be different for each way of life.

Cultural theory's claim of universality—that no matter what the material or technological position of people, or where they are located geographically, or in what historical time they live, their objectives can be derived from their socially induced biases—does *not* mean that history is irrelevant. On the contrary. Only history can tell us which means or instruments of policy are available and which ones will, based on the experience of these particular people, be seen as relevant to their circumstances. After the American Revolution, for instance, activists with egalitarian tendencies—anti-Federalists, Jeffersonians, Jacksonians—believed that the central government was a source of artificial inequality. Following the disputes between the party of the king and the party of the country in England, they believed that the executive power would be used to undermine republican government. Therefore they sought to keep the central government small and weak.[31] Nowadays, after the advent of the industrial revolution and corporate capitalism, their cultural successors, liberal Democrats, given their quite different circumstances and reading of history, believe that the central government is (or, at least, can and should be) an instrument for reducing inequalities. The objectives of egalitarians remain constant over time—reduce differences—but the means they adopt to that end differ with changing historical circumstances.

Without theory, history cannot speak; without history, theory is dumb. Cultural biases know nothing of specific historical events. Like the natural scientist who knows the principles involved, yet would be at a loss to say how many leaves will blow off a tree in the next storm,[32] theorists of cultural biases can state the principle—people will try to further their way of life—but will not, in the absence of information about the historical situation, be able to predict the means, such as the instruments of policy, that will be used to achieve this end.

Cultural biases rule out certain courses of action as incongruent with a way of life, but they do not necessarily rule in a specific alternative.[33] The theory leads us to predict, for instance, that egalitarian followers will not accept strong, overt leadership, but only a knowledge of the leader's personality can tell us which of the possible options—the dissembling behind-the-scenes leadership of a Thomas Jefferson versus the up-front mobilization of a mass public against inequality of an Andrew Jackson—will be selected.

The grid-group typology is a deliberately rough-and-ready frame of measurement. It is not aimed at filling in all the fine, specific detail of an individual's social environment but, rather, at sketching a broad picture that, thanks to its lack of particularistic detail, can be compared to others from widely different historical settings. Far from exempting the investigator from studying the vicissitudes of history, cultural theory gives us reason to take notice of history (and, more helpfully, what parts of history to notice) by demonstrating the past's relevance to the present.

Given the important part played by historically specific circumstances, our claims for cultural theory's universal applicability may appear unwarranted or at least exaggerated.[34] Only time will tell whether qualification proceeds faster than explanation. Our view is that knowing how people choose to live with others allows one to explain a great deal about human behavior, whether in thirteenth-century Italian city states,[35] eighteenth-century America, or twentieth-century China.

How much behavior in a given domain can be explained by recourse to cultural theory is an empirical question that cannot be settled by fiat. If a theory's fruitfulness can be gauged only through its empirical payoff and comparison with rival theories, why, the reader may wonder, aside from numerous illustrations, have we not done that here? Because, we answer, our strategic judgment is that at this stage exposition of the theory ought to be our first priority. Sufficient unto the book is the damage thereof. The bibliography that follows provides some indication of the theory's scope of application. No doubt criticism of the theory will help improve the many applications that are being carried on now and that we expect to conduct in the future.

What would count as evidence against our theory? Most damaging would be a demonstration that values are little constrained by institutional relationships. If the same cultural biases thrived in dissimilar social contexts or, conversely, if dissimilar biases existed in similar social contexts, then our faith in cultural theory would be greatly weakened. A study that showed, for instance, that beliefs about human or physical nature bore little or no relationship to how people organized their lives would draw into question the basic assumptions of the theory. Cultural theory, in generating proposals for research projects by which its validity can be tested, as well as in providing a position from which the major theoretical trends in social science can be surveyed, criticized, and compared, does what a theory has to do.

NOTES

1. Robert Brown, *Explanation in Social Science* (Chicago: Aldine, 1963), 169; emphasis in original.

2. Mary Douglas, "Notes and Queries About Analysis of Cultural Bias," typescript.

3. See Aaron Wildavsky, "The Soviet System," in Wildavsky, ed., *Beyond Containment, Alternative American Policies Toward the Soviet Union* (San Francisco: Institute for Contemporary Studies, 1983), 25–38.

4. Richard Ellis and Aaron Wildavsky, *Dilemmas of Presidential Leadership: From Washington Through Lincoln* (New Brunswick, N.J.: Transaction Publishers, 1989), 118–20. Also see Major L. Wilson, "The Concepts of Time and the Political Dialogue in the United States, 1828–1848," *American Quarterly,* 1967, 619–44, esp. 644; and Rush Welter, *The Mind of America, 1820–1860* (New York: Columbia University Press, 1975), esp. 193–95.

5. Eugene O'Neill, *The Iceman Cometh* (New York: Vintage, 1957), 30.

6. See Lewis Perry, *Radical Abolitionism: Anarchy and the Government of God in Antislavery Thought* (Ithaca: Cornell University Press, 1973); and Blanche Glassman Hersch, *The Slavery of Sex: Feminist Abolitionists in America* (Urbana: University of Illinois Press, 1978).

7. Harry Eckstein, *Division and Cohesion in Democracy: A Study of Norway* (Princeton: Princeton University Press, 1966), Appendix B.

8. Jon Elster, ed., *The Multiple Self* (Cambridge: Cambridge University Press, 1985), 4.

9. See Edmund S. Morgan, *American Slavery, American Freedom: The Ordeal of Colonial Freedom* (New York: Norton, 1975); and George M. Fredrickson, *White Supremacy: A Comparative Study in American and South African History* (New York: Oxford University Press, 1981).

10. The phrase is taken from Alasdair MacIntyre, *Whose Justice? Which Rationality?* (Notre Dame, Ind.: University of Notre Dame Press, 1988), 397.

11. Robert E. Lane, *Political Ideology* (New York: Free Press, 1962).

12. Ernest Gellner, "Relativism and Universals," in Martin Hollis and Steven Lukes, eds., *Rationality and Relativism* (Oxford: Basil Blackwell, 1982), 185.

13. MacIntyre, *Whose Justice?* 350.

14. Ibid., 351.

15. Ibid., 364.

16. Ibid., 361. Also see Alasdair MacIntyre, "Epistemological Crises, Dramatic Narrative, and the Philosophy of Science," in Gary Gutting, ed., *Paradigms and Revolutions: Appraisals and Applications of Thomas Kuhn's Philosophy of Science* (Notre Dame, Ind.: University of Notre Dame Press, 1980), 54–74.

17. John Henry Newman, *An Essay on the Development of Christian Doctrine* (Harmondsworth, Middlesex, UK: Penguin Books, 1974).

18. MacIntyre, *Whose Justice?* 366.

19. Ibid., 398.

20. See, e.g., Jurgen Habermas, *Legitimation Crisis* (Boston: Beacon Press, 1975), and *Communication and the Evolution of Society* (Boston: Beacon Press, 1979).

21. Clifford Geertz, "The Anthropologist at Large," *New Republic,* May 25, 1987, 34, 36–37.

22. Mary Douglas, *Natural Symbols: Explorations in Cosmology* (London: Barrie and Rockliff, 1970).

23. Mary Douglas, *How Institutions Think* (Syracuse: Syracuse University Press, 1986).

24. Gerald Mars, *Cheats at Work: An Anthropology of Workplace Crime* (London: Allen and Unwin, 1982).

25. David Bloor, "Polyhedra and the Abominations of Leviticus: Cognitive Styles in Mathematics," in Mary Douglas, ed., *Essays in the Sociology of Perception* (London: Routledge and Kegan Paul, 1982), 191–218.

26. We are indebted to Dennis Coyle for this point. A parallel example is given in Douglas, *How Institutions Think,* 7–8.

27. Talcott Parsons and Edward A. Shils, *Toward a General Theory of Action* (Cambridge: Harvard University Press, 1951), 63.

28. See the discussion by Kenneth Boulding in "Toward the Development of a Cultural Economics," *Social Science Quarterly,* 1974, 267–84.

29. See Michiel Schwarz and Michael Thompson, "Beyond the Politics of Interest," and Karl Dake and Aaron Wildavsky, "Comparing Rival Theories of Risk Perception," forthcoming in *Daedalus.*

30. See Dennis Coyle and Aaron Wildavsky, "Requisites of Radical Reform: Income Maintenance Versus Tax Preferences," *Journal of Policy Analysis and Management* 7, 1 (Fall 1987): 1–16.

31. See Lance Banning, *The Jeffersonian Persuasion* (Ithaca: Cornell University Press, 1978); and Aaron Wildavsky, "Industrial Policies in American Political Cultures," in Claude E. Barfield and William A. Schambra, eds., *The Politics of Industrial Policy* (Washington, D.C.: American Enterprise Institute, 1986), 15–32.

32. May Brodbeck, "On the Philosophy of the Social Sciences," in John O'Neill, ed., *Modes of Individualism and Collectivism* (London: Heinemann, 1973), 99.

33. On the logic of this mode of explanation in which one causal process limits the alternatives to some feasible set and another selects among the alternatives, see Arthur L. Stinchcombe, *Constructing Social Theories* (New York: Harcourt, Brace & World, 1968), 196–98.

34. This distrust is particularly evident among contemporary anthropologists who seem resigned to "Ethnography as Art." See the profile of Clifford Geertz by John Horgan in *Scientific American,* July 1989, 28–31.

35. Carolyn Webber and Aaron Wildavsky, *A History of Taxation and Expenditure in the Western World* (New York: Simon and Schuster, 1986).

Bibliography of Cultural Theory

Bloor, David. "Polyhedra and the Abominations of Leviticus: Cognitive Styles in Mathematics." *British Journal for the History of Science* 11, 39 (1978): 245–72. Reprinted in Mary Douglas, ed., *Essays in the Sociology of Perception.* London: Routledge and Kegan Paul, 1982, 191–218.

———. *Wittgenstein: A Social Theory of Knowledge.* London: Macmillan, 1983.

Bloor, David, and Celia Bloor. "Twenty Industrial Scientists: A Preliminary Exercise." In Mary Douglas, ed., *Essays in the Sociology of Perception.* London: Routledge and Kegan Paul, 1982, 83–102.

Caulkins, Douglas. "Networks and Narratives: An Anthropological Perspective for Small Business Research." Scottish Enterprise Foundation Occasional Paper no. 01/88. University of Stirling, Scotland, January 1988.

———. "Is Small Still Beautiful? Images of Success Among Scotland's High Technology Entrepreneurs." Central States Anthropological Society, St. Louis, March 25, 1988.

———. "From Coal Tips to Silicon Chips: Entrepreneurship and Technology Transfer in England's Industrial Northeast." American Anthropological Association Meetings, Phoenix, November 18, 1988.

Douglas, Mary. *Purity and Danger: An Analysis of Concepts of Pollution and Taboo.* London: Routledge and Kegan Paul, 1966.

———. *Natural Symbols: Explorations in Cosmology.* London: Barrie and Rockliff, 1970.

———. *Implicit Meanings: Essays in Anthropology.* London: Routledge and Kegan Paul, 1975.

———. "Cultural Bias." London: Royal Anthropological Institute, Occasional Paper no. 35, 1978. Reprinted in Douglas, *In The Active Voice.* London: Routledge and Kegan Paul, 1982, 183–254.

———. *Risk Acceptability According to the Social Sciences.* New York: Russell Sage Foundation, 1985.

———. *How Institutions Think.* Syracuse: Syracuse University Press, 1986.

———, ed. *Essays in the Sociology of Perception.* London: Routledge and Kegan Paul, 1982.

Douglas, Mary, and Jonathan L. Gross. "Food and Culture: Measuring the Intricacy of Rule Systems." *Social Science Information* 20 (1981): 1–35.

Douglas, Mary, and Baron Isherwood. *The World of Goods: Towards an Anthropology of Consumption.* London: Allen Lane, 1979.

Douglas, Mary, and Aaron Wildavsky. *Risk and Culture: An Essay on the Selection of Technical and Environmental Dangers.* Berkeley: University of California Press, 1982.

Ellis, Richard, and Aaron Wildavsky. *Dilemmas of Presidential Leadership: From Washington Through Lincoln.* New Brunswick, N.J.: Transaction Publishers, 1989.

_____. "A Cultural Analysis of the Role of Abolitionists in the Coming of the Civil War." *Comparative Studies in Society and History* 31, 1 (1990): 89–116.

Gager, John G. "Body-Symbols and Social Reality: Resurrection, Incarnation and Asceticism in Early Christianity." *Religion* 12 (1982): 345–63.

Gross, Jonathan L. "A Graph-Theoretical Model of Social Organization." *Annals of Discrete Mathematics* 13 (1982): 81–88.

Gross, Jonathan, and Steve Rayner. *Measuring Culture: A Paradigm for the Analysis of Social Organization.* New York: Columbia University Press, 1985.

Isenberg, Sheldon R., and Dennis E. Owen. "Bodies, Natural and Contrived: The Work of Mary Douglas." *Religious Studies Review* 3 (1977): 1–17.

Johnson, Branden B. "The Environmentalist Movement and Grid/Group Analysis: A Modest Critique." In Branden B. Johnson and Vincent T. Covello, eds., *The Social and Cultural Construction of Risk.* Dordrecht, Holland: D. Reidel, 1987, 147–75.

McLeod, Katrina C.D. "The Political Culture of Warring States in China." In Mary Douglas, ed., *Essays in the Sociology of Perception.* London: Routledge and Kegan Paul, 1982, 132–61.

Malecha, Gary Lee. "Understanding Agrarian Fundamentalism: A Cultural Interpretation of American Populism." Paper delivered at the 1988 Annual Meeting of the American Political Science Association, Washington, D.C., September 1–4, 1988.

Malina, Bruce J. *The New Testament World: Insights from Cultural Anthropology.* Atlanta: John Knox Press, 1981.

_____. *Christian Origins and Cultural Anthropology: Practical Models for Biblical Interpretation.* Atlanta: John Knox Press, 1986.

Mars, Gerald. *Cheats at Work: An Anthropology of Workplace Crime.* London: Allen and Unwin, 1982.

Mars, Gerald, and Valerie Mars. "Classifying Cuisines: Epicures, Isolates, Messmates and Cultists." In *Proceedings of the Oxford Food Symposium 1985: Cooking, Science, Lore and Books.* London: Prospect Books, 1986.

_____. "Taste and Etiquette in the Victorian Household." In *Proceedings of the Oxford Food Symposium 1987: In Taste.* London: Prospect Books, 1988.

Mars, Gerald, and Michael Nicod. *The World of Waiters.* London: Allen and Unwin, 1983.

Mars, Valerie. "Classifying Cooking Oils: The Boundaries Between Epicures, Isolates, Messmates and Cultists." In *Proceedings of the Oxford Food Symposium 1986: The Cooking Medium.* London: Prospect Books, 1987.

———. "Some Reasons Why There Was a Change from a Service à la Française to Service à la Russe in 19th Century England." Second International Food Symposium, Istanbul, 1988.

Neyrey, Jerome H. "Body Language in I Corinthians: The Use of Anthropological Models for Understanding Paul and the Apostles." *Semeia* 35 (1985): 129–70.

———. "The Idea of Purity in Mark's Gospel." *Semeia* 35 (1985): 91–128.

Olroyd, David. "By Grid and Group Divided: Buckland and the English Geological Community in the Early 19th Century." *Annals of Science* 41 (1984): 383–93.

Pagels, Elaine. "The Politics of Paradise: Augustine's Exegesis of Genesis 1–3 Versus that of John Chrysotom." *Harvard Theological Review* 78 (1985): 67–79.

Rayner, Steve. "The Classification and Dynamics of Sectarian Forms of Organization: Grid/Group Perspectives on the Far Left in Britain." Ph.D. Dissertation, University of London, 1979.

———. "The Perception of Time and Space in Egalitarian Sects: A Millenarian Cosmology." In Mary Douglas, ed., *Essays in the Sociology of Perception.* London: Routledge and Kegan Paul, 1982, 247–74.

———. "Disagreeing About Risk: The Institutional Cultures of Risk Management and Planning for Future Generations." In Susan G. Hadden, *Risk Analysis, Institutions, and Public Policy.* Port Washington, N.Y.: Associated Faculty Press, 1984, 150–69.

———. "Sickness and Social Control." *Listening: Journal of Religion and Culture* 19, 2 (Spring 1984): 143–54.

———. "Management of Radiation Hazards in Hospitals: Plural Rationalities in a Single Institution." *Social Studies of Science* 16 (1986): 573–91.

———. "The Politics of Schism: Routinization and Social Control in the International Socialists/Socialist Workers' Party." In John Law, ed., *Power, Action and Belief: A New Sociology of Knowledge.* Sociological Review Monograph 32. London: Routledge and Kegan Paul, 1986.

———. "The Rules that Keep Us Equal." In James G. Flanagan and Steve Rayner, eds., *Rules, Decisions, and Inequality in Egalitarian Societies.* Aldershot: Avebury, 1988, 20–42.

———. "Learning from the Blind Men and the Elephant, Or Seeing Things Whole in Risk Management." In Vincent T. Covello et al., eds., *Uncertainty in Risk Assessment, Risk Management, and Decision Making.* New York: Plenum Press, 1987.

Rayner, Steve, and Robin Cantor. "How Far Is Safe Enough? The Cultural Approach to Societal Technology Choice." *Risk Analysis* 7 (1987): 3–9.

Raynor, Steve, and Loutillie W. Rickert. "Perception of Risk: The Social Context of Public Concern over Non-Ionizing Radiation." In M. H. Repacholi, ed., *Non-Ionizing Radiations: Physical Characteristics, Biological Effects and Health Hazard Assessment.* Melbourne: International Radiation Protection Association, 1988, 39–48.

Schwarz, Michiel, and Michael Thompson. *Divided We Stand: Redefining Politics, Technology and Social Choice.* Hemel Hempstead: Harvester-Wheatsheaf, 1990.

Segal, Alan F. "Ruler of This World: Attitudes About Mediator Figures and the Importance of Sociology for Self-Definition." In E. P. Sanders, ed., *Jewish and Christian Self-Definition,* Vol. 2. Philadelphia: Fortress Press, 1981, 245–68.

Spickard, James. "Relativism and Cultural Comparison in the Anthropology of Mary Douglas: An Evaluation of the Meta-Theoretical Strategy of Her Grid-Group Theory." Ph.D. Dissertation, Graduate Theological Union, 1984.

———. "A Guide to Mary Douglas's Three Versions of Grid/Group Theory." *Sociological Analysis* 50, 1 (1989).

Stiles, Julie L., and Douglas Caulkins. "Prisoners in Their Own Homes: A Structural and Cognitive Interpretation of the Problems of Battered Women." Paper presented at the Iowa Academy of Science Meetings, Storm Lake, Iowa, April 22, 1989.

Thompson, Michael. *Rubbish Theory: The Creation and Destruction of Value.* Oxford: Oxford University Press, 1979.

———. "The Aesthetics of Risk: Culture of Context?" In R. C. Schwing and W. A. Albers, eds., *Societal Risk Assessment.* New York and London: Plenum, 1980, 273–85.

———. "The Problem of the Centre: An Autonomous Cosmology." In Mary Douglas, ed., *Essays in the Sociology of Perception.* London: Routledge and Kegan Paul, 1982, 302–27.

———. "A Three-Dimensional Model." In Mary Douglas, ed., *Essays in the Sociology of Perception.* London: Routledge and Kegan Paul, 1982, 31–63.

———. "A Cultural Basis for Comparison." Postscript to H. Kunreuther, J. Linneroth, et al., *Risk Analysis and Decision Processes: The Siting of Liquefied Energy Gas Facilities in 4 Countries.* Berlin: Springer-Verlag, 1983, 232–62.

———. "Among the Energy Tribes: A Cultural Framework for the Analysis and Design of Energy Policy." *Policy Sciences* 17 (1984): 321–39.

———. "Hazardous Waste: What Is It? Can We Ever Know? If We Can't, Does It Matter?" In F. Homburger, ed., *Safety Evaluation and Regulation of Chemicals: Interface Between Law and Science.* Basel: Karger, 1986, 230–36.

———. "To Hell with the Turkeys: A Diatribe Directed at the Pernicious Trepidity of Current Intellectual Approaches to Risk." In D. MacLean, ed., *Values at Risk.* Totowa, N.J.: Rowman and Allanheld, 1986, 113–35.

———. "Welche Gesellschaftsklassen sind potent genug, anderen ihre Zukunft aufzuoktroyieren? Und wie geht das vor sich?" (Which social category is able to impose its vision of the future? And how does it do this?) In Lucius Burckhardt, ed., *Design der Zukunft.* Berlin: Dumont/International Design Centre, 1987, 58–87.

———. "A Breakthrough in the Bathroom: Why Culture and Technology Can't be Separated" (in Dutch). In M. Schwarz and R. Jansma, eds., *De Technologische Cultuur.* Amsterdam: De Balie, 1988, 97–102.

_____. "Socially Viable Ideas of Nature." In E. Baark and U. Svedin, eds., *Nature, Culture, Technology: Towards a New Conceptual Framework.* London: Macmillan, 1988.

_____. "Engineering and Anthropology: Is There a Difference?" In J. Brown, ed., *Environmental Threats: Reception, Analysis, and Management.* London, Belhaven, 1989, 87–94.

Thompson, Michael, and P. James. "The Cultural Theory of Risk." In J. Brown, ed., *Environmental Threats: Reception, Analysis, and Management.* London: Belhaven, 1989, 138–50.

Thompson, Michael, and M. Warburton. "Decision Making Under Contradictory Certainties: How to Save the Himalayas When You Can't Find Out What's Wrong with Them." *Journal of Applied Systems Analysis* 12 (1985):3–34.

Thompson, Michael, and A. Wildavsky. "A Cultural Theory of Information Bias in Organisations." *Journal of Management Studies* 23, 3 (1986): 273–86.

_____. "A Poverty of Distinction: From Economic Homogeneity to Cultural Heterogeneity in the Classification of Poor People." *Policy Sciences* 19 (1986): 163–99.

Thompson, Michael, J. D. Ives, and B. Messerli. "Research Strategy for the Himalayan Region: Conference Conclusions and Overview." *Mountain Research and Development* 7, 3 (1987), Special Issue on the Himalaya–Ganges Problem.

Thompson, Michael, M. Warburton, and T. Hatley. *Uncertainty on a Himalayan Scale: An Institutional Theory of Environmental Perception and a Strategic Framework for the Sustainable Development of the Himalaya.* London: Ethnographica, 1987.

Trosset, Carol. "Welsh Senses of Self." Ph.D. Dissertation, University of Texas–Austin, 1989.

Webber, Carolyn, and Aaron Wildavsky, *A History of Taxation and Expenditure in the Western World.* New York: Simon and Schuster, 1986.

White, Leland J. "Grid and Group in Matthew's Community: The Righteousness/Honor Code in the Sermon on the Mount." *Semeia* 35 (1985): 61–90.

Wildavsky, Aaron. *The Nursing Father: Moses as a Political Leader.* Birmingham: University of Alabama Press, 1984.

_____. "Choosing Preferences by Constructing Institutions: A Cultural Theory of Preference Formation." *American Political Science Review* 81 (1987): 3–21.

_____. "A Cultural Theory of Budgeting." *International Journal of Public Administration* 11 (1988): 651–77.

_____. "Frames of Reference Come from Cultures: A Predictive Theory." In Morris Freilich, ed., *The Relevance of Culture.* South Hadley, Mass.: Bergin and Garvey, 1989.

_____. "A Cultural Theory of Leadership." In Bryan Jones, ed., *Leadership: From Political Science Perspectives.* Lawrence: University Press of Kansas, 1989.

———. "On the Social Construction of Distinctions: Risk, Rape, Public Goods, and Altruism," in Michael Hecter, Lynn A. Cooper, and Lynn Nadel, eds., *Toward a Scientific Understanding of Values* (Stanford: Stanford University Press), forthcoming.

Wildavsky, Aaron, and Daniel Polisar. "From Individual to System Blame: Analysis of Historical Change in the Law of Torts." *Journal of Policy History* 1: 129–55.

Wynne, Brian. "Building Public Concern into Risk Management." In Jennifer Brown, ed., *Environmental Threats: Perception, Analysis and Management.* London, Belhaven, 1989, 118–37.

———. "Frameworks of Rationality in Risk Management: Towards The Testing of Naïve Sociology." In Jennifer Brown, ed., *Environmental Threats, Perception, Analysis and Management.* London: Belhaven, 1989, 33–47.

Index